A Lancastrian Mirror for Princes

A Lancastrian Mirror for Princes

The Yale Law School
New Statutes of England

Rosemarie McGerr

INDIANA UNIVERSITY PRESS

Bloomington & Indianapolis

This book is a publication of

INDIANA UNIVERSITY PRESS
601 North Morton Street
Bloomington, IN 47404–3797 USA

iupress.indiana.edu

Telephone orders 800-842-6796
Fax orders 812-855-7931

♾ The paper used in this publication
meets the minimum requirements
of the American National Standard for
Information Sciences – Permanence
of Paper for Printed Library Materials,
ANSI Z39.48–1992.

Manufactured in the
United States of America

Library of Congress
Cataloging-in-Publication Data

McGerr, Rosemarie Potz, [date]
   A Lancastrian mirror for princes :
the Yale Law School new statutes of
England / Rosemarie McGerr.
     p. cm.
   Includes bibliographical references
and index.
     ISBN 978-0-253-35641-3 (cloth : alk.
paper) 1. England. Laws, etc. (Nova
statuta) 2. Law – England – History –
To 1500 – Manuscripts. 3. Great Britain
– Politics and government – 1399–1485
– Sources. I. Title.
   KD130 1327c
   349.42 – dc22

                                2011007708

1 2 3 4 5   16 15 14 13 12 11

In memoriam

MICHAEL CAMILLE & JEREMY GRIFFITHS

"And every statut koude he pleyn by rote."

GEOFFREY CHAUCER

Prologue to the *Canterbury Tales*

Contents

Preface

In the portrait of the "Sergeant of the Lawe" in the Prologue to Chaucer's *Canterbury Tales*, the narrator includes the information that this pilgrim can cite every statute from memory – an impressive professional credential, to be sure – yet the irony of the passage might make us wonder what this accomplishment really means. We might expect that knowledge of all the statutes would increase a lawyer's ability to solve a particular legal problem; but we might also wonder how knowledge of all of the statutes might shape a person's understanding of the relationship of the English monarchy and Parliament, as well as the history of particular laws and the concepts of justice that laws reflect. From the hundreds of medieval English statutes manuscripts that survive, we know that English lawyers often owned copies of the statutes; yet we also know that a growing number of readers in late medieval England who were not lawyers also owned copies of statute books. And we might ask, "Why?" A collection of medieval statutes may not seem like a very exciting kind of book to read; but a medieval manuscript of statutes may tell a very interesting tale. When the text begins with a narrative justifying an English prince's removal of his father from the throne, we begin to recognize that a statute book might serve many purposes. Some of what engages us when we read such a manuscript, however, comes in the margins of the central text – spaces where visual and verbal texts bring "other" voices into dialogue with the voices of the central text. Painted images, marginal comments, or ownership inscriptions may all come into play with the statutes, creating allusions to contemporary history, literature, or religious thought and revealing the cultural value the manuscript's earlier readers found within its covers.

I first came across the Yale Law School manuscript of the *New Statutes of England* or *Nova statuta Angliae* when I was searching for manuscripts made for Henry VI of England, in hopes of finding additional work by the scribes and artists who produced a manuscript of *The Pilgrimage of the Soul* inscribed with Henry VI's name. While the Yale *Nova statuta* did not provide the kinds of leads I hoped to find, I nonetheless became intrigued by several aspects of this statutes manuscript. First among these were the manuscript's historical links with two very interesting women: Margaret of Anjou, Henry VI's consort, and Margaret Elyot, wife of the humanist author Thomas Elyot. While recent scholarship on Margaret of Anjou has allowed us to understand more about her actions and their context, none of the studies of this queen has taken into account what her connection to this copy of the *New Statutes* might reveal about her knowledge of English law or her construction of her role as queen. Especially if, as I hope my study demonstrates, Margaret did not receive the Yale manuscript as a wedding gift, but had it made as a gift for her son, the manuscript has much to tell us about the extent of Margaret's participation in Lancastrian royal image-making. Less scholarship has focused on Lady Margaret Elyot (*née* Margaret Aborough or Margaret à Barrow), who was educated at the home of Sir Thomas More before she married into the Elyot family and came into possession of this manuscript. Knowledge of her link to this copy of the *New Statutes* adds greatly to our understanding of her adult life and the intellectual context in which Thomas Elyot composed his treatises.

Equally intriguing to me were the unique illustrations in the Yale Law School manuscript, which had not yet been fully reproduced, described, or analyzed. Although it is clear that this manuscript's texts and illustrations were produced by scribes and artists who worked on other copies of the *New Statutes*, the illustrations in this copy follow a different iconography from those found in the other surviving manuscripts, and these illustrations require a different form of reading process from what modern scholars might expect. To begin with, while the images of kings are "portraits" of the English kings whose statutes appear in the manuscript, the images borrow from discourses of justice and grace found in other visual and verbal genres to construct a commentary on kingship. The use of coats of arms in the margins of this manuscript also frames a reading of the statutes that is different from the readings suggested by the other surviving copies of the *New Statutes*. The Yale *New Statutes* manuscript thus demonstrates how medieval legal records could be framed in such a way as to inscribe multiple meanings and open the legal text to dialogue with works in other genres.

My project in this study is therefore both to offer a new reading of the Yale Law School *New Statutes of England* and to illustrate the value of reading medieval legal texts in new ways that become possible if we engage them in their manuscript context and their cultural context, including history, literature, and the visual arts. This study is not a critical edition of the texts that appear in the Yale Law School manuscript, but an analysis of the shaping of these texts as they appear in this fifteenth-century book. The present study goes considerably further than my preliminary treatment of the illustrations in the manuscript, in an article in *Textual Cultures*, vol. 1, no. 2 (Autumn 2006), pp. 6–59. Here I offer a full codicological description of the Yale manuscript; I also discuss in greater detail the relationship of the Yale manuscript to other copies of the *New Statutes*, to other legal texts associated with the Lancastrian court, and to other representations of kings that were part of public discourse during the fifteenth century. This study also analyzes the representation of Margaret of Anjou in the Yale manuscript, the relationship of this "portrait" to other representations of her from the 1440s to the 1470s, and the role that this manuscript may have played in her attempts to support her husband's claim to the throne of England and her son's right to inherit it. In addition, my analysis here goes considerably further than my article in showing links between the Yale statutes manuscript and other mirrors for princes, or works of advice about kingship, associated with the Lancastrian court. Finally, this study considers the different forms of value that a legal manuscript may have had for its owners after its initial production.

Many individuals and institutions made it possible for me to undertake and complete this project. First, I wish to express my gratitude to Mike Widener, Rare Book Librarian at Yale Law School's Lillian Goldman Law Library, for his generous assistance over the course of the project. I also want to recognize Guy Holborn, Librarian at Lincoln's Inn Library, and Jerome Farrell, Archivist at the Leathersellers' Company, who helped me greatly with images and information over several years. My thanks go also to the staff members of the British Library Manuscript Room, the Harvard Law School Rare Books and Early Manuscripts Collection, the Inner Temple Library, the Library of Congress, and the Houghton Library for their assistance during my visits.

Many libraries and institutions kindly granted me permission to reproduce images of items in their collections: the Bibliothèque nationale de France, the Bodleian Library, the British Library, Columbia University Rare

Book and Manuscript Library, Durham Cathedral Library, Eton College, the Fitzwilliam Museum, the Free Library of Philadelphia, the Harry Ransom Humanities Research Center at the University of Texas at Austin, the Huntington Library, Jesus College (Oxford), King's College (Cambridge), the Leathersellers' Company, the Honourable Society of Lincoln's Inn, the Lillian Goldman Law Library (Yale Law School), the London Metropolitan Archives, the Metropolitan Museum of Art, the National Archives of the United Kingdom, the National Portrait Gallery (London), the Pierpont Morgan Library, the Royal Collection of Her Majesty Queen Elizabeth II, St. John's College (Cambridge), St. John Baptist College (Oxford), and the Skinners' Company.

My sincere thanks also go to the many colleagues who assisted me in aspects of my research or analysis. First among these must be Kathleen Scott and Jeremy Griffiths, who generously shared their own research on manuscripts of the *New Statutes of England*. Without their work, my own would have been much more difficult. Many other colleagues also assisted me with information or responses to drafts of the project, which allowed me to resolve problems both material and intellectual: John Hamilton Baker, Michel-André Bossy, Michael Camille, Dario Del Puppo, Tony Edwards, Matt Giancarlo, Richard Green, Tom Hahn, Jim Marrow, Lister Matheson, Helen Maurer, Alastair Minnis, Derek Pearsall, Fred Robinson, Pamela Robinson, Wendy Scase, Joel Silver, Eric Stanley, Wayne Storey, and Paul Strohm. I join with many who work on medieval manuscripts in mourning the loss of Jeremy Griffiths and Michael Camille; their scholarship in this field continues to challenge us to read medieval books in new ways.

I also greatly appreciate the funding from Indiana University that helped to defray the costs of research and publication of this book. The Henry H. H. Remak Professorship I received in 2008 made the largest financial contribution to my research and also made it possible for me to provide color as well as black-and-white images to illustrate my analysis. I am grateful to Henry Remak's student Larry Lee, who chose to honor Remak's intellectual achievement and dedication to teaching by supporting the work of current faculty at his home institution. Additional funding for my research came from the College of Arts and Sciences, the Department of Comparative Literature, and the West European Studies Program.

Finally, I want to thank Jane Behnken and Sarah Wyatt Swanson of Indiana University Press, who have guided the book smoothly through all aspects of production, and Shoshanna Green, for her expert work on the copyediting. Special thanks to the Art Department, which has ably met the challenges of preparing the images for the book. I also want to thank Wayne Storey, the editor of *Textual Cultures*, and Indiana University Press for allowing me to include some material here that first appeared in my article about the Yale manuscript in that journal.

A Lancastrian Mirror for Princes

The Margin and the Center

FRAMING A READING OF A LEGAL MANUSCRIPT

Among the rare books in Yale Law School's Lillian Goldman Library is a fifteenth-century manuscript of the *Nova statuta Angliae* or *New Statutes of England*, covering the period from 1327 until 1484.[1] While significant as a record of medieval laws, the manuscript is even more important for the unique decoration and illustration it contains and for what they suggest about the framing and interweaving of discourses within and among texts in the fifteenth century. Although published references to the Yale copy of the *New Statutes of England* go back to the nineteenth century, scholars have only begun to analyze this manuscript and its relationship to other visual and verbal texts in the late Middle Ages.[2] Thus far, more art historians have published research on the manuscript than legal historians or other scholars, and there has been little consensus on the manuscript's origins or significance. As I hope to show, the manuscript's visual and verbal texts are most productively read from more than one disciplinary perspective. Using an interdisciplinary approach, the following study brings together research in several fields to present a new reading of the Yale Law School *Nova statuta*. This study is the first to offer a full codicological analysis of the manuscript, as well as a detailed discussion of its significance as a cultural artifact.[3] My project in the following chapters is to explore how the discourses found in the centers and margins of this manuscript contribute to its constructions of English law and history, kingship and queenship, justice and grace. In more general terms, the goal of this study is to offer a new exploration of what kind of "work" a fifteenth-century legal manuscript might do and what forms of representation and rhetorical strategies it might share with medieval manuscripts in other genres. Such an analysis is necessary for understanding the true importance of the Yale manuscript, and others like it, now as well as in the past.

Many images of royal power, grace, and justice appear in the Yale *Nova statuta* manuscript – some verbal, some visual, some in the central text, some in the margins. The relationship between the margin and the center has become an important focus of inquiry for scholars in many disciplines, including the study of medieval manuscripts, for the margins and centers of the leaves of medieval manuscripts, in addition to the flyleaves and pastedowns that surround a manuscript's central leaves, can be read as cultural space, as well as textual space. Like other margins, the margins of medieval manuscripts have been theorized as locations of difference or otherness, frames that both define and challenge centers. Michael Camille has argued, "Things written or drawn in the margins add an extra dimension, a supplement, that is able to gloss, parody, modernize and problematize the [central] text's authority while never totally undermining it. The centre is . . . dependent upon the margins for its continued existence" (Camille 1992, 10). The margins of medieval manuscripts may also be theorized as thresholds or locations of mediation between others, inside or outside an individual manuscript book. Images or texts that recur in the margins at different points in a manuscript can serve to highlight links between the texts on those leaves, even when the texts come from different genres or treat different subjects. Margins are often the spaces where we find a mixture of images and texts that come from categories traditionally considered different or even opposed (public vs. private, religious vs. secular, courtly vs. popular). The margins of a manuscript are also where we often find images that cross boundaries in such a way as to create imaginative or even "monstrous" scenes or creatures, as well as texts that do not fit into traditional categories of literature (such as fragments of other texts, informal commentary on the central texts, recipes, mottos, curses, prayers, and civic or family records). Often, these texts have been added by a manuscript's owners, rather than inscribed by the artisans who originally produced it, and these texts have traditionally been considered marginal to a manuscript's central texts; yet these additions highlight the "open" nature of the textual and cultural spaces of medieval manuscripts, which were often constructed in pieces over the course of years or added to by different owners. The margins of medieval manuscripts can thus be read as spaces of ambiguity and dialogue that allow for interrogation of constructions of otherness, hybrid areas resistant to traditional systems of classification. Even in cases where the marginal texts of a manuscript seem to reflect the nature of the manuscript's central texts, rather than offering what Camille calls the "exquisite incongruity of medieval marginal art" (Camille 1992, 12), the visual and verbal marginal texts of a manuscript have a voice in the economy of the manuscript as a whole, suggesting links to visual and verbal texts inside and outside the manuscript, offering readers additional contexts in which to read the manuscript's central texts.

Scholars have become more concerned about cultural context in describing the relationship of the central and marginal texts, as well as the visual and verbal texts, in medieval manuscripts. For example, Andrew Taylor has used the model of the medieval market to describe the artistic, intellectual, and social interactions occurring in the spaces surrounding the central text in an English manuscript of papal decrees (A. Taylor 2002, 158–59). For his part, Michael Camille has suggested the polyphony of late medieval music as another analogy for the interplay of visual and verbal texts in an English psalter (Camille 1998, 268). Both Taylor's and Camille's readings of medieval manuscripts have been shaped by Mikhail Bakhtin's theory of the interweaving of multiple discourses in the novel, which he traces back to medieval traditions of holiday transgression of official boundaries, such as those that took place during celebrations of Carnival just before Lent.[4] The arguments presented by Taylor and Camille also reflect the theories of Arnold van Gennep and Victor Turner, who define passages through boundaries as sites of between-ness and redefinition and show how other liminal spaces and times in a culture mirror these spaces.[5] As a result of working with the Yale *New Statutes* manuscript, I would like to suggest the medieval parliament as an additional model for the interplay of discourses in the margins and centers of late medieval manuscripts. Matthew Giancarlo has recently discussed the important ways in which parliament as a locus of dialogue, as well as legal process, played a significant role in the representation of voice in the literature of late medieval England: his study documents the development of the "sense of parliament as a *notional forum*, a place or site for the representation of conflict and colloquy and a fitting form for the tensions and debates of the day," as well as a discourse for exploring the process of representation, both legal and aesthetic (Giancarlo 2007, 14). The negotiations of textual and cultural authority that we can see in the relationship between margins and centers in late medieval manuscripts have parallels in the negotiations of authority that took place in parliamentary practices and discourses in England during the late Middle Ages. As these models for the complex relationship between margins and centers suggest, studies of medieval manuscripts become most fruitful when we read their components in terms of dialogue, both within the individual codex and within the culture that produced and consumed these texts.

The multidimensional relationship of the margin and the center provides the framework for my study of the Yale Law School manuscript of the *Nova statuta Angliae*. This manuscript presents the Statutes of the Realm enacted during the reigns of six kings, beginning in 1327 and ending in 1468, with a later addition of statutes from 1482 to 1484. In addition to the *Nova statuta*, the manuscript contains a copy of the *Modus tenendi Parliamentum*, the *Tractatus de senescalsia Angliae*, and an alphabetical index to the statutes. This copy of the *Nova statuta* also includes visual images of six kings during whose reigns the statutes presented in the manuscript were passed, but these images differ from the illustrations found in other manuscripts of this text. In the following chapters, I suggest that work on the original parts of the manuscript began by 1460 and ended in 1471, a period of great crisis in English history as a result of the conflict between the Lancastrian and Yorkist parties over rights to the English throne.[6] My analysis of this legal manuscript reads it as a document shaped by the debates between these two political factions, both in Parliament and through texts in diverse genres and media, including royal portraits, legal records, philosophical treatises, allegorical narratives, devotional texts, and civic pageants. Antonia Gransden argues, "Because of the insecurity of their dynasties, both Lancastrians and Yorkists used all known means to rally popular support, particularly that of the expanding middle classes. The spread of literacy made written propaganda more effective than ever before" (Gransden 1996, 251). Other scholars who study fifteenth-century English history and literature have noted that concerns about defining true kingship appear directly expressed or indirectly reflected in many different kinds of visual and verbal texts during this time. Anne Clark Bartlett considers fifteenth-century England "notorious" for the large number of texts produced during this time in the genre of "the literature of statecraft," or guides for kings and princes (Bartlett 2005, 53). Along with the ideal models of kingship depicted, however, we find anxieties and tensions stemming from the deposition of Richard II by the first Lancastrian king, Henry IV, in 1399. Scholars have now identified a wide range of texts from the fifteenth century in which the legitimacy of the Lancastrian line of kings remains an issue.[7] Simon Walker has shown how different depictions of Richard II were put to political use in the seventy years after his deposition and death, and Ralph Griffiths has noted the large number of texts offering divergent views of Henry VI that appeared both during his long reign and after his deposition in 1461 and death in 1471.[8] Maura Nolan has analyzed John Lydgate's poems during the time of Henry VI's minority in relationship to the Lancastrian campaign to assert the young king's sovereignty, and Anthony Gross has shown how treatises on legal issues from the middle of the fifteenth century also comment on challenges to Lancastrian rule (Nolan 2005, Gross 1996).[9] Nevertheless, the Lancastrians and Yorkists were not the first English political parties to debate ideals of kingship and justice through literature and the visual arts. Art historians have shown how earlier English monarchs and their supporters used the visual arts to suggest positive readings of royal power when threats to that power emerged.[10] In the chapters that follow, both the debates about Henry VI's kingship and the medieval traditions of representing kings and queens in the arts will provide interpretive frames for my analysis of the images and narratives of royal power in the Yale Law School manuscript of the *New Statutes of England*.

Lancastrian and Yorkist discourses are just some of the competing discourses at play in the Yale Law School *Nova statuta*. Others involve linguistic, social, generic, iconographic, and gender differences. Both the number of discourses inscribed in this manuscript and their fluid relationships suggest that the manuscript required its readers to possess a complex form of literacy. Not only did they need knowledge of French and Latin to make full use of the manuscript, but they needed the ability to read the different parts of the manuscript in relationship to each other and in relationship to visual and verbal texts outside the manuscript. For example, while the decoration and illustration found in the Yale Law School manuscript might seem entirely marginal to the meaning of the verbal texts, we will see that this manuscript intertwines its visual and verbal texts by using historiated initials. Historiated initials contain pictures, so these large letters, which appear at the beginning of major portions of the statutes text, participate in both the verbal and visual texts of the manuscript. The historiated initials serve as liminal spaces between different genres, as well as forms of representation, for constructions of kingship, grace, and justice. By echoing iconography strongly associated with King David, five of the six historiated initials present the kings of England as successfully fulfilling the primary medieval model of good kingship and suggest that the one king who is depicted differently has departed from that model. In addition, these five visual depictions of kings suggest that true justice derives from the king's relationship with God, rather than the king's relationship with his subjects. By extension, the allusion to King David in five of the royal portraits also brings the statutes text into dialogue with the statements about justice and kingship in the Book of Psalms, attributed to King David.

The border decoration in the Yale Law School manuscript contributes another layer of iconographic associations to the central text. The marginal decoration contains coats of arms that represent people who are discussed within the verbal texts, so that the visual texts of the margins mirror the verbal texts of the statutes, echoing but also reversing the images of power within the statutes by highlighting the roles of women. The woman inscribed into the text by the manuscript's original marginal decoration is Henry VI's queen, Margaret of Anjou, whose role in England's legal, political, and military battles of the mid-fifteenth century continues to be debated by historians.[11] Though Margaret's official power as queen was marginal, she used an array of legal tools, including petitions to Parliament, to pursue her goals, especially after her husband's illness gave his opponents greater opportunity to appropriate royal authority for their own purposes. She also used the discourses of visual images and public ceremonies to support the view that Henry VI and his son Prince Edward of Lancaster embodied the grace and justice needed for England's peace and prosperity. While the negative readings of Margaret's actions have often received more prominence in historical commentary, the Yale Law School manuscript serves to remind readers that Margaret also had strong support for her attempts to defend the rights of her incapacitated husband and young son. In addition, the presence of Margaret's arms on the leaf that opens the text of the *Nova statuta Angliae* in this manuscript serves to highlight for readers the role of an earlier English queen in helping to resolve the conflict between an ineffective king and his subjects. The statutes text opens with an account of how Edward III came to the throne after his father, Edward II, had been corrupted by false advisors, and the passage comments positively on the actions of Edward III's mother, Isabelle of France, including taking her son with her to France and returning with an army to help him restore justice to the realm (fol. 55r–v).[12] With the presence of Margaret's arms on the opening leaf, the manuscript's early readers would have been more likely to recognize that Edward II's queen, Isabelle of France, had been instrumental in preparing her son to become a king who would provide just leadership for his people – the king whose laws became the starting point for a new narrative in English legal history, the *New Statutes of England*. At the same time, with Margaret's arms inscribed on this leaf in visual parallel with the royal arms of England (as established by Edward III), readers would have been encouraged to recognize the parallel between the crisis the English monarchy faced in the 1320s and the crisis it faced in the 1450s – and the potential model for a solution to the later crisis that this parallel reveals. The tension that arises between the manuscript's positive depiction of Henry VI and the recognition that England might again profit from replacement of an ineffective king by his better prepared son sets the Yale manuscript in parallel with other Lancastrian texts that are characterized by ambivalence and instability.

The inscription of Margaret's arms also highlights the role of grace in the statutes text, since medieval queens were often depicted as representatives of divine grace, both as providers of heirs to maintain royal lines and as intercessors for others with representatives of royal justice. As we will see, contemporary evidence verifies Margaret's association with grace in England's public discourse, so that the presence of her arms in the manuscript's border decoration encourages readers to become more aware of the roles that grace plays in the statutes text. The fact that a medieval writer has twice added "Grace be our guide" in Middle English in the manuscript's margins indicates that at least one early reader recognized the importance of grace in the manuscript's constructions of justice and royal authority. At the same time, the inscriptions witness to the role of individual perspective in defining concepts such as grace. "Grace be our guide" suggests that readers of the manuscript and those participating in crafting England's laws could share a unified vision and purpose; yet the central text of the statutes reveals the many kinds of difference that require negotiation in establishing justice for the nation. The marginal references to grace in the manuscript serve to raise questions about how we read the references to grace in the central text. Through its construction of multiple frames for the text of the statutes, therefore, the Yale Law School manuscript reveals how the *Nova statuta* could be read, not only as a legal reference work, but also as a narrative of English history and as a "parliament" giving voice to differing views of kingship, queenship, justice, and grace at play in fifteenth-century English culture.

The Yale Law School *Nova statuta* offers an excellent example of the ways in which a medieval manuscript could encourage reading across discourses by interweaving different languages within its texts, as well as genres of verbal text with genres of visual text. The interplay of competing discourses in the manuscript reflects the different cultural forces shaping the reading of law in England during this time. Judgment about which linguistic discourses were marginal and which central was still in flux in England during the fifteenth century, varying from genre to genre and even from copy to copy of the same text. The most prolific English court poet at the turn of the century, John Gower (ca. 1330–1408), composed in Latin, French, and English. Although in the first half of the fifteenth century literature in English received considerably more court patronage than it had in the past, the nobility continued to read many kinds of texts in French and Latin: for example, in the late 1460s Sir John Fortescue wrote his treatise on English law for Henry VI's son in Latin, while in 1471 Edward IV received a gift copy of Jean de Waurin's history of England written in French.[13] There was also not yet consensus on the language of English law in the fifteenth century. Latin remained the primary language of legal record; but French had replaced Latin for parliamentary records and courtroom pleading in the fourteenth century, and English was newly authorized as a legal discourse.[14] In 1362, Parliament passed the Statute of Pleading, which designated English as the language for conducting all courtroom proceedings, though this was not enforced and the records were still usually kept in Latin. Petitions presented in Parliament in English begin to be included in the official record in English in the 1380s, and the records sometimes indicate that Parliament conducted its proceedings in English; yet the statutes continued to circulate primarily in Latin and French until the end of the fifteenth century. Of the surviving manuscripts of the *Nova statuta Angliae*, the overwhelming majority present the statutes in French, with rubrics in Latin; yet a few manuscripts present the statutes in English or in a combination of French, Latin, and English.[15] The Yale Law School manuscript presents the statutes in French, but surrounds the French text with a frame of Latin rubrics indicating the beginning and ending of each monarch's reign, the date and place of each session of Parliament, and the beginning of each statute passed in that session. The manuscript also prefaces the collection of statutes with two Latin treatises that construct another frame for interpreting the statutes that follow: *Modus tenendi Parliamentum* (*The Method of Holding Parliament*) and *Tractatus de senescalsia Angliae* (*Treatise on the Seneschal of England*). Later owners have also added marginal texts in Latin and in English, creating other social as well as linguistic frames: some marginal inscriptions offer comments on the text of the statutes and treatises, while others document the role of the manuscript as a gift. Each linguistic frame suggests different perspectives from which the laws of the land might be read.

In terms of modern assessments of the literatures of fifteenth-century England, a text like the *Nova statuta Angliae* might seem quite marginal; yet, in terms of readership, this work became more culturally central than other medieval legal texts. Copies of the *Nova statuta* began to circulate in the fourteenth century among members of the nobility, as well as among members of the legal profession; and, in the second half of the fifteenth century, ownership of highly decorated statutes manuscripts spread more widely among wealthy

English readers, including those who owned luxury copies of texts in courtly and religious genres.[16] As a result, the *Nova statuta* text entered into a wider reading context than most other medieval legal texts, and this context must be considered if we are to understand the text's potential significance for its audience. Scholars have demonstrated that medieval literary, legal, and political genres were less clearly demarcated than modern readers might assume. David Lawton has famously argued, "There is little theoretical room in the fifteenth century . . . for a distinction between literature, society and history. Fifteenth-century English writing is, for want of a better word, a culture. It is in that light that we should examine its paradigms of public discourse" (Lawton 1987, 771). For her part, Emily Steiner has shown how English literature in the fourteenth and fifteenth centuries shared discourses with legal documents, offering opportunities for exploring the interrelationship of language, identity, and authority. She argues that "documentary culture was shaped, in part, by the formal, ethical, spiritual, and political aspirations of late medieval English writers," and in turn "documentary culture helped shape an identity for English literature: the work it performs, the stories it tells, and the authority that it claims for itself" (Steiner 2003, 10). Not only did many English literary works in the fourteenth and fifteenth centuries borrow the discourses of parliaments, charters, lawsuits, petitions, and wills, but the authors of legal documents in the same period used literary techniques to suggest the justice and authority of their statements and to imply alliances and precedents that might otherwise have been questioned. A clear example can be found in Henry IV's writ to Parliament (dated 26 February 1401) authorizing the burning of heretics: in this document, he refers to himself as a *cultor* of the Catholic faith, which means a cultivator of soil or crops (like Langland's allegorical hero, Piers Plowman), as well as someone who supports a cause or worships as a member of a cult.[17] By using this term in the process of seeking Parliament's support for a radical change in the administration of justice for his subjects, Henry IV suggests an alliance between the king and his lowliest subjects, as well as more highly ranked supporters of the Roman Catholic Church, united together with the clergy to fight heresy.

In my view, the frames in which the Yale Law School manuscript sets the *New Statutes of England* encourage a reading of the text as a form of the "mirror for princes" – the *speculum regis* or *Fürstenspiegel*. Medieval texts offering advice to rulers took a wide variety of generic forms during the late Middle Ages, including treatises, chronicles, romance narratives, lyric poetry, and allegory.[18] Many of the texts in this tradition (such as John of Salisbury's

Policraticus, De regimine principum by Giles of Rome, Dante's *De monarchia,*
Christine de Pizan's *Livre des fais d'armes et de chevalerie,* and Hoccleve's *Regement of Princes*) present their advice explicitly; yet other texts offer their advice
to rulers more implicitly, through accounts of kings or princes whose conduct
is successful or not, or through commentaries on moral principles that relate
to the uses of political or military power. In England in the fourteenth and
fifteenth centuries, as scholars such as Judith Ferster, Nicholas Perkins, and
Maura Nolan have argued, works treating models of kingship created textual
spaces for both reflecting the image monarchs wished to project and exploring
the tension between royal authority and the power of other groups in society
(Ferster 1996, Perkins 2001, Nolan 2005).[19] Like the Yale Law School manuscript, many of the fifteenth-century English texts that address ideals of kingship transform older genres of literature into forms of political discourse – a
process Nuttall describes as "politicizing pre-existing languages."[20] We will
see, for example, how a book of hours (London, British Library MS Cotton
Domitian A xvii) given to Henry VI in his boyhood interweaves religious and
political discourses to become a mirror for princes that addresses concerns
about his leadership. With the birth of Henry VI's son, Edward of Lancaster,
in 1453, a new round of texts arose for educating the young prince; but the
Yorkist attempts to restrict Henry VI's power during these same years made
the new discussions of good kingship a commentary on the prince's father
as well. If we read the Yale Law School *Nova statuta* against Fortescue's *De
laudibus legum Angliae,* for example, we can see that their constructions of
English kings and English laws run parallel. Another of the interesting parallels between these texts is the role given to Queen Margaret: unexpected as
this might be in a mirror for princes, it supports the analysis of Anne Clark
Bartlett, who argues that, although female readers have rarely been seen as
important audiences for advice to rulers, records of book ownership and patronage indicate that women owned, commissioned, and bequeathed guides
for the education of princes, which circulated widely in various redactions,
adaptations, and translations during the Middle Ages (Bartlett 2005, 53). As
we will see, Margaret of Anjou fits Bartlett's profile in several ways.

The following study reads the Yale Law School *New Statutes* manuscript
both as a record of English law and as a text presenting ideals of kingship,
queenship, justice, and grace. To some readers, it may appear that the ornate
manuscripts of the *Nova statuta Angliae* are not significant to the history of
English law. J. H. Baker has argued that these books "were hardly working
copies. They may be considered rather as status symbols, and were doubtless

marketed as such" (Baker 1999, 422). Anthony Musson also argues, "The size and intricate ornamental design of some statute books signifies that they were what we would term 'coffee-table' books or the medieval equivalent of a set of the *Encylopaedia Britannica* – mainly there for show and only occasional[ly] referred to"; yet he goes on to suggest that "such volumes were probably viewed as possessing an inherent (perhaps even sacred) authority that was passed on and shared by the book's owner" (Musson 2001, 22). Certainly, illustrated copies of the *New Statutes of England* like the Yale Law School manuscript were not originally made only as legal reference works, and they never held the status of official records, like the statute rolls. These manuscripts do need to be read in comparison with ornate manuscript copies of other texts produced and consumed in England during this period – sometimes by the same artisans or for the same patrons. Yet the ornamentation of these copies of the *New Statutes* does not mean that their "work" was limited to marking social status. Indeed, decoration and illustration did not disqualify documents from having legal authority in the fifteenth century, as we will see from the royal charters and the records of the King's Bench during this time. Several aspects of the Yale Law School *Nova statuta* indicate that the manuscript was meant to be consulted for information about specific English laws and was indeed so consulted; yet, as we shall see, other aspects of the manuscript suggest that it could also be read as a narrative of English history and a commentary on royal justice and grace.

Exploring the multiple discourses of the Yale Law School *New Statutes* manuscript requires several methods of reading this codex. Chapter 1 discusses the physical aspects of the manuscript (presented in detail in appendix 2) and their significance as evidence about the manuscript's original production. This chapter examines the Yale Law School manuscript's links to at least ten other copies of the text, as well as the unique qualities that set the Yale Law School manuscript apart from other copies of the *New Statutes*. The chapter also discusses the different forms in which fifteenth-century English readers had access to the Statutes of the Realm, the increased numbers of highly ornate manuscript copies of the *New Statutes of England* made during the second half of the fifteenth century, and the widening range of readers associated with them.

Chapter 2 examines the royal portraits and coats of arms in the *Nova statuta* portion of the manuscript as an iconographic frame for the statutes recorded in the text – a frame that works to support Lancastrian claims of legitimacy and undermine the arguments of the Yorkist party against Henry VI and his son, Edward of Lancaster. After exploring the role played by the coats of arms in the border decoration, the chapter discusses the iconography of the manuscript's royal portraits in relationship to the iconography in other statutes manuscripts, in other royal portraits in England and France during the fifteenth century, and in devotional manuscripts. The chapter shows how the portraits construct a narrative of English kingship and royal justice that challenges the narrative suggested by the statutes themselves, revealing anxiety about royal authority at the same time that they defend it.

Chapter 3 discusses the relationship between the Yale Law School manuscript of the *New Statutes* and Margaret of Anjou's efforts to defend the legitimacy of her husband's and son's claims on the English throne through legal and artistic means. Records indicate that Margaret played a significant role in the production of literary, religious, and legal texts in the late 1440s and the 1450s (as either audience or commissioner), even before her husband's illness led her to become an active agent in protecting the interests of her young son, Edward of Lancaster. This chapter discusses important parallels between the iconography of the Yale *Nova statuta* manuscript and that found in texts associated with Margaret or with her family in France, who were among the leading secular patrons of French manuscript production in the fourteenth and fifteenth centuries. The crisis of her husband's incapacity may have led Margaret to recognize similar crises in English and French history, in which queens took active roles in renegotiating royal power for their husbands or sons, including the replacement of Edward II by Edward III. Margaret's personal history suggests that she understood the value of books as cultural symbols and potential weapons for defending her husband and son. The chapter also explores Margaret's knowledge of earlier books for princes that transform works in other genres into books of instruction on kingship.

Chapter 4 examines the relationship of the Yale *Nova statuta* manuscript to the Lancastrian literature on kingship and law that appeared in the late 1450s and 1460s. Several Lancastrian authors produced texts in the tradition of the mirror for princes that present themselves as instruction for Prince Edward, but also serve to defend his father from Yorkist attacks. Works by the most prominent of these authors, George Ashby and John Fortescue, who served as tutors to Prince Edward, have close links with the imagery of the Yale Law School manuscript. In particular, evidence from Fortescue's *De laudibus legum Angliae* strongly supports the idea that the Yale Law School manuscript is the copy of the *New Statutes* made for the prince. In addition, the royal portraits first added to the *Coram rege* Rolls of the King's Bench under Fortescue's supervision offer another parallel to the themes expressed in the royal portraits of the Yale Law School manuscript.

Chapter 5 examines the history of the manuscript's survival after the defeat of the Lancastrian forces in 1471 and its evolving significance as a cultural artifact, as well as legal resource. After its initial production ceased, the manuscript was expanded with statutes for the years 1482–83 in another hand and style. More importantly, it passed into the hands of readers who preserved it, despite elements that made its possession potentially dangerous until Henry VII restored the honor of his deposed predecessor. The inscriptions added to the manuscript provide information about how the manuscript was read, as well as who read it. In particular, the Middle English inscriptions of "Grace be our guide" allow us to explore how later readers interacted with the manuscript's presentation of royal power and justice. This chapter traces the manuscript's circulation among several prominent owners who were trained in law and served in the English government, as well as among women who seem to have had unusually high levels of education and independence. Though printed copies of the statutes became available by the late fifteenth century, the Yale Law School manuscript continued to be valued as a legal resource, visual work of art, and history book, as well as a personal gift, for generations, until it entered the antiquities market.

Paul Strohm's comment on the relationship of the margins and centers of medieval verbal texts applies in the study of the Yale Law School manuscript as well: the "historical meaning [of a text] lies not at its heart but at its edges and unacknowledged affiliations" (Strohm 1998, 214). Playing multiple roles as a gift, political statement, legal resource, artistic artifact, and historical evidence, the Yale Law School *New Statutes of England* offers an opportunity for readers in the twenty-first century to discover how the margins of one medieval manuscript help to construct discourses of royal justice and grace that both responded to a particular historical moment and continue to resonate over time.

ONE

The Yale *New Statutes* Manuscript and Medieval English Statute Books

SIMILARITIES AND DIFFERENCES

The Yale Law School manuscript of the *Nova statuta Angliae* (Goldman Library MS MssG +StII no.1) contains almost four hundred leaves, so it offers many margins and centers for readers to explore. Modern readers coming to a manuscript copy of a medieval text discover the complexity and the potential to empower that the reading process offered in earlier times: letter forms and abbreviations in handmade books could be ambiguous, words might be rearranged or missing, and authorship could be uncertain; but medieval readers could select what texts, decoration, and illustrations were put into new manuscript books, and medieval readers often added to or removed texts or images from their books over time. Examining the layout and content of the text and decoration in a medieval manuscript, as well as the structure of the manuscript as a whole and the relationship of its components to other manuscripts, can help modern readers understand when, where, and for whom a medieval manuscript was made, as well as the process by which the texts within the manuscript were read. As Malcolm Parkes and Ian Doyle have argued, "Layout and decoration [in a medieval manuscript] function like punctuation: they are part of the presentation of a text which facilitates its use by a reader" (Parkes and Doyle 1978, 169). In this chapter, we will examine what evidence the Yale *Nova statuta* manuscript offers about when and where it was made, who made it, and how the parts of the manuscript construct several frames for its presentation of English law.[1] We will also consider its relationship with developments in the history of medieval English statutes manuscripts. In the process, we will begin to see how the Yale manuscript transforms the *New Statutes of England* into a Lancastrian mirror for princes.

There has been little consensus among scholars about the origins, contents, or significance of the Yale manuscript of the *New Statutes of England*. In 1975, noting the manuscript's luxurious decoration and the appearance of Margaret of Anjou's coat of arms in the border decoration, art historian Jane Hayward argued that the book was a wedding gift from Henry VI to Margaret in 1445 (Hayward 1975, 142). Hayward suggested that the statutes in the codex from the Parliaments after 1444–45 are additions that Margaret herself commissioned before she returned to France as a widow in 1476. Since Hayward published her comments, other scholars have offered alternative interpretations of the manuscript's origins and significance. In 1978, art historians Walter Cahn and James Marrow dated the early parts of the manuscript to around 1460, fifteen years after Margaret's marriage to Henry (Cahn and Marrow 1978, 240–41). As we will see, this dating of the manuscript fits the evidence much better than Hayward's estimate. Though noting the appearance of Henry's and Margaret's arms, Cahn and Marrow did not link the presence of these arms with any royal commission or ownership of the manuscript. Cahn and Marrow also parted from Hayward in arguing that the manuscript's series of historiated initials is similar to illustrations in other English statute books. While Cahn and Marrow revealed some of the links between the Yale *Nova statuta* and other copies of the text, their description masked important distinguishing features of the Yale manuscript, as well as possible connections between this manuscript's illustrations and other medieval iconographic traditions.

Differing statements about the manuscript's dating and illustrations have continued to appear. In his catalogue of English legal manuscripts in the United States, legal historian John Hamilton Baker dated the core of the Yale *Nova statuta* to the 1450s, with later additions to 1484, and gave a full account of the manuscript's post-medieval provenance; but he erroneously described this copy of the *Nova statuta* as containing six miniatures of kings in Parliament (Baker 1985, 73–74). The most extensive work on this manuscript thus far, however, has been by art historian Kathleen Scott. Over the course of several publications, she has pointed out associations between the Yale *Nova statuta* manuscript and other English manuscripts from the second half of the fifteenth century, including a group of *Nova statuta* manuscripts that follow a standardized layout for illustration and decoration.[2] Scott's work, along with that of paleographers Malcolm Parkes, Jeremy Griffiths, and Pamela Robinson, suggests that one of the scribes and two of the artists who made the Yale manuscript of the *New Statutes* also worked on at least eleven other copies of this text. Scholars have now christened this scribe the "*Nova statuta* scribe."[3] Research by Jeremy Griffiths locates this scribe's work in several more manuscripts of the *New Statutes* and suggests that this scribe may have played a role in organizing production of copies of this text (J. Griffiths 1980).[4] Recognizing the similarities between the Yale manuscript and these other copies of the *New Statutes* helps to demonstrate what elements of the Yale manuscript are conventions of fifteenth-century statutes manuscripts. Nevertheless, it is precisely because the Yale Law School manuscript was made by these same scribes and artists that its differences from the other copies of the *Nova statuta* are significant, for these differences provide clues about the purpose for which this particular codex was made.

The Yale manuscript of the *New Statutes of England* is part of a complex and politically charged proliferation of legal information that took place in England in the fourteenth and fifteenth centuries. Based on the number of surviving manuscripts, scholars have determined that this period saw a significant increase of interest in owning copies of the Statutes of the Realm: more than four hundred manuscript copies of English statutes survive from the period between the end of the thirteenth century and the end of the fifteenth, when the statutes begin to appear in print (Skemer 1999, 113). The largest number of statutes manuscripts come from the second and third quarters of the fifteenth century: of the 125 surviving manuscripts of the *New Statutes*, thirty-three come from the 1430s and 1440s, yet Don Skemer argues that the third quarter of the fifteenth century probably saw even greater numbers of statutes manuscripts produced (Skemer 1999, 129–30). The expansion in the market for statute books was probably partly due to growth in the legal profession during this period. Nevertheless, Skemer presents the fifteenth-century proliferation of statutes manuscripts as fueled to a large degree by desire for education on the part of persons without professional legal training, such as land holders, who sought to learn about the laws through private reading. Skemer also recognizes a political dimension to the widening interest in knowledge about England's statutes, especially during the mid-fifteenth century: "Faced with a weak central government during the long minority and chaotic reign of Henry VI, and by the widespread lawlessness and the dynastic struggles of Lancaster and York, members of the landed gentry like the Paston family defended its property interests by every means available, including legal knowledge gained from school and from reading statute books" (Skemer 1999, 128–29). As we will see, political concerns other than protecting property rights may also have shaped the use of statute books during the fourteenth and fifteenth centuries.

The wider transmission of statutes texts brought changes in the content and format, as well as the ownership, of the books that recorded English statutes. None of these manuscripts has the same content or form as the official records of English statutes: the Great Roll of the Statutes, which was kept in the Tower of London, and the Rolls of Parliament.[5] Yet production of the statute books required access to the official records for fair copies to be used as models, as well as verification of individual copies by scribes: for example, Neil Ker found six statutes manuscripts from between 1330 and 1450 with scribal notes about statutes having been checked against the official rolls (Ker 1969–2002, 1:41–42, 127–28, 157, and 3:263–67, 519–20, and 660–65).[6] The need for access to official documents and the evidence in the manuscripts themselves both suggest that production of statutes manuscripts was centered in the London area and most likely involved scribes who had training in legal records (Scott 1980a, 48–58; Skemer 1999, 115–22).[7] The earliest collections, the *Old Statutes of England* (the *Statuta Angliae, Vetera statuta*, or *Statuta antiqua*), were a selection of important statutes from prior to the reign of Edward III, rather than an inclusive or chronological collection. The *Statuta antiqua* almost always begin with the *Magna carta* and almost always present the statutes in Latin. In the fourteenth century, however, changes took place in the form and content of statute collections that suggest a transformation in the purposes of statute books and interest in the statutory process itself. Beginning with the reign of Edward III (1327–77), statute books were produced that contain all of the statutes for each of a king's Parliament sessions, organized chronologically and recorded in Law French. The use of French for these statutes certainly made them accessible to a wider audience than the earlier Latin statutes, and inclusion of all of the statutes made the collection useful for a wider range of English society: each reader could decide for himself or herself which statutes were more or less important, according to personal concerns. The *New Statutes* were less of a collection and more of a continuous text; yet it was a text that continued to grow, with leaves often left blank at the end of the codex for addition of new statutes as time went on. In several senses, then, the *New Statutes of England* was a much more "open" text than the earlier statutes books had been.

Given the larger amount of text in the *New Statutes*, greater numbers of organizational tools were used in the *New Statutes* manuscripts – including initials of several different sizes and colors, scripts of different size and formality, and notations of kings, regnal years, and statute numbers in the margins – in order to facilitate reading and locating information. Additional reading aids were also developed, such as chronological lists of statutes and then alphabetical indexes of subjects covered in the statutes. During this time, new copies of the older statutes also began to present the laws in chronological order, with a table of contents and headings that indicated the king and regnal year associated with each law, and some manuscripts contain both the Latin *Statuta antiqua* and French *Nova statuta*. With the chronological and inclusive format of the *New Statutes of England*, the statutes can be read sequentially, like a history book, or read for statutes of a particular Parliament or on a particular topic, like a reference work. Reader interest in the parliamentary process itself may have led to the inclusion of additional texts in some manuscripts of the *New Statutes*. One of these is the Latin treatise *Modus tenendi Parliamentum (The Method of Holding Parliament)*, a fourteenth-century text that Matthew Giancarlo has discussed as a mythologizing account of the origins and procedures of Parliament (Giancarlo 2007, 2).[8] This anonymous treatise offers the earliest known discussion of Parliament as a part of English government, and scholars continue to debate the date and purpose of its composition.[9] The *Modus* is divided into sections that discuss such topics as the process by which the king calls Parliament into session, who among the clergy and laity should be summoned to a session of Parliament, who should keep the records of the session, what the order of business should be, and how decisions should be made about difficult problems. The discussion of the role of the high steward or seneschal in the *Modus tenendi Parliamentum* links it to a second Latin treatise that sometimes also appears in manuscripts of the *New Statutes* after the *Modus: De senescalsia Angliae (On the Seneschal of England)*.[10] The origins of this text are also somewhat obscure: Claire Valente argues that Thomas, Earl of Lancaster, had the treatise drawn up in order to justify his use of military power against the favorites of Edward II in 1321 (Valente 2003, 128, 137). Other scholars have associated this treatise with Lancastrian sympathizers in the later fourteenth and fifteenth centuries, since the tract supports the claim that, after the king, the seneschal has the power and responsibility to maintain justice in the realm of England, including presiding over trials in the

House of Lords (J. Taylor 1987, 314–16; and Weber 1998, 160). If the treatise on the seneschal was perceived to stem from the problems that led to Edward II's loss of the throne and his replacement by his son Edward III, medieval readers may have found it an appropriate preface for the opening of the *New Statutes*, which begin with the statutes of Edward III after a preamble that accounts for the king's replacement of his father. Both treatises appear in the Yale manuscript (fols. 2r–8v).

The wider audience for statutes books in the fourteenth and fifteenth centuries is also reflected in the wide range of workmanship and decoration in these manuscripts, both of which reflect a range of expenditure on the part of the owner. Copies of both the *Old Statutes* and *New Statutes* in the fourteenth and fifteenth centuries appear in smaller and less decorated forms, as well as larger and luxuriously decorated forms.[11] The Yale manuscript of the *New Statutes*, with its gold leaf, painted initials, images of kings, and decorated borders, falls into the latter category (plates 1–24). The smaller and simpler copies were probably made for professionals who needed information about the content of the statutes and perhaps could not afford expensive decoration. Some of the simple copies of the *Nova statuta* contain only a pen-drawn initial to open each king's reign: examples include New York, Columbia University Rare Book and Manuscript Library Plimpton MS 273 (plate 25); London, Inner Temple Library MS Petyt 505; and Oslo and London, Martin Schøyen Collection MS 1355.[12] Though the simpler format is more common among earlier copies of the *Nova statuta*, this format remained an option during the middle of the fifteenth century: for example, Schøyen MS 1355 contains the statutes through 23 Henry VI (1444–45) and Inner Temple Library MS Petyt 505 contains the statutes through 29 Henry VI (1450–51). Some of the less decorated copies of the *Nova statuta* use a large initial in paint and gold leaf, as well as border decoration, to mark only one king's reign, most often that of the first monarch, but sometimes the monarch reigning when the manuscript was made: for example, London, British Library MS Lansdowne 468 has a large painted initial and border for the opening of the statutes of Edward III and only pen-drawn initials for subsequent reigns, while London, British Library MS Additional 81292 uses a painted initial and border decoration for the opening of statutes passed under Henry VI, but uses only pen-drawn initials for the reigns of the other kings.[13] Some of the more elaborately decorated copies of the statutes have a large decorated initial in paint and gold leaf and border decoration for the beginning of each new king's reign, but no historiated initials: examples include Philadelphia,

Free Library MS Carson LC 14. 10 (plate 26); London, British Library MS Lansdowne 470; Kew, National Archives MS E 164/10; and Cambridge (MA), Harvard Law School Library MSS 10, 29–30, 42, and 163.[14] Use of these large illuminated, but not historiated, initials continued even after copies of the *Nova statuta* with historiated initials began to become more widespread: for example, Carson LC 14. 10 contains the statutes through 3 Henry VII (1487–88). It seems clear, therefore, that levels of luxury in presentation of text and in decoration in *Nova statuta* manuscripts were adjusted throughout the fourteenth and fifteenth centuries to suit the desires or circumstances of the person commissioning the copy.

The most elaborately decorated statutes manuscripts usually include illustrations in the form of historiated initials, and the image that appears most often in these initials is an image of a king. In the second half of the fourteenth century, we begin to find manuscripts of the *Nova statuta* that include initials with images of kings: London, British Library MS Arundel 331, which contains the statutes from 1 Edward III to 15 Richard II (1391–92) and is thought to date from shortly thereafter, uses an initial depicting an enthroned king for the opening of the reign of Edward III (plate 27).[15] This use of a single image of a king at the opening of the statutes parallels several manuscript copies of the *Vetera statuta*, including Philadelphia, Free Library MS Carson LC 14. 20.5 and Cambridge (MA), Harvard Law School Library MSS 58 and 177.[16] At about the same time in the late fourteenth century, copies of the *Nova statuta* were made with an historiated initial for the beginning of each king's reign. This is the case, for example, in Cambridge (UK), St. John's College Library MS A. 7, a manuscript combining the *Vetera statuta* and the *Nova statuta* up through 12 Richard II (1388–89): this manuscript signals its production during the reign of Richard II by portraying Richard in the act of receiving a book, presumably the statutes (plate 28).[17] San Marino, Huntington Library MS HM 19920, another manuscript that combines the *Vetera statuta* and the *Nova statuta* through 8 Henry IV (1406–1407), originally contained one historiated initial depicting a king at the opening of the old statutes and then historiated initials depicting each of the kings during the new statutes (plate 29).[18] Several mid-fifteenth-century *New Statutes* manuscripts, such as London, British Library MS Stowe 389 (plate 30) and Cambridge (MA), Harvard Law School Library MS 21, continue to use historiated initials showing the king seated and alone.[19] Other fifteenth-century copies use historiated initials that present images of the king in different poses and settings: for example, the initials in London, Lincoln's Inn Library MS

Hale 194 (plate 31) show the king enthroned under a canopy and discussing a written document (presumably the statutes) with a small group of robed officials, while the initials in London, British Library MS Yates Thompson 48 show each king standing alone and holding scepter and orb (plate 32).[20] The initials in London, British Library MS Harley 5233 show either the king from the waist up or just the king's head.[21]

During the 1470s, as Kathleen Scott has shown, some manuscripts of the *New Statutes of England* began to use historiated initials that all depict the king in the same format, enthroned at center under a canopy, facing forward and flanked by groups of advisors, as if in court or at a session of Parliament. The historiated initial for the statutes of Edward IV in the Yale manuscript is similar to this model (plate 6); but the first five historiated initials in the Yale manuscript are not, since they depict the king at prayer (plates 1–5). Some manuscripts of the *New Statutes of England* feature this type of standardized depiction of the king in most or all of their historiated initials: these include Philadelphia, Free Library MS Carson LC 14. 9.5 (plate 33); Kew, National Archives MS E 164/11 (plate 34); Holkham, Holkham Hall, Library of the Earl of Leicester MS 232; London, British Library MS Cotton Nero C i; and London, British Library MS Hargrave 274 (plate 35).[22] However, like the Yale manuscript, some copies move from another format to the standardized format with the reign of Edward IV, whose first statutes became available for copying shortly after 1468. For example, Oxford, Bodleian Library MS Hatton 10 uses the standardized scene only for the last two of its eight historiated initials, and its first six initials feature each monarch's badge animal instead.[23] Cambridge (MA), Houghton Library MS Richardson 40 and Oxford, St. John's College MS 257 (plate 36) have the standardized scene only for the initial that opens the statutes of Edward IV.[24]

Despite the increasing standardization of the illustration of *New Statutes* manuscripts, some copies of this text have initials that do not depict kings at all. One example is the *New Statutes* manuscript made for Sir Thomas Fitzwilliam of Mablethorpe, Lincolnshire, a lawyer who became recorder of the City of London: each of the six large initials that mark the opening of the royal reigns contains the arms of the Fitzwilliam family impaled with those of a family with whom the Fitzwilliam men married, so that the series as a whole records the marriages of six generations of Fitzwilliam men ending with that of Sir Thomas himself.[25] Likewise, the *New Statutes* manuscript made for Sir Gregory Adgore (London, Lincoln's Inn Library MS Hale 71) uses his arms inside the initials that begin each royal reign.[26] Some of these non-standardized illustrations may predate the spread of the standardized images of kings found in many *New Statutes* manuscripts. Although Sir Thomas Fitzwilliam died in 1497, Alfred Higgins argues, on the basis of its contents, that the *Nova statuta* manuscript with the Fitzwilliam family arms may have been made for Sir Thomas when he became a justice of the peace for Lincolnshire in 1460–61 (Higgins 1900–1901, 5). Nevertheless, the date of production alone does not explain the replacement of images of kings and royal arms with an alternative form of illustration. Such deviation from conventions of illustration can also occur through the influence of patrons.[27] In the Fitzwilliam and Adgore manuscripts, it seems as if the patron chose to replace the traditional images of kings with his family arms, as if to read the history of English statutes in parallel with his family's history. Higgins argues that the Fitzwilliam manuscript uses the coats of arms to celebrate the Mablethorpe branch of the Fitzwilliam family, which began during the reign of Edward II and rose to greater prominence in successive generations through marriage and through service in government roles: in addition to serving as justice of the peace for Lincolnshire and recorder of the City of London, Sir Thomas at different times represented London and Lincolnshire in Parliament and was elected speaker of the House of Commons (Higgins 1900–1901, 9–10). Something similar, I would argue, is the case with the Yale manuscript of the *Nova statuta*, for its illustrations differ from those in all other surviving copies of this text, despite the fact that it was made by some of the same professionals who worked on several of those other manuscripts.

Use of a shared model for historiated initials across several manuscripts of the *New Statutes* does suggest that there was a market for copies that could be made quickly, perhaps even in advance of commissions, for an audience that could afford a highly decorated copy, yet perceived conformity of presentation as a positive value. Copies of the *Modus tenendi Parliamentum* and *Tractatus de senescalsia* seem to have been available as matching "accessories" to supplement the statutes text: this is suggested by the fact that these texts appear to have been copied in separate gatherings in many manuscripts of the *New Statutes* and also survive as separate manuscripts: one example is Chicago, Newberry Library MS 32.1, a copy of the two Latin treatises that Scott and Baker believe was once part of a single volume with Oxford, Bodleian Library MS Hatton 10, and London, British Library MS Additional 24079.[28] Since the subject index to the *New Statutes* does not appear with every copy, this may have been another optional "accessory" that could also be partially prepared in advance and then completed to accompany a decorated copy.

Nevertheless, defining a standardized format for *New Statutes* manuscripts and dating its development have proved challenging, especially since some of the manuscripts only partly follow the standardized format of illustration. Scholars differ somewhat on how many aspects of a manuscript (texts, borders, initials, illustrations) are involved or are most important in this standardization process. For example, manuscripts such as London, London Metropolitan Archives MS COL/CS/01/007 (plate 37), with historiated initials that show the enthroned king flanked by officials but do not use the same exact model as the most standardized copies, seem only tangentially related to this process.[29] There also seems to be evidence for an alternate standardized model for *New Statutes* manuscripts, with large illuminated initials and full borders for the beginning of each king's reign: examples include Kew, National Archives MS E 164/10 and Philadelphia, Free Library MS Carson LC 14. 10 (plate 26). Dating the production of standardized *New Statutes* manuscripts is also difficult because some scholars define the group less rigidly than others and because so many manuscripts do not follow the most standardized form of historiated initials continuously. For example, Baker has described a group of "beautifully executed" *Nova statuta* manuscripts, including the Yale copy, as coming from the third quarter of the fifteenth century (Baker 2003, 505), while Skemer describes the scribe whose work appears in many of the manuscripts of the *Nova statuta*, including the Yale copy, as active between 1483 and 1496 (Skemer 1999, 130). More recently, Malcolm Parkes has suggested that this scribe began his work on statutes manuscripts in about 1470 and continued to work until about 1492 (Parkes 2008, 44–45). There is clearly more work to be done on understanding when and by whom the growing numbers of *New Statutes* manuscripts in the second half of the fifteenth century were made.

Certainly, the manuscripts that change from one style of historiated initial to the standardized model for the statutes of Edward IV strongly suggest that this model was first integrated into production of *New Statutes* manuscripts during the reign of that king, whose statutes first became available for copying shortly after 1468. Nevertheless, historiated initials are just one aspect of the production of statutes manuscripts and, as we have seen, many options for the form and content of *New Statutes* manuscripts remained in use, even after the introduction of the standardized image of the king. At the heart of the difficulty in dating manuscript copies of the *New Statutes of England*, moreover, is the fact that many of these codices were made in stages, sometimes over many years, as groups of new laws became available for copying. In some cases, the same scribes and artists continued with the previous models; but, in other cases, either different scribes and artists continued the work or the old scribes and artists followed newer models. As Scott herself has argued, "It is not useful or even accurate to date a manuscript on the basis of the last occurring statute; a series of dates would be more appropriate, based on a close study of the stints of scribes and illuminators" (Scott 1980a, 46 n. 3). Accordingly, Scott has argued that the work of the scribe and artists responsible for the quires of the Yale manuscript containing the statues of Edward IV dates to ca. 1470; but she dates the earlier parts of the manuscript to ca. 1452 (Scott 1996, 2:346). Baker seems to concur that the Yale manuscript was made in stages, since he describes it as having an original part made in the 1450s, with extensions to 1484, though without explanation for this distinction (Baker 1985, 73): his dating includes the final quire, which uses a different script and layout, has no decoration or illustration, and was most likely added by a later owner. To Scott's list of pertinent forms of evidence for dating, I would add the evidence provided by the relationship of the manuscript's contents to historical, literary, and artistic developments. In the following discussion, I hope to show that the evidence in the Yale *New Statutes* manuscript suggests that work on most of the manuscript took place prior to 1461; after that, work resumed between 1468 and 1471, when it was influenced by the standardized historiated initials. After 1471, the original plan for the manuscript was abandoned: the contents and form of the last quire of the manuscript indicate that it is the work of a different scribe for a different owner in the mid-1480s.

The physical evidence of the Yale manuscript of the *New Statutes of England* presented in appendix 2 and plates 1–15 makes clear that the earlier parts of the codex were planned and executed according to high standards. The manuscript is similar in many ways to the other deluxe copies of the *New Statutes* that survive, made with concern for high quality in form and content. The manuscript contains the *New Statutes of England*, in Law French with Latin headings, continuously from I Edward III until 7 Edward IV, in which year the text breaks off and there is a gap, after which the final quire presents the final statutes from 22 Edward IV and the first statutes from I Richard III, beginning and ending imperfectly. The manuscript prefaces the statutes with the two Latin treatises that often appear in the deluxe copies of the statutes

(*Modus tenendi Parliamentum* and *De senescalsia Angliae*), as well as the subject index for the statutes from 1 Edward III to 23 Henry VI.

Although the book is large, with almost four hundred leaves, and it has suffered some damage over time, the quality of the original materials and workmanship is very high. Forty-seven of the fifty gatherings in the manuscript have a regular structure of four bifolia, which indicates that careful planning went into the work on the book: the differences in the first and forty-third quires suggest adaptations to accommodate changes needed during the process of making the book, and we will consider their significance shortly. The highly irregular structure of the final gathering in the manuscript, however, is part of the evidence that this part of the current manuscript was not part of the original plan for the book. The structure of the original parts of the book does indicate that it was put together in sections that may have been made by different people or at different times, though under a cooperative arrangement: the two Latin treatises at the front of the manuscript make up a separate gathering, and the subject index that precedes the statutes is also separate from the quire in which the statutes begin. Despite the structural divisions within the original parts of the manuscript, the impression they create is one of unity, clarity, and beauty. These parts of the codex show careful preparation of the page and careful completion of text and decoration, while the last quire has irregular preparation of the page and no work completed on reading guides (paraphs and initials) or decoration of the page (borders and illustrations), again suggesting that it was not part of the original parts of the codex.

The texts in this manuscript appear to be the work of three scribes. Scribes A and B use Bastard Anglicana bookhands for the primary text they copy and Textura Semi-Quadrata script for highlighting certain words on the page (headings, chapter numbers, and the first word of each new statute) to guide readers. As discussed in appendix 2, the two hands show variation on several letter forms and abbreviations. Nevertheless, the hands of the two scribes are very similar and could represent two scribes with similar professional training or one scribe continuing work on the manuscript after a hiatus or under different time constraints.

Scribe A, whose work appears in plates 6–8, copied the Latin treatises on fols. 2r–8v and the statutes text from the middle of fol. 344v through the bottom of fol. 381v, where the text breaks off with the end of the quire. Since Scribe A's work concludes in mid-sentence, it is not clear whether he continued his work in a new gathering that has been lost or ended his work there.

Scribe A is the scribe whose hand, with its regular use of the split-stem **t**, has been identified in at least ten other manuscript copies of the *New Statutes of England*. According to Malcolm Parkes, these manuscripts are the following:

1. Cambridge (MA), Houghton Library MS Richardson 40
2. Holkham, Holkham Hall, Library of the Earl of Leicester MS 232
3. London, British Library MS Cotton Nero C i
4. London, British Library MS Hargrave 274 (plate 35)
5. London, London Metropolitan Archives MS COL/CS/01/007 (plate 37)
6. London, Inner Temple Library MS Petyt 505
7. London, Lincoln's Inn Library MS Hale 194 (plate 31)
8. Kew, National Archives MS E 164/11 (plate 34)
9. Oxford, Bodleian Library MS Hatton 10
10. Philadelphia, Free Library MS Carson LC 14. 9.5 (plate 33)

In addition, Parkes suggests that the same scribe may have worked on Oxford, St. John's College MS 257 (plate 36) (Parkes 2008, 44–45).[30] Neil Ker first noted the presence of this scribe's hand, which he called a "fancy legal anglicana," in five of the copies of the *Nova statuta* identified by Parkes.[31] Nevertheless, Pamela Robinson's paleographical research challenges the inclusion of Lincoln's Inn Library MS Hale 194 in this list of manuscripts, if the "*Nova statuta* scribe" is the scribe of Inner Temple Library MS Petyt 505.[32] She does agree with Parkes that the scribe who copied Petyt 505 also worked on National Archives MS E 164/11; but she argues that London, Lincoln's Inn Library MS Hale 71 should be included in the list of this scribe's work, as Jeremy Griffiths suggested (Robinson 2003, 1:57, 64).

More detailed discussion of the hands in these manuscripts and greater understanding of the variations in a single scribe's work over time are both needed in order to determine the extent of the *Nova statuta* scribe's work and influence. As in the Yale codex, Scribe A did not copy all of the text in each of the manuscripts in Parkes's list; yet the presence of this scribe's work in so many copies of the *New Statutes* does suggest that he was active in the production of legal manuscripts in London or Westminster and may have been involved in the standardization that allowed for more efficient production of statutes manuscripts by the end of the third quarter of the fifteenth century. Since Inner Temple Library MS Petyt 505 contains the statutes only through 1451 and does not share the same format as the other manuscripts, Scott argues that it probably represents this scribe's early work, possibly dating from as early as 1452 (Scott 1980a, 48). For his part, Parkes suggests that this scribe's work can be found as late as 1492, which would be a remarkably long career for a professional scribe. Nevertheless, since the statutes for Henry VI that date from after 1451 were probably not available for copying until 1461, Petyt 505 may have been copied toward the end of the 1450s, rather than ca. 1452. At least part of Scribe A's work in the Yale manuscript must have taken place after 1468, when the first statute roll for Edward IV became available to copyists. Scribe A's copying of the Latin treatises may also date from after 1468: even though the treatises appear at the beginning of the manuscript, they form a separate quire that could have been added to the codex after the other parts of the manuscript were copied.

It was Scribe B who copied the bulk of the text in the Yale manuscript, from fol. 10r through fol. 344v (plates 1–5, 9–15). This portion of the manuscript includes the subject index to the statutes, as well as the *Nova statuta* text from 1 Edward III through 29 Henry VI. The extent of Scribe B's work in the manuscript suggests that this scribe had primary responsibility for the codex and devoted a considerable amount of time to it. The fact that the opening leaves of the statutes for Richard II, Henry V, and Henry VI all occur within a quire, rather than at the beginning of a new quire, suggests that the scribe had the time to copy continuously and did not plan to have each reign copied or decorated separately in order to save time. The smaller amount of variation in the letter forms used by this scribe also suggests an attempt to produce a more formal-looking copy of the text than that found in some other manuscripts, as do such practices as highlighting the first words of each statute with larger, darker, and more formal script. The unusual way that Scribe B's work ends on fol. 344v (in the middle of the verso of a leaf, just after the beginning of a new quire) (plate 15) does not fit with the careful practices followed by this scribe elsewhere in the manuscript, and this suggests an unforeseen interruption in his work.

Scribe C (fols. 382r–389v) (plates 16–18) uses a less formal Anglicana script in the body of the statutes, with many cursive elements, but uses a more formal script for the headings at the top of the leaves. Scribe C's work also follows a different format from the one found in the earlier parts of the statutes text: the number of lines in the text block varies, the right margin is irregular, the first words of each statute do not appear in formal script, and there are no numbers for statutes in the outer margins. In addition to these changes, the gap in the statutes between the quires copied by Scribe A and Scribe C and the irregular structure of the quire in which Scribe C's work appears also suggest that Scribe C was not part of the team that prepared the rest of this manuscript. Finally, since Scribe C's work begins in mid-sentence, this quire may have been made for a different copy of the statutes but got separated and added to the rest of this codex by a later owner. We will therefore focus our attention on the earlier parts of the codex in the rest of our examination.

Although the text copied by Scribes A and B is of high quality, the beauty of the original parts of the Yale *New Statutes* manuscript comes from their decoration. Painted initials and border sprays, all illuminated with gold leaf, mark the opening of each preliminary text, with smaller versions of these initials and sprays showing the reader the beginnings of subsections within all of the texts (plates 7–15). The true distinction of the Yale manuscript, however, comes from the historiated initials and full borders that mark the opening of each king's reign in the *New Statutes* (plates 1–6). The decoration of these leaves is important for two reasons. First, some of the artists who worked on these leaves also worked on several other manuscripts of the *New Statutes*, suggesting that the Yale manuscript was produced by a group of professionals who had ties to the standardized manuscripts of this text. Second, despite these links to other copies, the six historiated initials in the Yale manuscript differ from all of the other surviving copies of the *New Statutes* in their depictions of these kings, which suggests that the manuscript was created to reflect a very specific set of concerns. The first five historiated initials show the kings at prayer, rather than standing or sitting alone or enthroned with officials, as the images of kings in other *New Statutes* manuscripts show. Even the historiated initial for Edward IV (plate 6), which was clearly influenced by the standardized model found in at least ten manuscripts, differs from this model in important details. Chapter 2 will discuss the sources and significance of the iconography of the royal images in the Yale manuscript. Here, we will focus on the relationships of the initials and borders in the Yale manuscript to those in other copies of the *New Statutes*.

The attention to detail in the images of kings in the Yale codex suggests that the sequence of historiated initials was a high priority for the person commissioning the manuscript: although none is a royal portrait aiming for historical accuracy, each of these images has details that do not occur in the rest of the sequence and so suggest some characterization of the individual monarch. According to Scott, the historiated initials show the work of three illustrators (Scott 1980a, 46 n. 8). Illustrator A painted the initial for Edward III on fol. 55r (plate 1), as well as the initial depicting Richard II on fol. 139r (plate 2). Illustrator B painted the initial depicting Henry IV on fol. 198r (plate 3), as well as those of Henry V on fol. 235*v* (plate 4) and of Henry VI on fol. 261*r* (plate 5). Illustrator C painted the initial for Edward IV on fol. 358*r* (plate 6). The work of Illustrators A and B is very well coordinated: care was taken to continue the details of the setting and certain aspects of the image of the king across the first five initials, while introducing some changes that create distinctions among them. The introduction of additional figures to the scene is the major distinction between the images painted by Illustrators A and B; but no two images are exactly alike in their depictions of the king or the additional figures. The balance between similarity and difference in the sequence maintains the interest of the reader in ways that the standardized scenes do not.

Scott argues that Illustrators A and B have very similar styles and were perhaps trained in the same shop; but she considers Illustrator B the more skilled artist (Scott 1996, 2:346). She has identified Illustrator B as the same artist who executed historiated initials in two other *New Statutes* manuscripts: London, Lincoln's Inn Library MS Hale 194, fol. 34*r* (plate 31) and London, London Metropolitan Archives MS COL/CS/01/007, fols. 37*r* and 95*r* (plate 37) (Scott 1996, 1: plates 481–83 and 2:346).[33] Although the images painted by Illustrator B in the Yale manuscript differ from those in these other manuscripts in their depictions of the kings, the images painted by him in all three manuscripts depict the king's counselors in a similar manner, in the robes of legal officials. Scott also argues that Illustrators A and B, as well as the illustrators from the London Corporation manuscript and Hale 194, were influenced by or trained by the first illustrator in London, British Library MS Harley 2287, a book of hours made before 1467 (Scott 1996, 2:300). Since both Hale 194 and the London Corporation manuscript also contain work by Scribe A of the Yale manuscript, these two illustrators seem to have had a continuing professional relationship with this scribe or the group of scribes with whom Scribe A worked. At the same time, since the work of Illustrator B appears in parts of the Yale manuscript copied by Scribe B, this illustrator appears to have been involved in production of this manuscript before Scribe A became involved.

Scott has not found any other manuscript illustrations that she attributes to Illustrator A; nor has she identified any other illustrations executed by Illustrator C, despite the fact that this illustrator's work links him to the standardized historiated initials of the *New Statutes* (Scott 1980a, 50). Illustrator C's work must date from after 1468, when the first statutes of Edward IV became available to copyists; but it is not clear whether the addition of Illustrator C to the Yale manuscript resulted from the first two illustrators no longer being available, the need to complete work on the manuscript quickly, or the desire to appear to conform to a visual representation of kingship that had the support of the party in power. If the manuscript was indeed copied in two or more stages, years could have elapsed between the work of Illustrator C and that of the earlier artists. He worked after 1468, a time when the Lancastrians would have had very limited access to London scribes and artists who could complete the Yale *Nova statuta*; Lancastrian sympathizers remaining in England after 1461 were unlikely to find many artists willing to run the risk of working on a manuscript with Lancastrian associations, like Margaret of Anjou's coat of arms, especially after Edward IV began to torture and execute individuals convicted of sympathizing or having contact with members of the Lancastrian party in the mid-1460s.[34] We should nevertheless not necessarily ascribe the changes in artistic style and iconography in the depiction of Edward IV to a change in the plan or the goals governing the manuscript's production. More likely, the changes in style and iconography reflect a change to a new artist who knew about the standardized initials in other copies of the *Nova statuta* and who may not have been given access to the earlier parts of the Yale manuscript that contain the other royal portraits and Margaret's coat of arms.

Illustrator C's work is the only initial that falls within a part of the manuscript copied by Scribe A, the scribe whose work also appears in several manuscripts with the standardized image of the king: Philadelphia, Free Library MS Carson LC 14. 9.5 (plate 33); Kew, National Archives MS E 164/11 (plate 34); Holkham, Holkham Hall, Library of the Earl of Leicester MS 232; London, British Library MS Cotton Nero C i; London, British Library MS Hargrave 274 (plate 35); and Oxford, Bodleian Library MS Hatton 10. As a result, the fact that Illustrator C's work in the Yale manuscript does *not* follow the standardized scene completely is further evidence that the Yale manuscript was shaped by a different set of goals from those that shaped other copies of the *New Statutes*. Chapter 2 will discuss the iconography of all of the historiated initials in greater detail.

The borders on the leaves with historiated initials provide additional evidence about the relationship between the Yale *New Statutes* manuscript and other copies of this text. Scott has suggested that each border accompanying an historiated initial was executed by a different border artist (Scott 1980a, 46 n. 8). The possibility that six or more artists, in addition to the illustrators, worked on the manuscript accords with the variation in small initial styles, as well as the number of border spray styles found in the manuscript. Scott has identified the artist responsible for the border on fol. 358r in the Yale manuscript (plate 6), and possibly the spray initials in the rest of the statutes of Edward IV, as one who worked on several other copies of the *New Statutes*: six borders in Philadelphia, Free Library MS Carson LC 14. 9.5, including fol. 245r (plate 33); six borders in London, British Library MS Cotton Nero C i; four borders in London, London Metropolitan Archives MS COL/CS/01/007 (plate 37); six borders in Oxford, Bodleian Library MS Hatton 10; and two borders in Holkham, Holkham Hall, Library of the Earl of Leicester MS 232 (Scott 1980a, 45–48; Scott 1996, 2:354). This border artist is one whose work Scott has found in several other manuscripts containing religious and secular texts, and she dates this artist's work from the late 1460s to about 1480 (Scott 1996, 2:352–55). Though she does not give details, Scott also states that one of the Yale manuscript's other border artists worked on some of the borders of London, Lincoln's Inn Library MS Hale 194 (plate 31) (Scott 1980a, 67). One of the shared features of the borders in the Yale manuscript and Hale 194 is the use of roundels at the corners of the frame on some of the leaves (compare plates 1–3 and plate 31). This border element is also shared with the Corporation of London manuscript (plate 37) and with London, British Library MS Yates Thompson 48 (plate 32). On some leaves in these manuscripts, the roundels appear in all four corners, while on other leaves the roundels appear in the upper corners only, or an additional roundel appears in one of the sides of the frame, as on fol. 139r in the Yale manuscript (plate 2). These links to other manuscripts of the *New Statutes* again suggest that the Yale manuscript was produced by a group of artists who worked on many copies of the *New Statutes of England*, which underscores the importance of the elements of decoration in the Yale manuscript that remain unique among the surviving copies of this work.

For example, the Yale *New Statutes* manuscript appears to be the only surviving copy that includes the coat of arms of a queen in its decoration, in this case the arms of Margaret of Anjou: on fols. 55r, 139r, and 198r in the Yale manuscript, Margaret's arms (her father's arms impaled with her husband's) appear in the upper-right roundel (plates 1–3). Whereas in the Corporation of London manuscript and the Yates Thompson manuscript the corner roundels remain empty, in both Hale 194 and the Yale manuscript these roundels house coats of arms. Both manuscripts display the arms of the kings of England chosen by Edward III (England quartered with France) in the top-left roundel, near the historiated initial; but only the Yale manuscript displays the arms of a queen in its decoration. On several of its leaves, Hale 194 uses the roundel in the top-right corner, as well as the bottom margin, for the arms of John Neville, Lord Montagu (or Montacute), so the manuscript is thought to have been made for him (Scott 1980a, 67; Robinson 2003, 1:58). Neville was rewarded for his service to Edward IV in battles against the Lancastrians by elevation to baron in 1463 and marquess in 1470, but he subsequently switched his allegiance and died fighting for the Lancastrians in 1471. His death date thus gives an endpoint for the production of this manuscript. One might also interpret the appearance of Margaret's arms in the Yale manuscript as evidence that the manuscript was made for her (Hayward 1975, 142); yet the evidence for royal coats of arms as marks of ownership in other copies of the *New Statutes* is not conclusive.

By the early fifteenth century, coats of arms were often displayed in the borders of statutes manuscripts, but the use of arms in these manuscripts does not follow a consistent pattern. The royal arms appear in the upper-right corner of the border decoration in San Marino, Huntington Library MS HM 19920, with owner's arms in the right and lower segments of the border decoration (plate 29). In the copies of the *New Statutes of England* in London, British Library MSS Stowe 389 and Yates Thompson 48, however, the border decoration contains no coats of arms at all (plates 30 and 32), even though the deluxe quality of Yates Thompson 48 suggests that it was designed for an owner of wealth and high social status. From other manuscript copies of the *New Statutes*, we can see more evidence that there was little consistency in whether any coats of arms appear, whether the coats of arms that appear are the monarch's or belong to another member of the nobility, or where coats of arms are placed when they do appear. The king's arms appear beside the historiated initials in Cambridge (UK), St. John's College Library MS A. 7 (plate 28) but in the bottom margin decoration of Kew, National Archives MS E 164/11 (plate 34) and Oxford, St. John's College MS 257 (plate 36). Alternatively, the arms of other members of the nobility or institutions appear in various positions in the decoration of other manuscript copies of the *New Statutes*. As we saw earlier, the painted initials of the *New Statutes* manuscript made for Sir Thomas Fitzwilliam of Mablethorpe, Lincolnshire, contain the coats of arms of succeeding generations of Fitzwilliam men impaled with those of their wives, and the arms of Sir Gregory Adgore appear in the initials of his copy of the *New Statutes* (London, Lincoln's Inn Library MS Hale 71). In addition, coats of arms other than the royal arms appear in the bottom margin decoration in other copies of the *New Statutes*: Philadelphia, Free Library

MS Carson LC 14. 9.5 (plate 33) contains the arms of the Molyneux family in several of its bottom margins (Baker 1985, 59); London, British Library MS Hargrave 274 (plate 35) shows the arms of the Gille family at the bottom of every border (Scott 1996, 2:347); and the lower borders in London, London Metropolitan Archives MS COL/CS/01/007 (plate 37) contain the arms of the City of London (Scott 1996, 2:346).

In some cases, such as the Yale Law School manuscript (plates 1–3, 5, and 6) and San Marino, Huntington Library MS HM 19920 (plate 29), we can tell that later owners of *New Statutes* manuscripts added coats of arms to the border decoration after original production of the manuscript was complete, because these coats of arms cover over parts of the original decoration. On fol. 55r in the Yale manuscript (plate 1), the arms of the Elyot and Delamare families now appear in the lower roundels, painted over parts of the original decoration of the manuscript, and the Elyot arms have been added to the center of the lower border decoration on fols. 139r, 198r, 261r, and 358r (plates 2, 3, 5, and 6) (Baker 1985, 73–74). The ownership of the manuscript by Sir Richard Elyot, who married Alice Delamare, is also attested by an inscription in the manuscript (fol. 1r), which will be part of the discussion of later owners in chapter 5. If other families' coats of arms appear underneath the Elyot and Delamare coats of arms on fol. 55r, this might indicate that a member of one of these families commissioned the Yale manuscript and decided to honor Henry and Margaret by including theirs. On the other hand, Henry's and Margaret's arms may have originally appeared in the bottom roundels, as well as the top ones.

By the 1470s and 1480s, placing the book owner's arms in the decoration of the bottom margin seems to have become a common practice that book producers accommodated or even encouraged. For example, in London, Lincoln's Inn Library MS Hale 183, the border decorators left empty shields in the bottom margins on the leaves that begin the statutes for the reigns of Edward IV, Richard III, and Henry VII, to be filled in later with the arms of owners; but these were never completed (Baker 1999, 422; and Ker 1969–2002, 1:138). Empty shields awaiting coats of arms also appear in the border decoration in the bottom margins of several of the leaves that begin new reigns in the copy of the *New Statutes* in London, British Library MS Additional 15728.[35]

In addition to the Yale Law School copy of the *New Statutes*, at least five manuscripts contain the arms of English kings, including Cambridge (UK), St. John's College Library MS A. 7 (plate 28); San Marino, Huntington Library MS HM 19920 (plate 29); London, Lincoln's Inn MS Hale 194 (plate 31); Kew,

National Archives MS E 164/11 (plate 34); and Oxford, St. John's College MS 257 (plate 36). Of these copies, Cambridge (UK), St. John's College Library MS A. 7 has the strongest evidence of being made for a king of England, in this case Richard II. The statutes contained in the manuscript end in 1388, during Richard II's reign, and his portrait is the only one that shows another figure presenting him with a book, which echoes the convention of a presentation miniature (plate 28). In addition, as Selby Whittington and Paul Binski have noted, the royal portraits in this manuscript have close stylistic affinities with the royal portraits in the *Liber regalis* (London, Westminster Abbey MS 38), as well as the portrait of Richard II in a 1389 royal charter in the Shrewsbury Guildhall Corporation Muniments (Binski 1995, 194; and Whittingham 1971, 15–16 and fig. 20). St. John's College Library MS A. 7, which presents the *Old Statutes* as well as the *New Statutes*, contains no other arms or inscriptions that indicate ownership, however, so scholars have not been able to trace its provenance more fully; but the evidence suggests that this manuscript was probably made for Richard II shortly after 1388.[36]

While St. John's College Library MS A. 7 may have been made as a royal presentation copy, the evidence offered by the other manuscripts with royal arms is more ambiguous. The other manuscript with royal arms that combines material from the *Antiqua statuta* and *Nova statuta* is San Marino, Huntington Library MS HM 19920 (plate 29). Like St. John's College Library MS A. 7, HM 19920 coordinates the version of the royal arms depicted with the particular king portrayed on the folio. This pattern does not appear in the Yale *Nova statuta*, however, which uses the arms of Henry VI and Margaret of Anjou on the leaves that contain the portraits of Edward III, Richard II, and Henry IV, but not on the leaf portraying Henry VI, where one might expect to see them. The Huntington Library manuscript was probably begun shortly after 1407, during the reign of Henry IV, but the later parts of this codex do not seem to have been made for this king: though the border decoration in the earlier parts of this codex originally included only the royal coats of arms, the arms of other owners are integrated into the border decoration plan beginning on the leaf that opens the reign of Henry IV (fol. 227r).[37] Despite the inclusion of the royal coat of arms in London, Lincoln's Inn Library MS Hale 194 (plate 31), as we have seen, this manuscript seems to have been made for Sir John Neville, Lord Montagu, since his coat of arms is part of the codex's original border decoration. The inclusion of the royal arms in the bottom border decoration of two copies of the *New Statutes* with the standardized historiated initials and borders – Kew, National Archives MS E 164/11 (plate 34) and

Oxford, St. John's College MS 257 (plate 36) – truly does suggest that inclusion of the royal arms in statutes manuscripts became conventional, perhaps as a way of displaying an owner's loyalty to the monarch. Given the ambiguity of the evidence, it seems best to conclude that the appearance of royal arms in a statutes manuscript does not serve as a sure indicator of royal ownership.

Unfortunately, the current binding of the Yale manuscript (plates 23–24) does not offer conclusive evidence of the manuscript's original owner. If the remnants of leather incorporated into the current binding come from an earlier binding of the same manuscript, the crowned escutcheons stamped on the front and back covers suggest that the book had a royal owner; but the crowned escutcheons are quartered like the royal arms of England, not impaled like Margaret of Anjou's arms. The crowned coat of arms has parallels with the presentation of Henry VI's coat of arms on several of the legal documents issued in his name, such as royal charters for King's College, Cambridge (plate 61) and Eton College (plate 62).

We will continue to examine the possible significance of Margaret of Anjou's coat of arms in the Yale codex as part of our investigation of the royal iconography in the manuscript in subsequent chapters; but we can recognize here that the appearance of Margaret's arms may play a role other than designating ownership of the manuscript: Margaret is queen, she is wife, and she is mother. Reading the coats of arms in the Yale *New Statutes* manuscript against the different uses of arms found in other copies of this text, we find that one of the patterns that emerge is the juxtaposition of the arms of husbands and wives. One example comes from the copy made for Sir Thomas Fitzwilliam, which presents the arms of six generations of Fitzwilliam husbands impaled with those of their wives, leading up to the generation of the owner. A similar example comes from Philadelphia, Free Library MS Carson LC 14. 9.5 (plate 33), which alternates the arms of Molyneux, Haydock, and Molyneux impaled with Haydock, for the marriage between Sir Richard Molyneux and Jane Haydock: since the manuscript contains statutes for more than twenty years after Sir Richard's death in 1454 and the initials in the manuscript use the standardized images of the king, the manuscript was most likely commissioned by or for one of his sons (Baker 1985, 59–60). In both cases, the mother's and father's arms provide the context for the next generation of readers of English laws.

When the original gatherings of the Yale manuscript were assembled, bringing together the deluxe copy of the *New Statutes* with the Latin treatises on parliamentary matters and the subject index to the statues, the codex created was one of legal record and education, past history and preparation for the future. It might well be considered a gift fit for a prince. The literal pattern created by the gatherings is one in which blank folios appear before the beginning of each of the major units of text in the manuscript, perhaps as space where large illustrations, gift inscriptions, or other prefatory materials could be added before final preparation of the codex for presentation. A leaf had to be added to the first quire in order to accomplish this, so the pattern does not seem to be coincidental. These leaves were not used for those purposes, however, which might suggest a change of plan or an unexpected end to work on the manuscript. Several other anomalies in the manuscript also suggest changes of plans. Scribe B also left fols. 334v–335v blank, and the quire in which this occurs is shorter than all the rest, as if the scribe were leaving space for new statutes or thought that some text might be missing. This differs from the pattern earlier in Scribe B's work, in which the statutes were copied in a continuous process, with several of the transitions to new reigns occurring within a quire, rather than at the beginning of a quire, even if only one leaf remained. Since the text in this quire ends with the statutes for the session of Parliament in 23 Henry VI (1444–45), Jane Hayward took this as evidence the manuscript was made as Henry VI's present to Margaret of Anjou on their wedding in April 1445 and so would have ended at this point. This scenario for the commission of the manuscript is unlikely, however, because the Parliament session called in 23 Henry VI was extended and did not end until April 1446, too late for the book to serve as a wedding gift for the queen (Skemer 1999, 130). In addition, since fifteen other copies of the *New Statutes* end with the statutes of 23 Henry VI (Skemer 1999, 129), this seems to have been a traditional point at which to end a copying stint. Perhaps this is where Scribe B expected that another scribe would take over the copying, or perhaps it was at this point that Scribe B's work on the manuscript had to be temporarily suspended, and he left a blank folio at the end to protect his work from damage.

Other hints of changes in plans also occur within the manuscript, despite the overall care shown for continuity and unity. After three borders in which the royal arms and Margaret's arms appear, the use of roundels and arms ceases in the original decoration. This change runs contrary to the care taken to maintain continuity in the series of five royal images. It is not clear whether this change occurred for artistic or political reasons. In addition, Scribe A began his work on the statutes in the middle of the text block on fol. 344v, in the midst of a quire. This again suggests that the two scribes worked sequentially, rather than dividing the text by gatherings or reigns in order to work concurrently; but the unusual transition point suggests that something unexpected may have happened to keep Scribe B from completing the leaf he had started. For his part, Scribe A also left fol. 357r–v blank at the end of the quire containing the final statutes for Henry VI, which might suggest that he was unsure about whether there would be more of Henry's statutes to include at a later time – an uncertainty that could have persisted until May 1471, when the Lancastrian forces suffered their final defeat and Henry VI was murdered in the Tower of London (R. Griffiths 1981, 885). Earlier in the manuscript, Scribe B did not leave the rest of a quire blank after the final statute for a king, even when there was only one leaf left in the quire, as long as the statutes of the next king were available (as in the case of the transition between Henry V and Henry VI). Just as Scribe A's work on the statutes begins abruptly, it ends abruptly in mid-sentence at the end of a quire (fol. 381v), though it is not clear if additional work by Scribe A might have been lost or if his work on the manuscript ended because all work on the manuscript came to an end. Despite the unusual transition, the change from Scribe B to Scribe A during the statutes does not alter the basic format of the text, which remains constant across the work of these two scribes and across the trauma of Henry VI's deposition. This continuity, as well as the continuity shown across the first five historiated initials, suggests that the scribes and the artists working on the Yale *New Statutes* manuscript were guided by a unified plan throughout their work, despite any delays or uncertainties they might have faced. Production of the Yale *New Statutes* manuscript thus reflects the political strategy of Margaret of Anjou and her circle. Even after Henry VI's deposition, continuity of form was an important tool for the Lancastrian party: "The Lancastrian advisers continued to protect their cause by working within patterns set while Henry was still king. After all, their position rested on the claim that that was still his rightful status" (Gross 1996, 38).

Given how similar the two hands in the original parts of the manuscript are in many respects, these scribes must have had very similar training; alternatively, the two hands may represent the same scribe working at different times. It is difficult to determine whether the primary scribe's work on the manuscript came to a stop because this scribe was no longer available, whether he was prevented from working on the manuscript for a period of time, or whether the copying process had to be hurried unexpectedly at the end, so that the care exhibited in the earlier copying was no longer possible. Since the portion of the manuscript copied by Scribe B ends during the statutes from 1450–51 and contains the arms of Margaret of Anjou, this portion of the manuscript must date from sometime after 1452, but before 1461, when Henry VI was deposed: as we will see, the iconography of the royal imagery in the manuscript and other types of evidence suggest that the early parts of the manuscript were probably made between 1457 and 1460. Because of the amount of text copied by Scribe B alone, it is unlikely that the manuscript as a whole was begun during Henry VI's brief restoration to the throne (October 1470–April 1471). Since the portion of the statutes copied by Scribe A includes the statutes through 1468, some of his work must have taken place after that date. It is unlikely, however, that Scribe A's work continued much beyond May 1471, when he could write with certainty on fol. 356v, "Expliciunt Statuta Regis Henrici Sexti" ("Here end the statutes of King Henry the Sixth"). The Lancastrian cause had come to an end with the deaths of Henry VI and Prince Edward, and nothing in the original parts of the Yale *New Statutes* manuscript has a definitive link with a later date.

While the texts presented in the Yale *New Statutes* manuscript are not unique, the frames that the manuscript creates for the reader's experience of these texts are unique, and they all contribute to presenting the history and significance of English law from a Lancastrian perspective in response to Yorkist attacks on the legitimacy of Lancastrian rule in the 1450s and 1460s. One of these frames is the pairing of Margaret of Anjou's coat of arms with the royal arms of England in the manuscript's border decoration. Although her arms only appear on the first three leaves with full frames (plates 1–3), these appearances set a pattern that reflects the original goals of making the manuscript. Whether or not she had any personal connection with the manuscript, the appearance of her arms associates the manuscript with the Lancastrian monarchy – as the royal arms themselves could not, because they are not unique to the Lancastrian kings. The appearance of Margaret's arms also serves to highlight the relationship of queens to justice and grace in English history, and we will explore this aspect of the manuscript further in chapter 3.

Another frame is created by the images of kings presented on the opening leaves for the reigns of each of the six monarchs from Edward III through Edward IV (plates 1–6). The historiated initials serve to construct a bridge (a location of interrogation and mediation) between text and decoration, since the initials participate in both. In addition, unlike the royal portraits in other copies of the *Nova statuta*, the portraits of the English kings in the Yale manuscript also construct an intertextual bridge to imagery of kingship that had become traditional in devotional texts such as psalters and books of hours, but also in medieval mirrors for princes, books of instruction on the ideals of kingship. In chapter 2, we will explore how the unique royal iconography in this manuscript sets the Statutes of the Realm in dialogue with other discourses of kingship, justice, and grace current in fifteenth-century England – especially those used by the Lancastrian regime to shore up its own authority.

Yet another frame is created in the Yale manuscript by the two Latin texts that preface the French text of the English statutes: the *Modus tenendi Parliamentum* (*The Method of Holding Parliament*) and *De senescalsia Angliae* (*On the Seneschal of England*). While the inclusion of these treatises at the beginning of a *New Statutes* manuscript is not unique, their appearance in a manuscript that highlights the authority of the Lancastrian monarchy gives them a role to play that they do not necessarily have in other manuscripts. These treatises here serve to remind readers of the role that the earls and dukes of Lancaster have played in fighting against injustice in earlier times in English history in the role of seneschal or high steward, demonstrating the worthiness of the house of Lancaster to rule as English kings in the fifteenth century. This is also an issue we will continue to explore in chapter 3.

As modern readers, we sometimes forget that medieval texts – including legal texts – take some of their meaning from their manuscript contexts. The frames created by the Yale manuscript of the *New Statutes of England* offer a powerful example of the ways in which a medieval manuscript can employ multiple discourses in order to open a text up to new meanings for its readers. Through its interplay of margins and centers, the Yale *New Statutes* manuscript both constructs ideals of justice and grace and associates them with Henry VI and Margaret of Anjou. Finally, though statutes manuscripts might appear to be marginal to the other literatures of medieval England, the Yale manuscript demonstrates that at least some statutes manuscripts participated in the central debates of the cultures that produced them.

TWO

Royal Portraits
and Royal Arms

Our comparison of the Yale Law School manuscript of the *New Statutes of England* with other English statutes manuscripts shows that two important features distinguish it from other surviving copies of this text: its inclusion of Margaret of Anjou's coat of arms in its border decoration (plates 1–3) and the iconography of its representations of the kings of England in the historiated initials (plates 1–6). In this chapter, we will explore the ways in which these features of the visual texts in the manuscript create frames for the verbal texts in the manuscript. Though the visual texts in the manuscript might seem entirely marginal to the significance of the verbal texts, the visual and verbal texts intertwine in important ways. First, the historiated initials are letters that contain pictures, so they participate in both the verbal and visual texts. The letters that introduce the kings whose reigns are the temporal frames for the statutes become visual frames for representations of these kings. As visual and verbal texts, historiated initials serve as hybrids, liminal spaces linking different forms of textuality; and, in this manuscript, the historiated initials become spaces to explore different perspectives on artistic and legal representation, as well as different perspectives on defining kingship, justice, and grace. In addition, the marginal decoration on the leaves with historiated initials features coats of arms that represent people who are discussed within the verbal texts, so that the visual texts of the margins echo the verbal texts of the statutes. The coats of arms in the marginal decoration also comment on the images of power found within the statutes, which are overwhelmingly associated with men: by pairing the coat of arms of a queen with the arms of the king of England, the marginal decoration that frames the statutes reminds readers of the roles that queens have played and might still play in England's legal history. The visual frames in the Yale Law School manuscript also help construct its commentary on the relationship of kingship, queenship, justice, and grace by linking the verbal texts of the manuscript to iconographic traditions that were current in England in the middle of the fifteenth century and were sometimes used for political purposes. Reading the historiated initials and border decoration in the Yale manuscript across discourses reveals much about how the visual texts of this manuscript help transform a record of English statutes and legal procedures into a Lancastrian mirror for princes.

From the evidence of the surviving statutes manuscripts, it appears that framing the verbal text of English statutes with the visual images of coats of arms was a tradition in statutes books by the middle of the fifteenth century, as it had been in manuscript copies of texts in many other genres, including books of hours, psalters, chronicles, and romances. In many cases, these coats of arms indicate ownership or a family relationship to the owner of the manuscript. Nevertheless, the fact that many copies of statutes manuscripts contain the arms of the English king, as well as the arms of other members of the nobility, suggests that the coats of arms in statutes manuscripts might have a significance other than or in addition to indicating book ownership. As art historians have shown, the appearance of royal arms in a medieval manuscript does not guarantee royal ownership, and the lack of royal arms in a manuscript does not preclude royal ownership: Anne Rudloff Stanton explains, "Books like the Tickhill Psalter and the Grey-Fitzpayn Hours are thick with heraldry, including royal arms, but were not made for the court. Conversely, not all illuminated books made for royalty included heraldry" (Stanton 2001, 195). We must take care, then, not to jump to conclusions about the significance of the coats of arms found in the Yale *Nova statuta Angliae*.

Since no other surviving copies of the *New Statutes of England* include a queen's arms, the depiction of Margaret's arms in the Yale manuscript strongly suggests an attempt to link the manuscript to her, rather than an accommodation to a conventional practice. Coats of arms had become a major visual sign of identity, social rank, and legal rights for members of the nobility, as well as merchants, landholders, and chartered groups such as cities, colleges, and

guilds.[1] Displays of arms became so widely used by the early fifteenth century
that in 1417 Henry V began to take steps to regulate who could receive permission to use coats of arms (Wagner 1956, 59–64). Margaret's arms, which
usually took the form of the arms of her father impaled or joined with the arms
of her husband, would have been part of public discourse, as well as private,
because of her role as queen. Given the official removal of her title as queen and
her conviction for treason after Edward IV's overthrow of Henry VI in 1461,
it is interesting to find that her arms were not all removed from their earlier
displays (Maurer 2003, 202; Given-Wilson 2005, 13:47). We will better understand the significance of her arms in the Yale Law School statutes manuscript
when we consider the range of contexts in which her arms were used.

      To begin with, Margaret's arms survive in several other manuscripts asso-
ciated with her. For example, her arms appear along with her portrait in a roll
of Latin prayers to the Virgin Mary that was made for her in England (Oxford,
Bodleian Library MS Jesus College 124) (plate 38).[2] Margaret's arms were also
added to the margin at the beginning of a Latin psalter that was originally
made for Henry Bolingbroke before he became Henry IV (Cambridge [UK],
Fitzwilliam Museum MS 38-1950) (plate 39).[3] Because Margaret's arms are
featured (without impaling) at the beginning of London, British Library MS
Additional 40851, some scholars believe that this manuscript copy of Thomas
Jenyns's *Ordinary of Arms* was made for her.[4] Margaret herself took actions
that brought representations of her coat of arms into public view. Without
impaling, Margaret's arms became the arms of Queens' College, Cambridge,
which she founded through Henry VI's grant in 1448 (Twigg 1987, 2–3). The
arms of Margaret of Anjou and Henry VI appeared together in a window
honoring the Virgin Mary commissioned by the queen for a chapel in Westminster Abbey in June 1453 (Myers 1957–58, 423–24). In addition, Margaret's
arms appeared with Henry VI's in the windows at the royal manor at Green-
wich. Other members of the nobility honored Margaret by displaying her
coat of arms along with the king's in the decoration of their own buildings:
examples can still be seen at Rycote Chapel in Oxfordshire, built by Sir Richard Quartermayne in 1449, and at Ockwells Manor (also called Ockholt Hall)
in Berkshire, built by Sir Edward Norreys about 1450 (Laynesmith 2004,
183; Eden 1933, 94–95; Marks 1993, 97). This evidence suggests that Margaret
herself used her coat of arms to signal her ownership and patronage, but also
that others expressed support for her by displaying her coat of arms.

      The appearance of Margaret of Anjou's coat of arms in the border deco-
ration on folios 55r, 139r, and 198r in the Yale Law School manuscript has

led some to argue that the codex was commissioned as a wedding gift for her by Henry VI.[5] Nevertheless, the manuscript itself offers no evidence of a link to the royal wedding. Despite its otherwise deluxe execution, the manuscript does not contain any inscription or miniature indicating that it was a gift to the queen or given in honor of the royal wedding. This contrasts with the elaborate and carefully planned ceremonies with which Margaret's betrothal, wedding, and coronation were celebrated.[6] Indeed, the Yale Law School manuscript differs considerably from the one book scholars agree Margaret did receive as a wedding present – a collection of French narratives and treatises on chivalry and heraldry given to her by Sir John Talbot, the first earl of Shrewsbury, which is now London, British Library MS Royal 15 E vi.[7] In addition to displaying the arms of both Margaret and Henry, the opening of the "Queen Margaret Anthology" honors the queen with a dedicatory poem, inscription, and miniature depicting Talbot's presentation of the manuscript (plate 40). Margaret's arms also appear next to the genealogy of Henry VI on the following leaf (plate 41), as well as on the opening leaf of each of the later texts in the collection. In the Yale Law School manuscript, however, Margaret's arms appear on only three of the six leaves that have full border decoration, and this does not include the leaf with the historiated initial that depicts Henry VI, where one would expect her arms to appear if the manuscript had been made as a wedding present. Nothing appears anywhere else in the codex that links the manuscript directly to her.

The reason Margaret's arms appear in the Yale Law School manuscript is therefore less obvious. As we noted in the previous chapter, the positioning of the queen's arms in the upper-right corner of the border decoration, parallel to the king's arms in the upper-left corner, puts her arms in the same location as the arms of the manuscript owner in London, Lincoln's Inn Library MS Hale 194 (plate 31); but this is not a consistent tradition in manuscripts of the *Nova statuta*, since royal arms appear in this same position in manuscripts for which we do not have evidence of royal ownership. Given the inconsistencies involved in the appearance of coats of arms in manuscript copies of the *New Statutes of England*, it is difficult to assign a single meaning to the royal arms that appear in several of the manuscripts. Without other evidence, therefore, the appearance of Margaret's arms in the Yale Law School *New Statutes of England* does not definitively indicate that she was the intended owner of this manuscript. Perhaps the queen's arms in the border decoration of the Yale Law School manuscript, paired with the royal arms on three leaves, represent a variant of the use of coats of arms in manuscript decoration to depict a patron's or recipient's family history, as in the case of the Fitzwilliam *Nova statuta* and the psalter made for Henry Bolingbroke (Cambridge [UK], Fitzwilliam Museum MS 38-1950) (plate 39): as Lucy Sandler explains, the coats of arms found in the decoration of the Bolingbroke psalter are "carefully composed to celebrate an alliance between members of the Bohun family and the Lancastrian branch of the royal family," incorporating the arms of three generations of each family (Sandler 1985, 367).

Indeed, the presence of Margaret of Anjou's coat of arms in the Yale Law School manuscript is significant for several reasons. Even if she was not the intended owner of the manuscript, the presence of her arms indicates that the Yale Law School manuscript was begun while Margaret was queen and was intended for ownership by someone who considered it appropriate to highlight her in a manuscript presenting England's laws. This suggests that at least the first three painted borders in the manuscript were produced prior to March 1461, when Henry VI was first deposed. Although we must postpone a full exploration of the association of the queen with English statutes for our next chapter, we must recognize here the importance of the pairing of Margaret's arms with the royal arms of England on three leaves of the manuscript: while the royal arms as depicted in this manuscript could refer to any of the six kings whose portraits appear in the manuscript, the pairing of the royal arms of England with Margaret's every time they appear suggests that the king signified by the royal arms is Henry VI. In addition, since the original parts of the Yale Law School manuscript include statutes enacted after Henry VI was deposed and Margaret was stripped of her title, the fact that Margaret's arms were not painted over suggests that the intended owner of the manuscript was loyal to her and her struggle to return Henry VI to the throne. Moreover, if the iconography of the coats of arms in the manuscript follows the "family history" model, the border decoration of the Yale Law School manuscript suggests that it was made for Prince Edward of Lancaster, Henry and Margaret's only child, who was born in October 1453.

Several aspects of the royal portraits in the Yale Law School manuscript also support the argument that the book was shaped for a purpose different from those of other statutes manuscripts – one reflecting Lancastrian concerns. The royal portraits in the Yale Law School manuscript incorporate iconography that does not appear in other manuscripts of the *New Statutes* with images of kings. Instead, as we will see, the Yale Law School manuscript borrows iconography from devotional manuscripts to bring a different set of associations to its depiction of kingship and justice. In addition, the royal portraits in this manuscript create patterns that suggest similarities and differences among the kings. If one reads the sequence of historiated initials as a "history of English kings," one can see that the iconography used in the portraits of Edward III through Henry VI (plates 1–5) presents these kings as an unbroken line of rulers who follow a religious ideal of just kingship, whereas the iconography used in the depiction of Edward IV (plate 6) suggests that he differs from his predecessors in his relationship to that traditional ideal. Even the distinctions between kings found in some of the other manuscripts of the *Nova statuta*, such as depicting Edward III as an elderly man (e.g., plates 27, 31, and 32) and Richard II as a young man (e.g., plate 29), are eliminated from the sequence of the first four kings in the Yale manuscript: all of the kings from Edward III through Henry V have similar dark hair and beards, making them very similar in age and appearance. Though Henry VI is depicted without a beard, other aspects of his physical appearance and setting link him to the previous kings. Through the similarity of its portraits of the kings from Edward III through Henry VI, the manuscript suggests a unified sequence of kings in which Henry VI participates, but Edward IV does not – a major theme of Henry VI's supporters. The narrative of English history created by the portraits in this manuscript glosses over Henry IV's deposition of Richard II on the basis of this king's failure to fulfill his responsibilities – a strategy similar to the narratives of legitimation that scholars have identified in other Lancastrian texts that were produced after the initial period of Lancastrian denigration of Richard II.[8] For example, Paul Strohm argues that, after Henry V inherited the throne from Henry IV, the Lancastrians symbolically appropriated Richard II as their royal ancestor, first by moving his body to Westminster Abbey and then by reinserting him into royal chronologies: "Richard may be encountered in this aspect in a host of genealogically inspired works of the mid-fifteenth century, in which his image is blandly reinserted in one or another argumentative chain or regal succession, the fact of traumatic rupture minimized or suppressed" (Strohm 1998, 124–25).[9]

In Henry VI's case, these legitimizing narratives of royal succession took several forms, and many combined visual and verbal texts. In addition to the genealogy of Henry VI in the anthology Sir John Talbot gave to Margaret of Anjou as a wedding gift in 1445 (London, British Library MS Royal 15 E vi) (plate 41), numerous genealogical rolls appeared from the 1420s through the 1450s that show Henry VI as the culmination of what appears to be an unbroken line of kings going back to ancient founder figures, such as Britain's legendary founder Brutus (e.g., London, British Library MS Additional 27342) or Noah (e.g., London, British Library MS Additional 18002). Many of these genealogies appear to have been made in association with a "milestone" in Henry's reign, such as his inheritance of the throne, his coronations in London and Paris, his marriage, and the birth of his son.[10] Chronicles in Latin, French, and English also circulated during Henry VI's reign that celebrate him as continuing the achievements of England's ancient royal heritage. While modern readers might not find it surprising that many medieval texts present the reigning monarch in a positive light, Antonia Gransden argues that the extensive use of historical narratives for political purposes during this period was new: "The period shows a marked development in the use of history as a propaganda instrument, both to persuade and to inform" (Gransden 1996, 252). Gransden and other scholars also stress that, despite their legitimizing discourse, many of these narratives interweave praise with allusions to previous or potential problems: the assertions of legitimacy reveal that questions existed and the approbations of royal actions and goals reveal unease about other interpretations or about royal capacity to achieve the ideals depicted. As Strohm points out, "Continually at strife with its own professions, the Lancastrian text is above all a hardworking text, always striving but never succeeding in reconciling its placid surface with its external entanglements and its internal contradictions" (Strohm 1998, 195).[11]

Some of these verbal narratives of Henry VI's royal heritage are versions of the *Brut*, while others present Henry VI's dual inheritance of the crowns of England and France.[12] Among the hardworking Lancastrian texts that present Henry VI as the culmination of an English royal heritage is John Lydgate's widely disseminated poem "The Reigns of the Kings of England," which covers the period from William the Conqueror to Henry VI and may have been composed for the celebration of Henry's knighting in July 1426, when he was four years old.[13] London, British Library MS Lansdowne 204 contains Henry VI's presentation copy of a chronicle of the kings of Britain from Brutus to Henry VI, composed by John Hardyng in 1457.[14] John Capgrave's *Liber de illustribus Henricis* (1446–47) presents Henry VI as the culmination of the kings of England named Henry as part of a three-book account of medieval leaders named Henry, dedicated to Henry VI (Gransden 1996, 389–90). Another kind of narrative of royal succession that celebrates Henry VI as the legitimate heir to England's unbroken royal descent is the set of statues of the kings from William the Conqueror to Henry VI on the magnificent choir screen or *pulpitum* at York Minster. Sarah Brown argues that the York screen is "the largest and most public of a group of works dating from the period c. 1440–60, making an uncompromising statement about the legitimacy of Lancastrian rule. . . . These monuments have in common the representation of the Lancastrian kings as . . . part of the unbroken succession of the English monarchy."[15] The sequence of royal portraits in the Yale Law School *Nova statuta* also parallels earlier English manuscripts that present visual "galleries of kings" through sets of miniatures.[16] Nevertheless, the Yale Law School manuscript portraits differ from other Lancastrian legitimizing texts in two important ways. First, the royal portraits appear in the context of the laws enacted under these monarchs. Second, the first five royal portraits suggest the legitimacy of Henry VI's rule through more than unbroken succession: using iconography that differs significantly from earlier depictions of royal legitimacy, these portraits link Henry VI to the previous four kings of England by depicting his continuation of their close relationship with God.

Through its introduction of a change in iconography after Henry VI, the series of royal portraits in the Yale Law School manuscript suggests that the line of pious and just kings has been broken, not by Richard II or Henry IV, but by Edward IV, who deposed Henry VI. Ironically, of all the royal portraits included in the Yale Law School manuscript, it is also the portrayal of Edward IV, enthroned at center and flanked by other figures, that ties the Yale Law School manuscript to the standardized copies of the *New Statutes* that Kathleen Scott and Jeremy Griffiths have situated in the 1470s and 1480s.[17] As James Marrow and Walter Cahn have noted, many *New Statutes* manuscripts feature an historiated initial depicting a king for the beginning of each new reign (Cahn and Marrow 1978, 240–41). Many of these initials depict a frontal view of the enthroned king flanked by his counselors, usually in groups of clerical and secular figures. The fact that eleven surviving manuscript copies of the *New Statutes* use the same composition for royal portraits by different artists – for at least one royal portrait in the manuscript, and in some cases for eight – does indeed suggest that book illustrators shared models and that a market had arisen for statutes manuscripts that followed these models by the 1470s. The manuscripts with the standardized historiated initials are

1. Cambridge (MA), Houghton Library MS Richardson 40
2. Holkham, Holkham Hall, Library of the Earl of Leicester MS 232
3. Kew, National Archives MS E 164/11 (plate 34)
4. London, British Library MS Additional 15728
5. London, British Library MS Cotton Nero c i

6. London, British Library MS Hargrave 274 (plate 35)
7. London, Lincoln's Inn Library MS Hale 183
8. London, London Metropolitan Archives MS COL/CS/01/007 (plate 37)
9. Oxford, Bodleian Library MS Hatton 10
10. Oxford, St. John's College MS 257 (plate 36)
11. Philadelphia, Free Library MS Carson LC 14. 9.5 (plate 33)

Since all but two of these manuscripts also contain work by Scribe A of the Yale Law School copy of the *New Statutes of England*, the use of such different iconography in the royal portraits of the Yale Law School manuscript becomes even more significant, suggesting that a very different plan guided the artists working on the Yale manuscript.

The standardized royal portraits in these *Nova statuta* manuscripts appear to be versions of the "king in majesty" or "king and counselors" scenes that can be found as illustrations in medieval texts of several genres. Scott sees a possible link between the standardized royal portraits and the illustrations in a manuscript copy of Lydgate's *Troy Book* and *Siege of Thebes* made in the 1450s or 1460s (London, British Library MS Royal 18 D ii), since some of the illustrations for these texts depict a king seated at center under a canopy, holding a scepter and consulting with advisors (plate 42) (Scott 1980b). The part of the manuscript containing these two works was commissioned by Sir William Herbert, Earl of Pembroke (d. 1469), and his wife Anne Devereux, possibly for presentation to Henry VI or Edward IV; but it was never completed. Similar depictions of a king in council with advisors also appear in earlier French manuscripts, such as a copy of the *Chroniques de France* dated to about 1400 (London, British Library MS Royal 20 C vii) (plate 43) (O'Meara 2001; Gilson and Warner 1921, 2:372–74; Hedeman 1991, 221–26).[18] An English manuscript from the late fourteenth or early fifteenth century that depicts a king consulting with advisors is London, British Library MS Royal 1 E ix (fol. 167r), a Bible that may have been made for either Richard II or Henry IV.[19] Another earlier English parallel is the depiction of a king consulting with advisors in the historiated initial at the beginning of a late fourteenth-century copy of the *Modus tenendi Parliamentum* (London, British Library MS Cotton Nero D vi, fol. 72r) (plate 44) (J. Taylor 1968, 679).

The standardized portraits of the monarch in the *Nova statuta* manuscripts might be read as highlighting the king's sovereignty as lawgiver, since the image shows the king with symbols of royal power (throne, crown, scepter, orb) and centralizes the king while marginalizing the other figures (Hayward 1975, 142). These figures often wear ceremonial robes that identify them as members of the clergy and secular lords, while in other cases some of these figures wear striped sleeves, which might identify them as lawyers.[20] In some cases, the figures include subjects without ceremonial robes, who might represent the king's common subjects. Despite the central position of the king in these images, the inclusion of other figures, whether these are read as royal advisors or members of Parliament, inscribes their presence into the depiction of royal justice. M. A. Michael has described this type of ruler portrait as a reflection of the complex balance of power between the monarchy and the body politic in medieval England: the image suggests the hierarchy of king over magnates and bishops, at the same time that the image underscores the good king's reliance on counsel (Michael 1994, 43–44).

By using a different composition for its first five royal portraits, therefore, the Yale Law School manuscript offers a different perspective on royal power and justice before turning to a "king and counselors" model: the portraits of Edward III and Richard II include no royal subjects (plates 1 and 2), and the portraits of Henry IV, Henry V, and Henry VI (plates 3, 4, and 5) include only one or two other people, so that they seem unlikely to represent large segments of the body politic. Because these initials are the three executed by the second illustrator, the introduction of additional figures could simply reflect the choice of the artist to whom these miniatures were assigned; but this runs counter to the care for continuity that the second illustrator generally exhibits. Since the additional figures appear only in the initials depicting Henry IV, Henry V, and Henry VI, they do serve to distinguish the Lancastrian kings from the first two kings in the series. The men's fur-adorned red robes associate them with the royal counselors or noble members of Parliament who flank Edward IV in the last initial; but the additional figures in the three illustrations of Lancastrian kings are not portrayed consistently across the three images: only the front figure in the initial depicting Henry VI has the miniver bars that indicate high rank among the secular lords. The figures do not appear to be tonsured or have other symbols of ecclesiastical office, so they do not appear to be members of the clergy. In addition, the position of these figures in the miniatures does not remain constant. The first figure peers from behind the curtained canopy in the initial depicting Henry IV (plate 3). Then, in the initial depicting Henry V (plate 4), a similar figure appears before the king and gestures as though addressing him. In the initial depicting Henry VI (plate 5), two similar figures appear to the side of the royal canopy, and the first of the two men gestures with his hands, but faces in the same direction as the king, as if joining him in prayer. Models for the three different configurations can be found in earlier texts associated with the English and French royal families in the late fourteenth and early fifteenth centuries. Images of John of France, Duke of Berry, and his wife in his devotional books sometimes show men partially visible behind the curtains that screen the duke or duchess during prayer (plates 45–47). The figures who hold a staff appear to be officials in the duke's household, and they hold the curtain back as if to mediate between our gaze and the private devotions of the duke and duchess; but some of the figures partially visible behind curtains are clergy participating in worship along with the duke. Perhaps a better parallel with the three scenes in the Yale manuscript can be found in an image that shows a king kneeling before a *prie-dieu* and being counseled by an advisor, while another figure kneels at the side of the king's curtained throne: this image depicts St. Edward, the martyred English king, in a composite illustration of his life in the breviary made for John of Lancaster, Duke of Bedford, while he was regent of France for Henry VI from 1422 to 1435 (Paris, Bibliothèque nationale MS Lat. 17294, fol. 432v) (plate 48). Here the illustration serves to reinforce St. Edward's reputation as a good king because, as William of Malmesbury's twelfth-century history of the kings of England describes him, he was pious and listened to good counsel.[21]

The changes in the additional figures across the three illustrations of Lancastrian kings in the Yale manuscript suggest a narrative, perhaps a sequence that depicts the role of a small number of trusted counselors during the reigns of the Lancastrian kings: the addition of a small number of counselors in these three initials suggests an intermediate step between kings who rely on themselves alone to understand God's counsel and kings who rely on human counsel rather than divine. One of the criticisms leveled against Richard II was that he did not listen to wise counsel, which in turn led the Lancastrian kings to present themselves as working closely with such counsel.[22] As the character Prudence teaches in Chaucer's "Tale of Melibee," a king should take counsel first from God, then from self-examination, and then from the most wise and trusted subjects of his realm, who will be very few in number (*Canterbury Tales* VII, 1115–71, in Benson 1987, 222–23).[23] The figures who appear in the portraits of the Lancastrian kings in the Yale manuscript could therefore be seen to reinforce the manuscript's celebration of the Lancastrian kings, especially Henry VI, as monarchs who fulfill the ideals of kingship enunciated by medieval mirrors for princes.

The fact that the first five portraits in the Yale Law School manuscript highlight the role of the king in the construction of English law and play down the role of representative bodies as advisors may reflect Lancastrian concerns about Parliament's power after 1453. Though the king held the right to call Parliament into session, Parliament could become a powerful tool in the hands of the king's opponents, if the king appeared to be unable or unwilling to exercise his authority. Such had been the case in the depositions of Edward II in 1327 and Richard II in 1399, who, while they were in the custody of their opponents, were presented to Parliament as resigning or forfeiting their right to rule, enabling Parliament to name successors.[24] An even more ambiguous set of circumstances arose with Henry VI in August 1453, when he became both mentally and physically impaired. When his incapacity could no longer be hidden, representatives of both Henry's supporters and his opponents appealed to Parliament to designate a loyal subject to act in the king's name: in March 1454 Parliament rejected Margaret of Anjou's petition for appointment as regent for her husband and appointed Richard of York Protector of the Realm instead.[25] After the king's recovery in December 1454 and the end of York's protectorate in February 1455, the Lancastrians tried to undermine the new power that York had achieved through his position, and York responded with military force: the duke and his supporters attacked the king and his entourage at St. Albans in May 1455, wounding the king, killing several Lancastrians, including members of the royal household, and arresting many of the Lancastrian leaders who survived. With the king's closest supporters either dead or in custody, York persuaded Henry to issue a pardon to the Yorkists who had participated in the battle. York's further consolidation of his power manifested itself in November, when Parliament again declared Henry incapacitated and again appointed York Protector of the Realm until the king recovered. Parliamentary battles between the Yorkists and Lancastrians continued through the end of the decade, until the Lancastrians persuaded Parliament to attaint the Duke of York and his followers in December 1459 and the Yorkists again turned to military force, capturing Henry VI in July 1460 and persuading him to inform Parliament in October 1460 that Richard of York, rather than Henry and Margaret's son Edward of Lancaster, was the rightful heir to the throne. After Richard of York died in battle against the Lancastrians in December 1460, the duke's son Edward led his army to London and claimed the title of king before any official transfer of power had occurred. Edward then appealed to Parliament to declare Henry in violation of the succession agreement that Parliament had accepted the previous October and to declare him the new king, as Richard's heir. Through Parliament's approval, on 4 March 1461 Edward of York became King Edward IV (R. Griffiths 1981, 854–82; Wolffe 1981, 315–32).

It seems appropriate, then, that the portrait of Edward IV in the Yale Law School *Nova statuta* depicts him flanked by secular and clerical lords, as if in Parliament (plate 6). Nevertheless, even in its portrait of Edward IV, where the Yale Law School manuscript is most like the standardized model of king and counselors, we still find important differences. Though the portrait of Edward IV in this manuscript appears at first glance to follow the standardized format, closer scrutiny reveals that this historiated initial does not follow the standard model in important details: instead of holding a scepter and orb, traditional symbols of the king's rightful rule, the image of Edward IV in the Yale Law School manuscript shows him holding only a sword. In addition, Edward holds this sword in his left or sinister hand, and his right hand points to the sword, calling the reader's attention to it. The other manuscript copies of the *New Statutes of England* that depict kings but do not use the standardized image – such as San Marino, Huntington Library MS HM 19920 (plate 29), London, British Library MS Stowe 389 (plate 30), London, Lincoln's Inn Library MS Hale 194 (plate 31), and London, British Library MS Yates Thompson 48 (plate 32) – do not replace the scepter or orb with a sword. The Yale Law School manuscript's differences from the standardized model in the portrait of Edward IV therefore suggest a deliberate choice on the part of the person or persons planning the illustration to play off of the standardized iconography to make a new point in a subtle manner: according to the Lancastrians, Edward IV may have had Parliament's approval for his claim to the throne, but he received this approval because of unjust use of military power.

Depictions of kings holding swords were certainly not unusual in the medieval period. In another context, the depiction of a seated king holding an upright sword might symbolize his authority as judge or embodiment of the law.[26] For example, Adelaide Bennett describes a depiction of King Solomon seated and holding an upright sword in the Windmill Psalter (New York, Pierpont Morgan Library MS M102, fol. 2r) (plate 49) as "an attitude typical of the ruler as judge" (A. Bennett 1980, 62). Nevertheless, the scene portrayed in this psalter, based on 1 Kings 3:16–28, reveals a complex view of the sword's role in royal justice. Solomon tests the claims of two women to be a child's true mother by calling for a sword (not the one in his hand, but the one held by a soldier on the right of the image) and offering to have the child cut in half, which causes the true mother to relinquish her claim so that the child may live, and Solomon gives the child to her. The sword's power in this narrative is strategic, and the passage ends with the people of Israel in awe of Solomon because they recognize that divine wisdom guides the king's judgment. Since the psalter presents this image within the initial that opens Psalm 1, the reader's interpretation of the image might also be shaped by the verbal text's praise of those who delight in the law of the Lord and meditate on that law day and night. Read together, the verbal text and visual image link King David's exhortation of human beings to learn from God's law with King Solomon's wise use of the sword in pursuit of justice. The visual and verbal contexts of this image of a king holding a sword therefore offer an example of the need to consider how even signs that seem conventional take on different meanings in different contexts. As Richard Mohr has argued about the semiotics of legal symbols, "The process of interpreting a sign may be understood through the contexts of meanings by which a sign is connected with various other cultural manifestations. The changing cultural, social, and political context refigures the meaning which we attribute to a sign. In other words, its meaning depends on the associations, cultural contexts and broader meaning frameworks by which we interpret it" (Mohr 2005, 180).

The sword's use as a symbol of justice seems to have come into medieval Europe through both classical and biblical traditions. The Egyptian goddess of justice Ma'at and the Greek goddess of justice Themis were associated with scales, but Roman personifications of Justicia were associated with scales and swords.[27] In medieval Christian iconography, swords play several roles: the Archangel Michael sometimes holds an upright sword, as well as a scale, in his depiction as agent of divine justice, and saints sometimes hold upright swords as symbols of their martyrdom (Kirschbaum 1968–76, under "Schwert," "Recht," "Justicia," and "Kaiser"). It may be for that reason that St. Paul holds an upright sword in his right hand on a seal created for the City of London in the fourteenth century.[28] St. Paul's sword may also have allegorical significance on the seal, representing his use of God's word, rather than earthly weapons, to defeat the forces of evil: in his famous description of the metaphoric armor of the faithful, Paul refers to the word of God as the sword of the Spirit (Ephesians 6:17). In the case of the iconography of the portrait of Edward IV, however, the Yale Law School manuscript does not seem to draw on an association of the king with St. Paul, martyrdom, or the word of God.

Swords were associated with some traditional images of English kings, including some found on royal seals. Attaching the visual image of the king to legal documents was a way of representing the judicial authority behind the verbal text of the document. Several English kings after the Norman Conquest used a Great Seal on which the king appears enthroned and holding an upright sword in his right hand on the obverse side and appears on horseback holding an upright sword in his right hand on the reverse side. Such is the case, for example, with the Great Seal of Richard I.[29] However, as Binski and Musson have shown, a significant change in the imaging of royal justice took place under Henry III (Binski 1999, 76–77; Musson 2001, 224–25). Whereas Henry III's first Great Seal continued the earlier imagery of the king holding a sword on both sides, in 1259 he commissioned a new seal that kept the image of a king on horseback with a sword in his right hand on the reverse side, but changed the image of the enthroned king on the obverse side (plates 50 and 51). In this new image, the throne uses iconography associated with King Solomon, yet the king's right hand holds not a sword but a scepter topped with a dove, linking Henry III to a biblical symbol of divine grace and to the sainted English king, Edward the Confessor, whose coat of arms included five doves (see, for example, plates 61 and 62). This new construction of royal power received contemporary approval: in the same year that Henry III's new Great Seal appeared, the *Liber de antiquis legibus* noted the change in the image on the royal seal and commented that this fulfilled Merlin's prophecy that the sword would be severed from the scepter (Binski 1999, 79). Subsequent English kings, including Edward III (plates 52 and 53) and Henry VI (plates 54 and 55), preserved the iconography of the 1259 Great Seal, maintaining the distinction between the king's two roles as military leader and embodiment of justice. A similar balance of the king's two roles can be seen in the kings holding upright swords and scepters on the York Minster choir screen, as well as in Lydgate's poetic depiction of St. Edmund holding scepter and sword to symbolize the monarch's two roles (Lewis 2005, 163). Portraits of English kings holding unsheathed swords did continue to appear, including the portraits accompanying a set of Middle English verses on the kings of England in London, British Library MS Cotton Julius E iv, and the opening historiated initial in some copies of the *Vetera statuta Angliae*, such as Cambridge (MA), Harvard Law School Library MS 58 and Princeton, Scheide Collection MS 30.[30] Nevertheless, images of English and French kings in majesty without swords became more prominent in the late fourteenth century. For example, the image of the king enthroned and holding orb and scepter is the model used for the portrait of Richard II made in the 1390s that now hangs in Westminster Abbey.[31] As Binski argues, the large size of the portrait and its depiction of Richard with symbols of royal authority, but without any visual context relating him to another figure, event, or place, suggest that it was made as a "manifest display of rank" and "audacious icon of power" (Binski 1995, 204). Yet no sword appears.

In the Yale Law School *New Statutes* manuscript, the portrayal of Edward IV with a sword in his left hand, rather than in his right, and unbalanced by a scepter or cross-topped orb in the other hand, suggests a subtle attempt to depict Edward IV as someone who confused the king's two roles, using military power to gain authority to rule. While the manuscript's depiction of Edward IV takes some of its significance from comparison with earlier depictions of the enthroned king in statutes manuscripts as well as in other contexts, it takes its most immediate significance from comparison with the series of five royal portraits that come before it (plates 1–5). Each of the first five kings in this manuscript appears kneeling before a *prie-dieu*, an image that does not appear in other surviving copies of the *Nova statuta*. Despite small differences in the physical characteristics of the kings that give the impression of individualized portraits and the appearance of figures in addition to the king in some of the images, this representation of kingship remains constant across the depictions of the first five kings: the images include symbols of sovereign rulership, such as scepter and crown, yet these illustrations depict all five kings on their knees in prayer, demonstrating their piety and humility before God. If the standardized portraits showing the king flanked by groups of his counselors are thought to emphasize the king's power as sovereign lawgiver, who nonetheless must seek counsel from his subjects, the first five portraits in the Yale Law School manuscript might be seen to challenge that construction, reminding readers that a king's power to rule derives from a divine lawgiver, who authorizes kings to act as earthly representatives of divine justice and to whom earthly monarchs who desire to embody true justice must appeal for counsel.

The full significance of the difference between the first five royal portraits in the Yale *New Statutes* manuscript and the last one becomes clearer when we recognize that the depictions of the first five kings echo the images of King David at prayer that appear in many liturgical and devotional books in the late Middle Ages.[32] Not only in illustrated Bibles, but also accompanying the Psalms in psalters, breviaries, and books of hours, images of King David became a traditional feature of devotional books, including images of David at prayer. Although some of these illustrations depict David praying in the wilderness, as we can see in the missal given by William Melreth to St. Lawrence Church in London in 1446 (London, British Library MS Arundel 109, fol. 8r) (plate 56), other illustrations present David in architectural settings, kneeling before an altar or a *prie-dieu*, sometimes with a throne behind him.[33] Examples of David praying at a *prie-dieu* in French books of hours include one in Austin, Harry Ransom Humanities Research Center MS HRC 5, fol. 96r (plate 57) and Jean Colombe's illustration for Psalm 124 in the *Très riches heures* of John of France, Duke of Berry (Chantilly, Musée Condé MS 65, fol. 53v). We know that this iconography was also part of English tradition in the fifteenth century, because several English manuscripts from this time show David kneeling in prayer before a *prie-dieu*: these include Oxford, Bodleian Library MS Don. d. 85, fol. 21v (plate 58); Cape Town, National Library of South Africa MS Grey 4 c 5, fol. 36r; Turin, Biblioteca Nazionale Universitaria MS I. I. 9, fol. 82v; London, British Library MS Royal I E ix, fol. 153r; and Nottingham, University Library Wollaton Antiphonal, fol. 213r.[34]

The Yale Law School manuscript's use of images of King David in prayer as a model for its first five illustrations suggests an attempt to associate these English monarchs, but not Edward IV, with the great biblical king. In the visual arts and literature of medieval and renaissance Europe, King David was depicted as one of the most important models for rulers, both because he represented the unification of secular and divine authority and because his story reinforced the importance of royal piety and humility.[35] Several medieval Latin and vernacular texts composed for courtly audiences in England, as well as in France, employ King David as the primary model of ideal kingship. For example, in his famous mirror for princes, the twelfth-century writer John of Salisbury calls David the best of the kings about whom he has read (*Policraticus*, bk. 8, ch. 20).[36] In his French poem *Les voeux du paon* (c. 1310), Jacques de Longuyon names King David as one of the Nine Worthies or chivalric heroes – three from classical literature, three from the Bible, and three from medieval literature – who appear widely in the literature and visual arts of the fourteenth and fifteenth centuries.[37] In the late fourteenth century, John Gower presents King David as the mirror and exemplar for all kings in *Le mirour de l'homme* (lines 22,873–84):

> Ly Rois David, comme dist l'auctour,
> Estoit des six pointz essamplour,
> Dont chascun Roy puet essampler. . . .
> As autrez Rois il fuist mirour.[38]
>
> (King David, as the author says,
> Was an exemplar of the six points,
> Which each king can follow. . . .
> To other kings he was a mirror.)

Because King David was considered the author of the Book of Psalms, the comments on justice in the Psalms were often presented as David's instructions to his successors on good kingship. For example, *L'avis aus roys*, an anonymous fourteenth-century French treatise that survives in New York, Pierpont Morgan Library MS M456, begins with a quotation from Psalm 2: "Reges intelligite erudimini qui iudicatis terram. Cest une parole que dit David qui fu Roy et prophete, laquele parole sadresce aus Roys et aus princes qui ont le monde a gourerner et iuger" ("Kings, understand, be instructed, you who judge the earth. This is a statement that David speaks, who was a king and prophet, which statement addresses itself to kings and to princes who have the world to govern and judge"). The miniature that accompanies the opening of this text shows King David instructing two other kings (plate 59).[39] An earlier French royal manuscript that presents David as the model for kings and also emphasizes the king's role as upholder of the law is the Latin Bible given to the young Carolingian king Charles the Bald by the Benedictine abbey of St. Martin at Tours in 845 (Paris, Bibliothèque nationale MS lat. 1).[40] The illustrations in this manuscript and the dedicatory poems addressed to Charles the Bald encourage the young king to consider King David as his model and to read the Bible as instruction in divine law, so that he may uphold justice in his own realm (Dutton and Kessler 1997, 44). The visual and verbal texts framing this copy of the Bible thus transform it into a mirror for princes. A fourteenth-century English royal manuscript that presents King David as the model of true kingship is London, British Library MS Royal 2 B vii. Anne Rudloff Stanton argues that this manuscript, which prefaces the Latin psalter with an illustrated summary of the Bible in French, was commissioned by Edward II's queen, Isabelle of France, as a book that would instruct their son, the future Edward III, to follow the model of King David: the prince would find lessons in good kingship in the words of the Psalms and in the manuscript's illustrations of the life of King David, including David instructing his own son, Solomon (Stanton 2001, 174–88, 231–44). As in the case of the Bible of Charles the Bald, Royal 2 B vii transforms a traditional devotional text into a *speculum regis* by highlighting King David as the model of true kingship.

In depicting five of its six kings in terms that reflect the iconography of King David, the Yale *Nova statuta* both associates the first five with an important medieval ideal of kingship and differentiates them from Edward IV, whose depiction involves very different imagery. As the visual texts accompanying the statutes, the first five illustrations also suggest to the reader of the statutes, not that kings are the sovereign givers of law, as Hayward argues, but that human laws and rulers are secondary to the divine law of the heavenly king. Though the human king is physically central to the image, he is shown on his knees in petition to a higher authority and so is shown paradoxically as both earthly ruler and spiritual servant of the heavenly king: the initial depicts the human king as the rightful arbiter of earthly justice because of his proper relationship with divine justice. Instead of depicting the king in consultation with earthly counselors, the first five portraits depict the kings in consultation with a heavenly counselor. As a result, in the context of the Yale Law School manuscript, the transition to the standardized depiction of the king with his court for Edward IV becomes an ironic commentary on this king's different relationship with divine justice, compared with that of his predecessors.

The Yale Law School manuscript emphasizes the difference between Edward IV and the king he deposed by depicting Henry VI with iconography closest to that of King David: Henry VI's portrait (plate 5) is the only one of the first five that includes the face of God that often appears in the depictions of King David in prayer. An important feature of many images of King David in medieval Bibles and devotional works is the depiction of God revealing his face to David, often with golden rays shining down on the king: we saw an English example in the Melreth missal made in 1446 (London, British Library MS Arundel 109, fol. 8r) (plate 56). In the Yale Law School manuscript, this feature of the traditional David iconography appears only in the initial depicting Henry VI. A circular blue area in the upper-right corner of this historiated initial has facial characteristics that represent the face of God, in the same visual style as we find in three depictions of King David in an English psalter that has been dated to the early fifteenth century (Oxford, Bodleian Library MS Don. d. 85, fols. 21v, 29r, and 42v): on fol. 21v (plate 58) and fol. 42v the outline of the face of God appears in a red circular area in the heavens, whereas on fol. 29r the area with the face of God is blue. The circular blue area in the historiated initial for Henry VI in the Yale Law School manuscript sends golden rays down upon Henry, just as the face of God more explicitly sheds gracious illumination in countless depictions of King David in late medieval Bibles, books of hours, and psalters. In using imagery that associates Henry VI so strongly with King David, the Yale Law School manuscript distinguishes Henry VI from the earlier kings in the series, as well as from his deposer, and suggests that he is both the recipient of divine grace and most like the medieval ideal of kingship.

Appropriating the iconography of King David in order to depict a living king was not a widespread practice in the late medieval period; but Scott's discussion of patron influence on fifteenth-century manuscript illustration suggests that there are parallels between the images of King David in prayer that accompanied the Psalms in late medieval manuscripts and the illustrations of unidentified praying figures in manuscripts from the same period, which might be considered patron portraits or more generic models of contemporary piety.[41] Representations of King David in psalters and books of hours do seem to have inspired many of the depictions of John of France, Duke of Berry, in his own devotional books: he is often portrayed kneeling before a *prie-dieu* with a depiction of God's face or Christ's face appearing in the clouds at the top of the illustration. Examples occur, for instance, in his book of hours called the *Petites heures* (Paris, Bibliothèque nationale MS lat. 18014), on fols. 106v, 117v, 119r, 121v (plate 60), and 145r.[42] The frequency with which these images of the duke appear suggests a keen desire to depict the duke reenacting the devotional model of King David – and perhaps to suggest that the duke would be a suitable candidate to reenact David's royal role as well. The use of some of these illustrations in conjunction with readings from the Book of Psalms further suggests the idea that the duke is portrayed as following the model of King David in his devotions. The duke's illustrated devotional manuscripts were famous in his own time and influenced artists and wealthy manuscript patrons in the early fifteenth century, including the English nobility who were part of the administration of English-controlled areas of France after 1415. Knowledge of the Duke of Berry's portraits at prayer may, for instance, have led to the inclusion of parallel images of King David at prayer and a French king at prayer, both with the face of God looking down from above, in the presentation copy of Pierre Salmon's *Dialogues*, a mirror for princes originally written for Charles VI of France (Geneva, Bibliothèque publique et universitaire MS fr. 165): since he helped the Duke of Berry collect books, in addition to serving as secretary to Charles VI, Salmon would most likely have seen the duke's elaborately decorated prayer books and have recognized iconography that he could use for his own purposes.[43] Nevertheless, the Yale manuscript's use of the iconography of King David at prayer as a model for the depictions of kings in a legal manuscript, rather than a devotional manuscript or traditional mirror for princes, is clearly a major innovation.

The depiction of Henry VI in the Yale Law School *Nova statuta* also differentiates him from the other kings in the series by showing him with a crown that is of a different style from those worn by the other kings in the manuscript. This crown has arches that cross over Henry VI's head and are topped with a cross. In their discussion of this portrait, Walter Cahn and James Marrow identify this crown as the Germanic *Bügel* type, which had imperial associations (Cahn and Marrow 1978, 240). Medieval illustrations of classical and medieval emperors often show them wearing an arched or closed crown: as a Christian emperor, Charlemagne appears with the cross-topped crown in the illustrations of the *Chroniques de France*. Some late medieval manuscripts use a similar cross-topped crown for Christ in depictions of the coronation of the Virgin.[44] In a study of the role of the imperial crown in depictions of English monarchs, Dale Hoak argues that this style of crown became an important symbol of royal power during the reign of Henry V, who associated it with St. Edward the Confessor; but Hoak explains that Henry VI was the first English monarch to be depicted wearing it during his lifetime, perhaps because he was the first English king also crowned as the monarch of France (Hoak 1995, 5). For example, Henry VI wears an arched crown in his portrayal in the royal charters for King's College, Cambridge, and Eton College, decorated by William Abel in 1446, and the arched crown also appears at the top of both documents with the royal arms that quarter the symbols of the French and English monarchs (plates 61 and 62).[45] Henry VI also wears an arched crown in the illustrated royal charter for the London Leathersellers' Company, dated 1444 (plate 63).[46] By combining the iconography of King David with the imperial crown, the Yale manuscript's depiction of Henry VI thus suggests that Henry VI represents the highest degree of divine favor and earthly authority of all the kings depicted in the manuscript.

The Yale Law School manuscript's representation of Henry VI as a king who has imperial majesty as well as divine favor accords with depictions of him as a saint in the 1470s and 1480s. Veneration of Henry grew rapidly after he was murdered in May 1471 while imprisoned by Edward IV in the Tower of London.[47] Edward IV had Henry's body quietly buried at the Benedictine abbey at Chertsey in Surrey; but pilgrims began to honor him there, as well as in churches in the north of England, including at his statue on the choir screen in York Minster. By 1473, Edward IV began to issue proclamations in London that royal authorization would be necessary for pilgrimages. By 1480, fueled by claims of posthumous miracles, the strength of Henry's cult caused Edward IV such concern that he asked the livery companies of London for aid in discouraging pilgrims from praying at Henry's tomb. In 1484, Edward's successor Richard III had Henry VI's body reinterred at St. George's Chapel at Windsor Castle, purportedly to honor his predecessor, but most likely also to regulate access to Henry's tomb. After Richard's own overthrow in 1485, his successor embraced the cult of Henry VI: Henry VII commissioned an account of the miracles associated with Henry VI in order to make a case for his canonization and planned a chapel at Westminster Abbey that would house his own tomb along with that of his martyred predecessor. Official sainthood never came, and Henry VI's body remained entombed at Windsor; however, images of Henry VI, such as the rood screen painting from ca. 1493 in St. Catherine's Church at Ludham, Norfolk, continue to honor him as a saint, combining the imperial crown with a halo. The large numbers of pilgrim badges for Henry VI that archeologists have uncovered suggest that only St. Thomas of Canterbury received more veneration than Henry VI before the Reformation limited public worship of saints in English religious life: Brian Spencer has catalogued more than ninety different designs of badges honoring Henry VI.[48] Most often, the badges portray Henry with orb and scepter, even when he is depicted on horseback, and he often wears an arched crown similar to the one he wears in the Yale manuscript.

Henry VII's support for official recognition of Henry VI as a saint both responded to and encouraged widespread devotion to Henry VI in the 1480s. Scholars now consider John Blacman's biography of Henry VI, which highlights the king's piety, as part of the effort to support canonization in the 1480s.[49] Kathleen Scott also notes evidence of the veneration of Henry VI in a *Nova statuta* manuscript that she dates to c. 1488 (London, British Library MS Hargrave 274) (Scott 1996, 2:347). The depiction of Henry VI in this manuscript (plate 64) presents him in the standardized format, except that it shows him wearing the imperial crown topped by a cross and flanked by angels descending from heaven with a heavenly scepter and crown. Scott has found work by the illustrator who painted this initial in three other copies of the *Nova statuta*, which she dates to the 1480s and 1490s; but none of these other copies singles Henry VI out for special treatment. Since this illustrator's work also appears in three additional manuscripts associated with Henry VII and his family, Hargrave 274 may also have been made for them, which would explain that manuscript's depiction of heavenly honors for Henry VI.

Though the Yale Law School manuscript's portrait of Henry VI as the recipient of divine favor parallels the saintly images of the king that appeared after his death, the Yale image of Henry VI is closer to the depictions of him as a devout and just king with divine benediction for his rule that appeared much earlier. These began in response to the unusual circumstances of his accession to the throne. Henry VI inherited the throne of England at the age of nine months, when his father Henry V died on 31 August 1422, and inherited the throne of France just six weeks later, as a result of the Treaty of Troyes, when his grandfather Charles VI died on 21 October 1422. Henry VI's uncles, the Duke of Gloucester and the Duke of Bedford, quickly took up the task of promoting images of the young king that emphasized the legitimacy of his rule of England and France on the basis of divine sanction and earthly law. As J. W. McKenna has demonstrated, over the next ten years, regency officials devised both literary themes and pictorial motifs to advertise this public image of Henry VI at home and abroad (McKenna 1965).[50] The strategic texts for public consumption included newly designed coins, some of which appropriated imagery from traditional depictions of the Annunciation for a new political purpose: "Since the figures on the coin [the angel Gabriel and the Virgin Mary] stand directly behind the two escutcheons [of England and France], the religious figures could be construed to personify the countries whose arms are directly in front of them. Understood in this fashion, the angel (England) is portrayed as announcing to the Virgin (France) the coming of a saviour" (McKenna 1965, 149). Also belonging to this campaign to claim divine sanction for Henry VI's inheritance of the crowns of France and England is the use of angels to present the two crowns to Henry in the pedigrees commissioned by the Duke of Bedford to accompany copies of Laurence Calot's poem on Henry's dual monarchy when it was displayed in French cathedrals (McKenna 1965, 151–52).[51] An image of Henry VI that suggests he received his English crown from the Virgin Mary herself appeared as the third tableau at Henry's English coronation feast in November 1429, as described by John Lygate's account in "The Sotoltes at the Coronation Banquet of Henry VI" – yet another example of the Lancastrians' "conflations of political and theological imagery" (MacCracken 1934, 623–24).[52]

Several other early visual and verbal portraits of Henry VI suggest divine sanction for his role as heir to the thrones of England and France by associating him with each nation's sainted kings of the past, especially Edward the Confessor and Louis IX. Lydgate's roundel celebrating Henry's coronation at Westminster depicts him as "Blode of Seint Edward and Seint Lowys," a theme Lydgate echoes in his ballade for the same occasion, in which he describes the young king as "Royal braunche descendid from twoo lynes / Of Saynt Edward and of Saynt Lowys, / Hooly sayntes translated in theyre shrynes."[53] Likewise, according to Lydgate's account, the first tableau that was presented as part of the English coronation banquet showed St. Edward and St. Louis escorting Henry VI (MacCracken 1934, 623–24).[54] Scholars like McKenna have noted that St. Louis also appears as a patron of Henry VI in the illustrations in London, British Library MS Cotton Domitian A xvii, a psalter given to Henry VI, perhaps by his mother, Katherine of Valois, in honor of his French coronation in 1431 (McKenna 1965, 158; Backhouse 1997, 153).[55] The depiction of St. Louis presenting Henry VI to Christ and Mary, while God the Father and the Holy Spirit look on from above, that appears on fol. 50r (plate 65) parallels the image of Richard II presented to Christ and the Virgin by St. Edward, St. Edmund, and St. John the Baptist in the Wilton Diptych (see Whittingham 1971 and Scheifele 1999). What critics have not commented on, however, is the role that this image of holy patronage plays in the sequence of illustrations within this manuscript – images that together transform the devotional book into a mirror for princes. Though the original manuscript appears to have been augmented for presentation to the young king, the resulting combination of illustrations and psalms offers a textual mirror for Henry VI that depicts him as pious in his own devotions, blessed with the patronage of several heavenly figures, and acting in parallel with King David. The manuscript intertwines images of King David with images of Henry VI so thoroughly that the parallels between them become clear. Before the miniature depicting Henry's presentation to Christ and the Virgin by St. Louis, the reader finds the opening of Psalm 1 on fol. 13r, illustrated by two miniatures (plate 66): the miniature at the top of the leaf depicts two scenes from the life of King David (fighting with Goliath and singing psalms), while the miniature at the bottom of the leaf depicts Henry VI kneeling at a *prie-dieu*, with his throne behind him and an altar before him, echoing many of the depictions of King David at prayer found in medieval books of devotion. The two miniatures thus create a frame for the opening of Psalm 1, which praises those who study and follow the law of the Lord. Images of Henry VI then appear at the opening of later psalms in the manuscript, where psalters often show images of King David, and banners in the images show the young king repeating words from David's Psalms. The parallel between Henry VI and King David finds reinforcement in the final illustrations in the manuscript: in facing miniatures on fols. 206v and 207r (plates 67 and 68), the left image depicts King David singing psalms in his court, while the right image shows Henry kneeling at a *prie-dieu* before Christ and the Virgin, who kneel in supplication to God the Father, as if interceding for the young king. The illustrations accompany the opening of Psalm 109 in the Vulgate Bible, which is often associated with coronations because it depicts the Lord's words of welcome to a king and expressions of support for the king's justice and power. Depictions of Henry VI in parallel with King David thus create a frame for the young king's reading of the Psalms, enacting the process of learning about good kingship from King David's words and actions that is suggested by texts like *L'avis aus roys*. Several other illustrations in the manuscript reinforce the idea that the young king follows the model of King David, since they show Henry VI leading members of his court in devotions or participating in public worship, just as David is shown leading his people in the Lord's praise. Many of the leaves that open a psalm in this manuscript also have a facing illustration showing a medieval religious community at worship, presumably singing the psalms of the daily office, perhaps suggesting the important role that these groups have in supporting the young king as he follows King David's model (plate 69). One interesting departure from the traditions of mirrors for princes that this manuscript offers is its depiction of women as participants in establishing the young king's spiritual authority. Following the image of Henry VI's presentation to Christ and Mary by St. Louis is a miniature showing the young king's presentation to Christ and Mary by St. Katherine, patron saint of Henry's mother, Katherine of Valois (fol. 75r) (plate 70), which suggests the importance of the queen herself as a spiritual guide to her son, as well as presenting the most recent blood link between Henry VI and the French royal line. In addition, the reader finds opposite this image a miniature depicting a community of nuns singing the divine office (fol. 74v) (plate 71) and another image of nuns at worship on fol. 177v, just as other miniatures in the manuscript show men in religious orders (including hermits) at worship. These additions of spiritual women to the visual portrayal of kingship in the manuscript, marginal though they might seem, present a significant parallel to the Yale Law School manuscript's depiction of the importance of good queens in the achievement of good kingship.

Associating Henry VI with King David was one of the ways in which the Lancastrians could associate their young king with the ideal of just kingship. This goal was also served in the pageant devoted to the subject of royal justice presented as part of the festivities that welcomed the young king to London in February 1432, after his coronation in Paris. In this case, we have John Carpenter's letter describing the events, as well as John Lydgate's poem, "King Henry VI's Triumphant Entry into London, 21 February 1432" (Mac-Cracken 1934, 630–48). This pageant depicts a young king seated on a throne and advised by three female figures (representing mercy, truth, and clemency), as well as two judges and eight sergeants at law. According to Lydgate's poem, the pageant's theme was that *iudicium* (law) and *iudiciam* (justice) will "a kyng preserve in lange prosperytee" ["preserve a king in prosperity for a long time"] (line 292). Robert Zajkowski describes this pageant as an expression of the most fundamental fifteenth-century beliefs about law and kingship: "Among the most important of these was the divine origin of the law, the close association of the king with the rule of law, and the further close connection of law and justice with the preservation of God-ordained social hierarchy, the estates, and the peace and harmony of society" (Zajkowski 2002, 121).

Associating Henry VI with just kingship and a divine mandate remained an important project for his supporters throughout his reign. In addition to attaching the king's image to legal documents in the form of the Great Seal, the Lancastrians often enhanced the power of the royal word by including a painted image of the king on the legal document itself. As Elizabeth Danbury and Anthony Musson have argued, the decoration of medieval legal documents often provided an ideological frame for the verbal text (Danbury 1989b; Musson 2001, 23). Some of these images link Henry's legal authority with his religious devotion. For example, the 1446 royal charter for King's College, Cambridge (plate 61) depicts Henry kneeling before a *prie-dieu* and presenting his charter for the educational foundation to the Virgin Mary and the Trinity. While the charter itself demonstrates Henry's use of his legal power to provide education that will benefit the spiritual life of his subjects, the decoration depicts Henry's act in terms of his personal relationship to heavenly patronage. St. Nicholas appears as a holy patron for Henry before the Virgin (since the king was born on the feast of St. Nicholas, December 6, and the saint was the patron of students), and the intercession of Edward the Confessor may be implied by the appearance of his arms next to Henry's at the top of the charter. Behind Henry, as if following his lead, kneel one group of men representing the temporal and spiritual Lords and another group of men representing the Commons. Though the charter presents the members of Parliament using their authority to support the royal foundation, it depicts them as subject to both the king's power and divine power. The 1446 Consolidation Charter for Eton College (plate 62) repeats the same imagery, except that it omits St. Nicholas's patronage, perhaps allowing St. Edward's symbolic patronage to come to the fore. These portrayals of the link between royal power and divine power place less focus on the king's authority than do other royal charters. For example, the images on the charter given to the Leathersellers' Company in London in 1444 (plate 63) focus on the relationship between Henry VI and his subjects: the historiated initial shows the king seated on a canopied throne and offering his royal charter to members of the company, who kneel before the king in humble supplication. Nevertheless, the words on the banners over the guild members might be read as an indication that these subjects also appeal to a divine king, to whom they pray, "Domine, saluum fac regem" ("O Lord, make safe the king") and "Christe, saluum fac regem" ("O Christ, make safe the king"). Medieval readers might recognize that the prayer for the king's safety echoes the words of King David in Psalm 19 in the Vulgate Bible. Greater focus on the king's sole embodiment of authority can be found in the visual imagery of London, British Library MS Harley Charter 51 H 6, which has an historiated initial portraying Henry VI, enthroned and holding his scepter. Since this charter was issued in Henry VI's name by the Duke of Gloucester much earlier in the young king's reign (1431), perhaps the visual image of the king alone served to highlight the idea that the authority behind the charter was indeed the king's (Scott 2002, 46).

Medieval iconography of justice became more complex when judicial systems developed in which subjects interpreted laws in the name of the king, whether in King's Bench proceedings or in Parliament, which by definition advised the king on matters of law as well as other policy and acted as a national court of appeals (Musson 2001, 186–87). Curtis and Resnik have argued, "The imagery of justice reflects the tensions inherent in defining what is just and what stance judges should take vis-à-vis their sovereigns" (Curtis and Resnik 1987, 1764). As questions about Henry VI's leadership of the government grew in 1449, for example, the Commons expressed concern about rising lawlessness, reminding the king that

> the honour, welthe and prosperite, of every prynce reynyng uppon his people, stondith moost principally upon conservation of his peas, kepyng of justice, and due execution of his lawes, withouten which no roialme may long endure in quyete nor prosperite.

> (the honour, wealth and prosperity of every prince governing his people stands most principally on the conservation of his peace, the keeping of justice, and the due execution of his laws, without which no realm may remain in quiet and prosperity for long.) (Given-Wilson 2005, 12:147)

Especially after Henry VI's illness led to more questions about his ability to govern and the conflict with York's party moved beyond parliamentary maneuvering to armed combat, the Lancastrians needed additional means to suggest the divine source for Henry VI's authority in the establishment and administration of earthly justice. This is the context in which we should read the iconography of the Yale Law School *Nova statuta Angliae*, which associates Henry VI with King David's divinely guided kingship and associates

Edward IV with violation of that ideal. Using a copy of the Statutes of the Realm to make this political argument expands upon, yet is consistent with, the Lancastrians' earlier transformation of religious and legal documents to serve political ends. Further support for this reading of the Yale Law School manuscript comes from another set of legal documents from this same period – the *Coram rege* Rolls, the records of cases heard before the King's Bench.

It is highly significant that a conjunction of royal portraits and allusions to King David similar to the one that occurs in the Yale Law School *Nova statuta* takes place in the records of the King's Bench during the crisis year of 1460. These records were copied under the supervision of Sir John Fortescue, the chief justice who played a central role in defending the Lancastrian monarchy in the 1450s and went into exile with the royal family on Henry VI's deposition. As Erna Auerbach points out in her study of the royal portraits in the *Coram rege* Rolls, elaborate decoration of the opening initial of the *Coram rege* Rolls (always "P" for "Placita") first appears in the roll for Easter session in 1443, shortly after Henry VI appointed Fortescue as king's chief justice and knighted him.[56] Auerbach reads the decoration of the *Coram rege* Rolls that began under Fortescue as a visual commentary on the relationship of the justices of the King's Bench to the justice embodied in the king: "The proceedings of the Court of King's Bench took place theoretically in the presence of the sovereign; and it was evidently this distinctive feature that caused the rolls of this Court, as of no other court, to be illuminated and to bear the likeness of the sovereign" (Auerbach 1954, 18). Nevertheless, the issue of royal representation did not lead to the addition of royal portraits in the *Coram rege* Rolls until 1460. As in the case of the Yale Law School *Nova statuta* manuscript, each historiated initial in the *Coram rege* Rolls creates a liminal space because it participates in both the central text of the manuscript and its decoration – a space where differing perspectives on justice come into contact and relationships among sources of legal authority are renegotiated. The addition of an historiated initial to the legal record engages the eye of the reader even more than the decorated initials in other rolls, and the interweaving of words within the initial requires the reader to explore the relationship of the added words to the visual image, as well as to the central text of the legal record. Because the historiated initials contain images of monarchs, the liminal space of the initials offers an opportunity to explore the relationship between the authority of the monarch and the authority of the judges who pursue justice in his or her name. As if to highlight how the representation of justice is negotiated in this court, the king's authority is not the only authority visually highlighted in the *Coram rege* Rolls with royal portraits. Decoration is also added to the name of the chief justice, which always appears on the first rotulet or sheet of the roll (Auerbach 1954, 19).[57] Though the *Coram rege* Rolls did not "circulate" in a traditional sense, they were documents constructed for the eyes of several audiences: the monarch to whom the justices of the King's Bench reported their decisions, the judges and lawyers who needed to know what precedents had been set by the King's Bench in the past, and possibly the subjects of the Crown who wished to appeal judgments made by the King's Bench.

It seems more than coincidence, therefore, that the first *Coram rege* Rolls that open with an initial depicting a monarch come from 1460, the year of great turmoil before Henry VI was deposed, and that the chief justice supervising the rolls was someone whose own compositions, as we will see in chapter 4, demonstrate his ability to marshal multiple discourses to construct an argument. Though they do not show the artistic skill of the portraits of Henry VI found in the charters and book illustrations of the time, the first historiated initials in the *Coram rege* Rolls use a complex interweaving of discourses – visual and verbal, as well as legal and religious – that echoes the interwoven discourses of the Yale Law School *Nova statuta* manuscript. In the initial in the Easter roll of 1460 (Kew, National Archives MS KB 27/796) (plate 72), the image shows the king enthroned under a canopy between two figures. The king holds a scepter in his right hand, and he holds his left hand open toward the scroll to his left with the words "recte iudicate" ("judge rightly"), an allusion to Psalm 57 as it is often found in medieval Latin psalters.[58] At the same time, the king looks toward the figure to his right, which suggests that the king addresses these words to both figures. Since the two figures wear caps similar to those worn by the judges of the King's Bench, the scene seems to represent the king's instructions to the judges who serve as his representatives in the legal proceedings recorded in the *Coram rege* Roll.[59] By presenting the words of King David as the king's words, just as we saw in the illustrations of the king in the Henry VI Psalter, the illustration at the opening of this *Coram rege* Roll associates Henry VI with the primary medieval model of just kingship. The illustration also contains two other verbal passages: over the canopy of the king's throne are the words "domine saluum fac regem" ("O Lord, make safe the king") from Psalm 19, and below the king's throne we find "domine fiat pax" ("O Lord, let there be peace") from Psalm 121 – both particularly relevant prayers at the time that the roll was inscribed, given the political situation. Since the text over the canopy refers to the king in the third person, it seems to represent the words of the judges in response to the king's instruction. The prayer for peace could represent a shared concern of both the king and judges. Through its integration of the visual image of the king and his judicial representatives with verbal allusions to the Book of Psalms, the opening initial of this document presents the king and judges speaking the same language, as it were: a biblical discourse of justice. As a frame for the *Coram rege* Roll record of judicial actions, therefore, the initial suggests that the justice practiced in Henry VI's court follows the ideals of justice put forth by King David. This certainly was the view of Henry VI's rule that the Lancastrians were trying to maintain, and the methodology of interweaving biblical and legal discourses accords with other textual defenses of Henry VI at this time, including the Yale Law School manuscript of the *New Statutes of England*. In this case, because the verbal passages inscribed in the initial come from the Book of Psalms, readers should find common ground in the initial's expressions of concern for justice, peace, and good kingship.

Likewise, in the historiated initial beginning the *Coram rege* Roll for Michaelmas 1460 (Kew, National Archives MS KB 27/798) (plate 73), we find a similar integration of word and image. Here, Henry VI sits enthroned and faces forward, but no other figures appear in the scene. Auerbach describes the image as emphasizing "the prestige and power of the royal figure as fountain of justice" (Auerbach 1954, 21). Instead of sitting between two judges, the king is flanked by two scrolls: the scroll to his right holds the words "Legem tenete" ("Keep the law"), and the scroll to his left holds the words "et recte iudicate" ("and judge rightly"), the phrase borrowed from Psalm 57 that appeared in the previous initial. As in that case, the king here holds a scepter in his right hand, and his left hand points to the scroll to his left, as if to indicate that this is his admonition, as well as King David's, inspired by God. If these elements have remained stable, what do we make of the differences? Gone is the visual suggestion of dialogue in the scene. Instead, the king seems to speak directly to the reader of the document, whether that person is a judge of the King's Bench or anyone else. Though the historiated initial includes another verbal text, this appears outside the scene depicting the king: in the stem of the "P" is a scroll with the words "justicia et pax osculati sunt" ("justice and peace have kissed"), which echoes Psalm 84 in the Vulgate Bible. Whose voice is represented by these words? In isolation, they stand as the words of King David's psalm, so they set up a parallel with the words of the king in the image, perhaps reinforcing his association with King David. Nevertheless, since these words appear more closely associated with the initial itself, rather than the image of the king, they suggest an association of the text of the legal document with the biblical ideal of justice. These words might therefore be read as the voice of the judges of the King's Bench, though they are not visually present in this initial, and parallel to the prayer for peace in the initial of the Easter *Coram rege* Roll.

Like other Lancastrian texts, however, this *Coram rege* Roll works hard to express confidence in the king, yet raises questions in the process: if the removal of the judges from the image serves to focus the reader on the authority embodied in the king, this also suggests a distancing in the relationship between the king and his judicial representatives, as well as his other subjects. The ambiguities in this initial reflect the political and legal crisis in England in the autumn of 1460. Henry VI had been captured by the Yorkists in July and, while in custody in October, would name the Duke of York as his heir, displacing Prince Edward. Chief Justice Fortescue would soon join Queen Margaret and Prince Edward near the border with Scotland to help plan the rescue of the king and try to persuade his countrymen with written works sent from exile that the Yorkists' claims were unjust. Fortescue would later be declared attainted by Parliament, along with the queen and prince; but his presence is already absent from the traditional inscription of the chief justice's name in the *Coram rege* Roll for Michaelmas 1460: the banner on which his name appeared in the Easter roll is here empty. It was indeed a threshold time, a time in which the margins and centers of power were in flux, a time in which definitions of justice were being renegotiated. The *Coram rege* Roll initials for that year use the authority of the Psalms to remind readers of an ideal of justice that was supposed to be shared by both sides in the conflict – and perhaps to suggest that, like David, divinely sanctioned kings require loyalty, despite their flaws.

But it is not just the depictions of Henry VI in the *Coram rege* Rolls that provide a parallel to the Yale Law School *Nova statuta* manuscript: the parallel continues in the depictions of Edward IV that appear in later rolls. After the initials of 1460, historiated initials with royal portraits do not appear in the *Coram rege* Rolls until 1466, when they appear in the rolls for the Hilary and Easter sessions (Kew, National Archives MSS KB 27/819 and 27/820) (plates 74 and 75). Just as the royal portraits in the Yale Law School *Nova statuta* show a change in iconography for Edward IV, showing him holding a sword instead of a scepter, the first *Coram rege* Roll that presents an image of Edward IV (Hilary session) also suggests that his performance of kingship differs from his predecessor's by showing Edward holding a sword instead of a scepter. In addition, though the Hilary initial integrates text and image by using words on a banner inside the stem of the initial, the text does not come from Holy Scripture: "Lex est regni ut rex regat" ("The law of the kingdom exists so that the king may govern"). Auerbach describes the king in this image as "grasping the sword of justice," and, in another context, so this image might be read (Auerbach 1954, 21). In comparison with the previous royal portraits in the rolls and the imagery of the royal seals, however, the visual imagery of this initial links Edward IV to military power, rather than the king's role as upholder of justice. Though the sword is balanced with an orb in the king's other hand in this image (whereas he holds a sword alone in the image in the Yale *Nova statuta*), the verbal text in this initial raises questions about reading the king's image as an upholder of justice, since the verbal text calls attention to the law, not the sword, as the tool by which the king should govern. In addition, the initial does not suggest that the words about kingship and law come from the king, since the banner with the verbal text decorates the initial itself. The words on the banner seem therefore to represent advice to the king that is linked to the central text in the legal document, yet no other figure appears in the initial: the source of the advice and the authority behind it are left unclear. In stressing the need for kings to use the law of the land as the means by which to rule, the passage echoes the distinction between ruling by law and ruling by arms that appears as the opening of the preface to the well-known Latin treatise on English law attributed to Ranulf de Glanville, *De legibus et consuetudinibus regni Angliae:* "Regiam potestatem non solum armis contra rebelles et gentes sibi regnoque insurgentes oportet esse decoratam, sed et legibus ad subditos et populos pacificos regendos decet esse ornatam" ("Not only must royal power be furnished with arms against rebels and nations which rise up against the king and the realm, but it is also fitting that it should be adorned with laws for the governance of subject and peaceful peoples") (Hall 1965, 1–2).[60] Perhaps a more direct source for the text in this *Coram rege* Roll initial will become known; but the move away from the quotations from Holy Scripture found in the earlier initials serves to distance the model of kingship offered by the image of the king in this initial even further from the model of King David alluded to by the earlier initials.

As if to underscore the potential critique implicit in depicting Edward IV with a sword in the Hilary initial, the historiated initial in the next *Coram rege* Roll (Easter session) returns to the iconography of kingship that appeared in the portraits of Henry VI in the rolls of 1460. Once again, the king is enthroned and holding a scepter, and the verbal text comes from Psalm 44 in the Vulgate Bible: "Virga directionis virga regni tui" ("The scepter of thy kingdom is a scepter of uprightness"). Gone, however, are the explicit prayers for divine protection and peace. In this case, the verbal text of the initial calls attention to the king's scepter and its association with justice, and the image of the king accords with the ideal expressed by King David, so the initial may suggest that Edward IV has begun to follow the model of just kingship provided by King David; but the initial also suggests that Edward's performance of the biblical ideal of justice has not yet been fully achieved. Since the words about justice are not attributed to the king in this image, but use the second person to refer to the king and appear on a part of the letter itself, the historiated initial associates the words of King David with the words of the justices of the King's Bench. The verbal and visual components of the initial together might thus work to offer the king advice about following a biblical ideal of justice.

Comparison of the two sets of historiated initials in the *Coram rege* Rolls shows an important transition taking place. While the images of Henry VI associate him with the teachings of King David and depict Henry VI as the instructor of his judges in the ideals of justice, the images of Edward IV distance the verbal precepts on justice from the king, instead addressing them to the king as instruction on kingship, but not attributing the instruction directly to any of the king's subjects. The return to using historiated initials in the *Coram rege* Rolls in 1466, after a hiatus of six years, raises questions about what might have caused such a return at that time. If the initials were meant to associate Edward with just rulership, their ambiguity undermines their effectiveness. Perhaps the fact that Edward's forces had finally captured the deposed king in July 1465 led some members of the judiciary to have concerns about Edward's plans for his predecessor.[61] Edward seems to have realized, however, that Henry was more valuable to him alive than dead, since Henry's death would have allowed his son, Prince Edward of Lancaster, a teenager who had already demonstrated more promise as a leader than his father, to make a direct claim on the throne.

As one might expect, the depictions of Edward IV's relationship with biblical models of kingship and justice in the *Coram rege* Rolls and the Yale Law School *Nova statuta* manuscript contrast sharply with the images of Edward IV that his supporters were circulating. Several of the manuscripts that celebrate Yorkist victory over the Lancastrians combine images of Edward IV with quotations from the Bible that suggest a divine mandate for Edward's accession to the throne. One of these (London, British Library MS Harley 7353) cites several passages from Psalm 2 in the Vulgate Bible to depict Edward as God's agent in punishing his enemies.[62] This manuscript also shows several illustrations of scenes from Edward's life in parallel with scenes from the lives of biblical heroes, including King David and Christ. Paul Strohm has pointed out that, in the image that shows Edward IV atop a wheel of Fortune, the figure of Reason, who stops the wheel from turning, is depicted in the robes of an English judge, as if to associate Edward's kingship with justice, as well as reason. At the same time, one might read the image as suggesting that the representatives of royal justice in the realm play a crucial role in determining how long Edward IV will remain enthroned at the top of the wheel or how soon he will follow his toppled Lancastrian predecessors when the wheel again begins to turn. Since MS Harley 7353 must date from after 4 March 1461, it postdates the depictions of Henry VI in the *Coram rege* Rolls; but the Harley manuscript may predate the portraits of Edward IV in the *Coram rege* Rolls, as well as the portrait of Edward IV in the Yale Law School *New Statutes* manuscript. Despite the celebratory aspects of Harley 7353, including the allusions to Psalm 2, the presence of the wheel of Fortune image in the manuscript seems to suggest an instability to Edward's kingship that he shares with his royal predecessors – unless he governs by law, as suggested also by the portraits of Edward IV in the 1466 *Coram rege* Rolls.

Clearly, both the Lancastrian and Yorkist parties sought to use the interplay of verbal and visual texts to associate their leaders with divine sanction and true justice; but the relationship of earthly laws and biblical ideals of just kingship was difficult for both parties to negotiate. Anxieties about the presence of royal justice and authority may explain the increased use of the face of the king on several sorts of legal documents during the fifteenth century, including statutes manuscripts and royal charters. By using iconography strongly associated with images of King David in fifteenth-century devotional texts, the first five royal portraits in the Yale Law School *New Statutes* manuscript suggest that divine guidance and biblical precept have been the basis of English kingship and royal justice throughout the reigns of Edward III through Henry VI; yet the iconography of the first five historiated initials also suggests that divine guidance and biblical precept should serve as frames for the reader's construction of English kings and laws. These frames challenge the focus on the human definitions of justice and negotiations of power recorded in the statutes text at the center of the manuscript, creating textual space for comparison of multiple perspectives on the laws of England. In effect, the visual frames in this manuscript reverse the relationship of margin and center found in traditional discussions of law and justice in medieval manuscripts, where the words of the Bible (often centered on the page and highlighted with larger or more formal script, or written in a different color of ink) provide the central textual authority, and the commentary by other voices takes a marginal role. By adding a frame with allusions to religious ideals of kingship and justice, the Yale manuscript comments ironically on the marginal role that the Bible's instruction on justice may have played in shaping the English laws that stand recorded in the manuscript, despite the references to God that occur in the statutes text, beginning with the prologue to the very first statute, where God is credited with bringing about a victory over injustice and misappropriation of royal power so that Edward III could become king (Tomlins et al. 1811–28, 1:251–52). The questions raised by the manuscript's framing of the statutes, suggesting the priority of divine justice and the king's role as mediator of divine justice to his people, reflect traditional medieval ideals of kingship and law, but they also echo the arguments of the Lancastrian regime as it struggled to maintain power.

The use of visual imagery in the *Coram rege* Rolls offers additional evidence that legal documents other than charters had become textual spaces for political discourse by 1460 and that allusions to King David and the Psalms were employed to comment on the relationship of earthly laws and divine ideals of justice. The iconographic parallels between the historiated initials in the *Coram rege* Rolls and those in the Yale Law School *Nova statuta Angliae* will become even more clear, however, when we look at the Lancastrian treatises on kingship and justice that took part in the debates about Henry VI's monarchy in chapter 4. As we will see, in the 1450s and 1460s Lancastrian texts in different genres, languages, and media defended Henry VI against the criticism of the Duke of York and his supporters; yet some of these texts depicted themselves as works of instruction for Henry's son, Prince Edward, who was presented to the public as preparing diligently to take on his rightful and sacred role as successor to his father. These works include verbal "portraits" of good and bad kingship that parallel the visual portraits of Henry VI and Edward IV in the Yale *Nova statuta*. In light of the other evidence provided by the Yale manuscript, I suggest that the iconography found there presents a complex textual program that both represents Lancastrian views on the relationship of royal power to divine justice and celebrates the extension of the Lancastrian royal line in Prince Edward, despite the interruption of the sword-wielding usurper, Edward of York.

THREE

The Queen and the Lancastrian Cause

THE YALE *NEW STATUTES* MANUSCRIPT
AND MARGARET OF ANJOU

The appearance of Margaret of Anjou's arms in the border decoration of three leaves in the Yale Law School manuscript of the *Nova statuta Angliae* (plates 1–3) is undeniable evidence that the manuscript was commissioned by a supporter of the Lancastrian monarchy who chose to link Henry VI's queen to England's legal history. While nothing in the manuscript indicates that it was made for presentation to Margaret herself, a close connection with the queen and her circle of supporters does explain the manuscript's unique features. As we have seen from our examination of the manuscript's historiated initials and border decoration, the manuscript creates a visual frame for the legal texts it contains – a frame that shapes the reader's perceptions of the legal texts of the manuscript and links the Lancastrian line of kings, especially Henry VI, to King David, the primary medieval model of just kingship. The Yale Law School *Nova statuta* therefore inscribes in its record of English laws a political statement that parallels other examples of Lancastrian discourse in defense of Henry VI, and the form that this political statement takes is particularly well suited to Margaret of Anjou's need for indirect methods to undermine the authority of those who questioned the legitimacy of Henry VI's rule. For the reader of the manuscript, the appearance of Margaret's arms in the border decoration of the first leaf of the statutes text also has important implications for constructing the role of English queens in preparing heirs to the throne to become just rulers, especially when justice needs to be restored to the realm: the preamble to the first statute in the collection gives an account of the unusual "transfer" of royal power from Edward II to Edward III in 1326–27, with the aid of his mother Queen Isabelle, and this account depicts Edward III and the queen as instruments of divine grace. Several other texts from the 1440s and 1450s also depict Margaret of Anjou as a representative of God's grace who brings peace and justice to England, which suggests that this association was part of Lancastrian discourse and that the parallel between the situations of Queen Isabelle and Queen Margaret might well be recognized by readers of the *Nova statuta Angliae*. Margaret's "presence" in the margins of the Yale Law School manuscript, as well as within its central text, might thus be read as a metaphor for her ambiguous role in the defense of the Lancastrian monarchy – officially marginal, yet in many ways at the center, as a voice for a king who was either literally or figuratively absent after his illness in August 1453 and for a prince who was either literally or figuratively absented by the Lancastrians' foes after his birth in October 1453.

Tensions between royal presence and absence and political margin and center are inscribed in the very origins of the *Nova statuta Angliae* as a text. What is "new" about the *New Statutes* is that they begin with the first year of the reign of Edward III in 1326–27 and present him as inaugurating a new beginning in English legal history, one in which records for each session of Parliament were made available to readers for the first time and the laws were recorded in French, instead of Latin, allowing for a wider readership. Nevertheless, this new beginning cannot entirely gloss over the political and legal fractures that brought Edward III to the throne and brought about a new form of legal text. In order to construct Edward II's removal from the throne and replacement by his son as necessary for the restoration of just rule to England, the *Nova statuta* text begins, not with the first statute of Edward III's reign, but with a narrative account, similar to a chronicle.[1] The account employs remarkable rhetorical strategies in order to explain that Edward III has become "the king that now is," whose first statute pardons all individuals who aided him and Queen Isabelle when they invaded England and removed Edward II from the throne.

When the account begins, it presents Edward II in terms of his relationship with Edward III, but in terms that require recognition of Edward III as rightful sovereign from the very start: "Roi Edward piere nostre Seigneur le Roi qore est" ("King Edward Father to our Sovereign Lord the King that

now is"). Even though most of the events described in the account take place
prior to Edward III's coronation, throughout the passage Edward III is identified as the one who is the sovereign – "nostre Seigneur le Roi qore est" ("our
Sovereign Lord the King that now is") – while his father is the one who had
the name of King Edward – "le dit Roi Edward" ("the said King Edward").
Edward III is thus the unnamed "center" for much of the account. Only when
the account finally refers to Edward III holding his first Parliament after his
coronation do we find him referred to by his name, and it appears as part
of a royal genealogy: "nostre Seigneur le Roi Edward qe ore est, fiuz du dit
Roi Edward, qe fut fiuz le Roi Edward fiuz le Roi Henri" ("our Sovereign
Lord King Edward that now is, [son of the said King Edward, who was son
of King Edward son of King Henry]"). Nowhere does the passage explain
what happened to Edward II that allowed his son to succeed him. In fact, the
use of the genealogy at this point helps the passage suggest that Edward III
succeeded his father as king in the traditional manner, at his father's death,
just as Edward II succeeded his father, Edward I, and Edward I succeeded
Henry III. The account also suggests, through its repeated use of linguistic
connectors such as "come" ("whereas"), "par quoi" ("wherefore"), and "dount"
("wherefore"), that Edward III's royal authority to call Parliament into session and enact the statutes that follow was arrived at by logical and legal
steps. Nevertheless, the account does not present the immediate cause for the
kingship of Edward III in terms of Edward II. Instead, Edward III becomes
king because he and his mother, Queen Isabelle, defeat the men defined by
Parliament as the enemies of the king and the realm:

> et velauntz qe eux ne poient remede mettre fors qe par force, taunt fesoient
> qil vindrent en Engleterre a graunt force des gentz darmes, et par la grace de
> Dieu ove cele force, et ove leide des grauntz et du poeple du roialme, unt ven-
> cuz et destrut les ditz Hughe et Hughe, Robert, Esmon Counte Darundelle.

> (and seeing they [i.e., Edward III and Queen Isabel] might not remedy the
> same unless they came into England with an army of men of war, and by the
> Grace of God, with such puissance and with the help of great men and Com-
> mons of the Realm, they have vanquished and destroyed the said Hugh and
> Hugh, Robert, and Edmond.)

The account is silent about both what happened to Edward II and how Edward III officially became the new king.[2] There is no mention of the imprisonment of Edward II, his persuasion to relinquish the throne in favor of his
son, or his death. The account also presents Edward III and his mother as

partners in saving England from the injustices that occurred under Edward
II: the account makes no mention of the queen's acting as regent or the role
played in the deposition by her lover, Roger Mortimer. Whereas other contemporary accounts raise questions about Queen Isabelle's ulterior motives in
challenging her husband's rule, this account associates her actions with just
rule and the grace of God.[3]

At the same time that the opening account elides the actual transfer of
power from Edward II to Edward III, the passage provides explicit evidence
for why Edward II needed to be removed from power. The passage first presents Edward II as a king who acts justly in condemning and exiling Hugh
Despenser the father and Hugh Despenser the son as traitors to the realm,
because he does so in agreement with his high steward or seneschal and with
Parliament: "a la suite Thomas adonqes Counte de Lancastre et de Leycestre,
Seneschal Dengleterre, par commune assent et agard des piers et du poeple
du roialme" ("at the Suit of Thomas then Earl of Lancaster and Leicester,
and Steward of England, by the common assent and award of the Peers and
Commons of the Realm"). Soon, however, according to this account, Edward
II turns his back on the counsel of his loyal seneschal and Parliament and becomes the victim of evil counsel, allowing the Despensers to return to England
without the assent of Parliament. He then allows the Despensers to take the
law into their own hands and pursue their enemies, killing the Earl of Lancaster and many others, as well as banishing, imprisoning, and disinheriting
more of the great and common people of England, without regard for their
rights. Through Edward II's heeding of evil counsel and disregard of the laws
of the land, according to this account, the Despensers and their allies usurp
the power of the king:

> et apres tieux mauveistez les ditz Hughe et Hughe, Mestre Robert de
> Baldok, Esmon jadis Counte Darundell acrocherent a eux roial poer, en tieu
> manere qe le dit Roi Edward rien ne fist, ne ne voleit faire, forsqe ceo qe les
> ditz Hughe et Hughe, Robert, Esmon Counte Darundell, luy conseilerent,
> ne fust ceo ja si grant tort.

> (and after such Mischief, the said Hugh and Hugh, Master Robert Baldocke,
> and Edmond late Earl of Arundel usurped to them the Royal Power, so that
> the King nothing did nor would do, but as the said Hugh, and Hugh, Robert,
> and Edmond Earl of Arundel did counsel him, were it never so great wrong.)

Although Edward II is briefly shown again acting with the assent of Parliament when he allows his son and wife to go to France to pursue a peace treaty,

this is the last act of just kingship that the account attributes to him. Instead, Edward II next gives his assent to the mischief and grievances that the traitors now perpetrate against his own son and queen, as well as the English people:

> Les ditz Hughe et Hughe, Robert et Esmon Count Darundell, continuauntz lour mauveiste, moverent le corage le dit Roi Edward contre nostre Seigneur le Roi son fiuz qore est, et la dite Roine sa compaigne, et par poair roial qil avaient a eux acrochez, sicome desus est dit, tantz de durte procurerent estre fait par lassent du dit Roi Edward, au dit nostre Seigneur le Roi qore est, et a la Roine sa miere, adonqes esteauntz dela la mier, qe eux y demorerent relinquiz du dit Roi Edward et come exilez hors du roialme Dengleterre.

> (The said Hugh and Hugh, Robert, and Edmond Earl of Arundel continuing their Mischief, encouraged the said King Edward against our Sovereign Lord the King that now is, his Son, and the said Queen his Wife, and by the Royal Power which they had to them encroached, as afore is said, procured so much Grievance, by the assent of the said King Edward, to our Sovereign Lord the King that now is, and the Queen his Mother, then being beyond the Sea, that they remained as forsaken of the said King Edward, and as exiled from this Realm of England.)

According to the account, because of this usurpation of royal power and its unjust use against the prince and queen, as well as the people of England, including members of the clergy, it becomes necessary for the future Edward III and Queen Isabelle to seek good counsel and take action to save the kingdom:

> Par quoi il covenist nostre dit Seigneur le Roi qore est, et la Roine sa miere, ensi mys a si grant meschefs de eux mesmes en estraunge terre, et attendauntz les destructions, damages, oppressions, et desheritisons qe notoirement furent faitz en dit roialme Dengleterre sur Seinte eglise, prelatz, Countes, Barons, et autres grauntz, et sur le poeple du roialme, per les ditz Hughe et Hughe, Robert, Esmon Counte Darundelle, par poair roial a eux issint acroche, mettre y le bon conseil qil perroient; et velauntz qe eux ne poient remede mettre fors qe par force, taunt fesoient qil vindrent en Engleterre a graunt force des gentz darmes, et par la grace de Dieu ove cele force, et ove leide des grauntz et du poeple du roialme, unt vencuz et destrut les ditz Hughe et Hughe, Robert, Esmon Counte Darundelle.

> (Wherefore it was necessary for our Sovereign Lord the King that now is, and the Queen his Mother, being in so great jeopardy of themselves in a strange Country, and seeing the Destruction, Damage, Oppressions, and Disherisons which were notoriously done in the Realm of England, upon Holy Church, Prelates, Earls, Barons, and other great Men and the Commonalty by the said

> Hugh and Hugh, Robert, and Edmond Earl of Arundel, by the encroaching
> of such Royal Power to them, to take as good Counsel therein as they might;
> and seeing they might not remedy the same unless they came into England
> with an army of men of war, and by the Grace of God, with such puissance
> and with the help of great men and Commons of the Realm, they have van-
> quished and destroyed the said Hugh and Hugh, Robert, and Edmond.)

The account very effectively intertwines religious and political discourses, depicting the military invasion of England as an act that results from good counsel and has the approval of the nobility and common people of England, as well as divine sanction. It is therefore not Edward III, with the help of his mother, who has usurped power from Edward II, but the condemned traitors Hugh Despenser father and son and their allies. The army that has landed is not a foreign invasion, but has come to help the people of England overthrow usurpers who have been depriving the English of their own lands and rights. Moreover, the language of this account of English laws reminds readers that French is one of England's own discourses, which suggests that the English people thus need not fear a queen from France bringing an army to confront an English king. Edward III and Queen Isabelle have only acted to restore peace and justice to England, after they were sent by the king and Parliament to seek peace with France, and the unspoken removal of Edward II from the throne becomes part of what was necessary in order to remedy the usurpation of royal power and fulfill God's will for England.

The positive depiction of Queen Isabelle in this account differs from the negative image of her in some other contemporary accounts (Weir 2007, xiii); but the narrative that opens the *Nova statuta Angliae* echoes the writs Isabelle herself issued upon arriving in England with her son in 1326: these depict her goal as removing the king's evil counselors and rescuing the kingdom from the terrible harm that they have done (Menache 1984, 111). M. A. Michael and Anne Rudloff Stanton have also argued that Queen Isabelle commissioned several manuscripts for her eldest son, including a copy of the *Vetera statuta Angliae*, that served to suggest he had received extensive education in good kingship before replacing his father.[4] Nevertheless, despite her success in placing her son on the throne, as Diana Dunn points out, Isabelle lost her association with justice and grace, was placed in forced retirement by her son, and eventually came to be read in parallel with Margaret of Anjou: Isabelle even shares the same epithet of "She-Wolf of France" with Margaret in later English literature.[5] Dunn finds the parallel between the two queens, if not the critique, appropriate because of the problems they both faced: "Comparisons with Margaret of Anjou are appropriate because Isabella also married a king who failed to fulfil the requirements of medieval kingship" (Dunn 2000, 147). Though the scholarship on Queen Isabelle does not cite the *Nova statuta Angliae* as evidence of a positive reading of her actions in a contemporary document, the Yale Law School manuscript of the *Nova statuta* offers an opportunity to examine contemporary readings of both queens and evidence of the ways in which both queens used legal documents to shape their public images.

Although the appearance of Margaret of Anjou's coat of arms in the border decoration of the Yale Law School *Nova statuta* serves to honor her as Henry VI's consort, the appearance of Margaret's arms on the leaf containing the account that introduces Edward III's statutes also serves to highlight Queen Isabelle's role in Edward III's replacement of his father on the English throne. For readers of the *Nova statuta* in the late fourteenth century, the account that opens the text offered a model for successful deposition of an English king that would again be implemented in the overthrow of Richard II in 1399 – the event that brought the Lancastrian monarchy into power, because Richard II had no son. By the middle of the fifteenth century, however, questions about the influence of Henry VI's advisors and his own fitness to rule became intertwined with questions about the legitimacy of the Lancastrian claim to the throne. Before Henry VI's son was born, the model for any thought about removing Henry VI would most likely have been the deposition of Richard II; but, with a Lancastrian heir to the throne in the picture, the model of Edward III's replacement of his misguided father came into play once more. The presentation of Queen Isabelle in the account that opens the *Nova statuta Angliae* could thus be read as a model for Henry VI's queen: Margaret of Anjou could become the queen who fulfills her proper role in preparing her son to restore justice and peace to the realm, acting in accordance with the grace of God.

Margaret was indeed publicly associated with divine grace and justice, as well as good counsel, at the time of her arrival in England. In a set of poetic pageants performed to welcome her when she came to London on her way to her coronation at Westminster in May 1445, an allegorical character says to the queen, "Grace conueie you forthe and be youre gide" ("Grace lead you forth and be your guide") (line 34).[6] Though the pageants are no longer attributed to John Lydgate, the surviving manuscript copies suggest that their anonymous author understood the power of interweaving multiple discourses – courtly, religious, and legal, as well as English, French, and Latin. As Gordon Kipling has argued, the theme of grace plays a major role in the pageants, and he links this theme to an attempt to portray Margaret as a type of the Virgin Mary (Kipling 1986–87). What Kipling's analysis does not discuss, however, is the role of legal discourse in the work's representation of grace and the implications of the legal discourse for linking the pageants to other representations of Margaret's role as queen. The interweaving of multiple discourses in these pageants takes several forms. Along with the Middle English poetic texts, the two surviving copies of the pageants include marginal texts in Latin that echo Bible passages and are thought to have been presented visually as part of the pageant performances. The surviving copies of the pageants also include marginal French texts identifying characters. Altogether, the Middle English poems and their marginal texts bring together the primary languages, as well as the discourses of religion, law, and courtly literature, of the dual kingdom over which Henry VI and Margaret of Anjou claimed to rule. In addition, as pageants, these written texts allude to performative and visual discourses that are part of their significance: the physical settings of the pageants and the roles into which they cast their audiences have implications for the potential interpretations of the verbal texts.

The first three pageants together construct a reading of Margaret as an agent of divine grace and justice on earth. The first pageant was performed at the Southwark end of London Bridge, the physical bridge that took Margaret across the Thames River and into the city of London. The opening speaker, Plenty, welcomes Margaret as "Moost Cristen Princesse, by influence of Grace / Doughter of Iherusalem" ("Most Christian Princess, by influence of Grace / Daughter of Jerusalem") (lines 1–2). With the phrase "by influence of Grace," Plenty probably refers to the divine grace by which Margaret holds the title Princess of Jerusalem, based on her father's claim to the title of King of Jerusalem. The phrase echoes the tradition of referring to sovereigns as achieving their ranks "by the grace of God," just as the opening passage for each king's reign in the *Nova statuta* text refers to the monarch as king "par la grace de Dieu." (See, for example, plate 2.) This same phrase is part of the goal of Margaret's journey through the city of London, on her way to her coronation in Westminster. At the same time, being the recipient of heavenly grace, Margaret could also be read as a daughter of Heavenly Jerusalem, a metaphoric emissary from the City of God to the City of London. When the first pageant continues, it suggests that, having received the "influence of Grace," Margaret now takes on the role of reflecting or mediating this divine grace for her subjects. Peace, the second speaker, announces that Margaret's people trust that, through her "grace" (line 10), peace between England and France will be achieved. Crossing the bridge over the Thames into London on her way to her coronation becomes a metaphor for Margaret's longer journey across the sea from France to become Henry VI's queen as part of the peace treaty negotiated between the two kingdoms. In making both journeys, Margaret performs the peace treaty, becoming the new bridge that creates an alliance between the English and the French. By taking part in this welcoming ceremony, the people of London perform their part in this process of achieving peace and prosperity with Margaret. In the pageant performance, Peace and Plenty do not arrive in England with Margaret: they are right there on London Bridge to welcome her with gifts and public expressions of welcome, suggesting English contributions to this alliance.

The first pageant also inscribes additional dimensions to Margaret's entry into her new role as queen. The Latin passage that accompanies the text of this pageant in the manuscripts – and is said to have been displayed visually as part of its performance – presents the command "ingredimini et replete terram" ("go in and fill the earth"), which echoes divine commands for human reproduction in the book of Genesis. This suggests a link between the peace and plenty described in the speeches and the biological fertility expected of the new queen, which will create a new biological link between the English and French royal families. But this marginal Latin passage conflates several of the divine commands to populate the earth in Genesis, which come from significantly different parts of this narrative. The first command is given to the newly created men and women on the sixth day of creation, when peace and plenty abound on the earth: Gen. 1:28 reads "multiplicamini, et replete terram" ("multiply, and fill the earth"). The other commands, given to Noah's family after the Flood, come after a time of destruction and death, when by the grace of God they remain alive and must populate the earth anew: Gen. 8:17 reads "ingredimini super terram: crescite et multiplicamini super eam" ("go in upon the earth: increase and multiply upon it"), Gen. 9:1 reads "multiplicamini, et replete terram" ("multiply, and fill the earth"), and Gen. 9:7 reads "ingredimini super terram, et implete eam" ("go in upon the earth, and fill it"). The conflation of the commands from different parts of Genesis thus suggests concerns underlying the Lancastrian project of using Henry's marriage to Margaret as a means to secure peace: the first pageant suggests the hope that Margaret, traveling over water to dry land, will help create peace and prosperity for England and France, but the pageant recognizes at the same time that she bears the burden of bringing forth new life after the destruction of war, in a fallen world rather than an Edenic one – a world in which human promises to refrain from further destruction are less sure than divine ones.

The parallel between Margaret's arrival and the story of Noah is made explicit in the second pageant, which took place farther along on London Bridge and featured a visual representation of Noah's ark. The speaker of this pageant is not identified in the manuscripts, but Kipling hypothesizes that an "expositor" or narrator presented the poetic text, rather than the figure of Noah. This pageant continues to link divine grace to Margaret, but the story of the Flood has now become central as the context for Margaret's welcome. Just as "Goddes myght and Grace" ("God's might and grace") (line 18) guided Noah to build the ark and sent a dove resembling Margaret's "symplesse columbine" ("dove-like humility") (line 26) to Noah with a "braunche of pees" ("branch of peace") (line 25), so Margaret, "conducte by Grace and Pure Diuine" ("guided by grace and power divine") (line 28), is a sign of peace by whose presence the "Sonne of Comfort gynneth faire to shyne" ("sun of comfort begins to shine fairly") (line 29). The potential for reading the "Sonne of Comfort" and "braunche of pees" as metaphors for the desired son who will extend the Lancastrian line of monarchs becomes clear when the speaker addresses Margaret as "right extendet lyne" ("directly descended lineage") in the rhyming line (line 31).

The manuscript copies of this pageant include another marginal comment in Latin that echoes the Bible's depiction of God's promise not to send another Flood to destroy life on earth: "Iam non ultra irascar super terram" ("No more will I show anger on the earth"). By implication, the pageant suggests that the divine covenant to refrain from destroying life on earth should be the model for earthly peace treaties, so that they will remain unbroken as well. Kipling identifies the source for the Latin text as Genesis 8:21:

> Odoratusque est Dominus odorem suavitatis, et ait: Nequaquam ultra maledicam terrae propter homines: sensus enim et cogitatio humani cordis in malum prona sunt ab adolescentia sua: non igitur ultra percutiam omnem animam viventem sicut feci.
>
> (The Lord smelled the pleasing aroma and said: "Never again will I curse the ground because of man, even though every inclination of his heart is evil from childhood. And never again will I destroy all living creatures, as I have done.")

Nevertheless, that passage does not match the wording of the Latin text of the pageant as closely as Isaiah 54:9:

Sicut in diebus Noe istud mihi est,
Cui iuravi ne inducerem aquas Noe
Ultra supra terram;
Sic iuravi ut non irascar tibi,
Et non increpem te.

(To me this is like the days of Noah, when I swore that the waters of Noah
would never again cover the earth. So now I have sworn not to be angry with
you and not to rebuke you.)

An even closer match for this pageant's marginal Latin text can be found in
the liturgy for the fourth Sunday in Advent in the English tradition, which is
based on Isaiah 54:9–10: "Juravi dicit dominus ut ultra jam non irascar super
terram: montes enim et colles suscipient justiciam meam. Et testamentum
pacis erit in hierusalem" ("'I have sworn,' says the Lord, 'that I will no longer
turn my anger upon the earth: for the mountains and hills will receive my
justice. And a covenant of peace will be in Jerusalem'"). The differences are
significant, because the liturgical passage links God's promise not to repeat
destruction like the Flood with the theme of divine justice. Through the allusion to the liturgy, this pageant sets up an association of grace and justice
that becomes explicit in the following pageant.

In the third pageant, grace plays its most prominent role yet, for the
surviving records indicate that the speaker of all three stanzas is none other
than the Grace of God personified. It is also the pageant in which Margaret
is most closely linked with justice. The opening stanza begins with a clear
enunciation of the theme of Margaret's guidance by divine grace:

Oure benigne Princesse and lady souereyne,
Grace conueie you forthe and be youre gide
In good life longe, prosperously to reyne.

(Our good princess and sovereign lady,
Grace lead you forth and be your guide
To reign prosperously, in good, long life.) (lines 33–35)

This prayer for Margaret's guidance by divine grace is followed in the first
stanza by imagery borrowed from one of the most famous allegories of peace
and justice in the Bible – the alliance of the Four Daughters of God from
Psalm 84:

Trouth and Mercy togedre ben allied,
Justice and Pees; these sustres schal prouide
Twixt reawmes tweyn stedfast loue to sette.

(Truth and Mercy are allied together,
[With] Justice and Peace; these sisters shall arrange
That steadfast love be established between two realms.) (lines 36–38)

Although Kipling's edition adds the Latin passage from Psalm 84:11 in the margin ("Misericordia et veritas obviaverunt sibi: / Iustitia et pax osculatae sunt" – "Mercy and truth have met each other: justice and peace have kissed"), the manuscript copies do not include this marginal annotation, despite the pattern suggested by the first two pageants. Perhaps the copyists (or their exemplar) omitted the marginal annotation by mistake; but it is also possible that the Bible passage alluded to was so well known that no marginal commentary was necessary.[7] According to the first stanza of this pageant, "God and Grace" (line 39) have joined England and France, just as they have allied Mercy, Truth, Peace, and Justice. Since the alliance of England and France parallels the marriage of Henry VI and Margaret of Anjou, the pageant suggests that God and Grace have brought Margaret to England to take up her new role as Henry's queen. The stanza also suggests that, if Margaret is guided by divine grace, she will be empowered to maintain the alliance among these four ideals, as well as between the realms of England and France.

Stanza two of this pageant elaborates on the authority of "Dame Grace" in terms that interweave the discourses of theological virtue and government documents. Grace is "Goddes Vicarie Generalle" ("God's chief representative") (line 42), who has sent the Four Daughters of God, "Foure patentes, faire, fressh, and legible" ("Four official documents, correct, newly copied, and clear") (line 44), and these official documents contain "iiii precepts" ("four instructions") (line 44) that these sisters "as mynystres further proclamen shalle, / T'encresen pees, werres to correcte" ("as representatives [of God] shall then make public / To increase peace, to correct wars") (lines 47–48). This parallel between the earthly representation of Divine Grace and the government of England finds support in the marginal identification of the speaker of the pageant: Dame Grace is here given a French title, "Ma dame Grace, Chauncelere de Dieu" ("My lady Grace, Chancellor of God"). A chancellor is the chief administrative officer of a figure of higher authority, and the use of the title in French links this pageant to the use of French in medieval English legal records like the *Nova statuta Angliae*. The marginal depiction of Grace as "Chauncelere de Dieu" reinforces the pageant's reference to Grace as "Goddes vicarie generall"; but it also links Grace to the office overseeing documentation of royal power in medieval England: the Lord Chancellor of

1. New Haven, Yale Law School, Goldman Library MssG +StII no.1, fol. 55r
Reproduced with the kind permission of the Lillian Goldman Law Library, Yale Law School

2. New Haven, Yale Law School, Goldman Library MssG +St11 no.1, fol. 139r
Reproduced with the kind permission of the Lillian Goldman Law Library, Yale Law School

3. New Haven, Yale Law School, Goldman Library MssG +Stii no.1, fol. 198r
Reproduced with the kind permission of the Lillian Goldman Law Library, Yale Law School

4. New Haven, Yale Law School, Goldman Library MssG +Stii no.1, fol. 235*v*

Reproduced with the kind permission of the Lillian Goldman Law Library, Yale Law School

5. New Haven, Yale Law School, Goldman Library MssG +St11 no.1, fol. 261r
Reproduced with the kind permission of the Lillian Goldman Law Library, Yale Law School

6. New Haven, Yale Law School, Goldman Library MssG +StII no.1, fol. 358r
Reproduced with the kind permission of the Lillian Goldman Law Library, Yale Law School

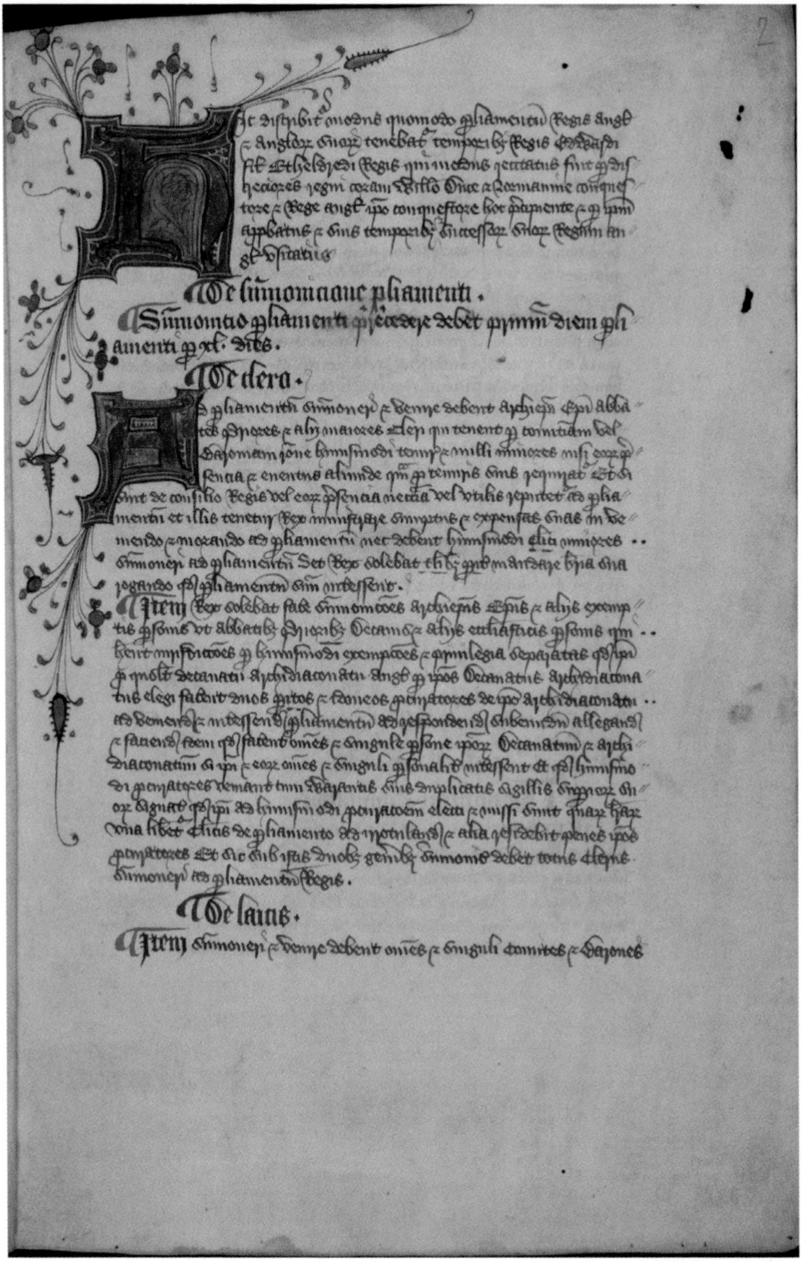

7. New Haven, Yale Law School, Goldman Library MssG +St11 no.1, fol. 2*r*
Reproduced with the kind permission of the Lillian Goldman Law Library, Yale Law School

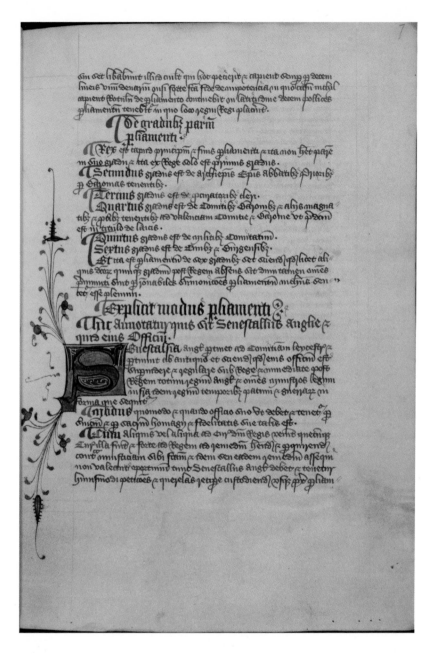

8. New Haven, Yale Law School, Goldman Library MssG +StII no.1, fol. 7r

Reproduced with the kind permission of the Lillian Goldman Law Library, Yale Law School

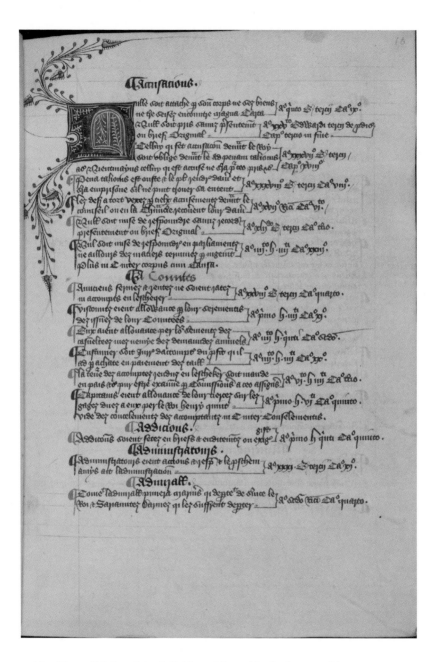

9. New Haven, Yale Law School, Goldman Library MssG +StII no.1, fol. 10r
Reproduced with the kind permission of the Lillian Goldman Law Library, Yale Law School

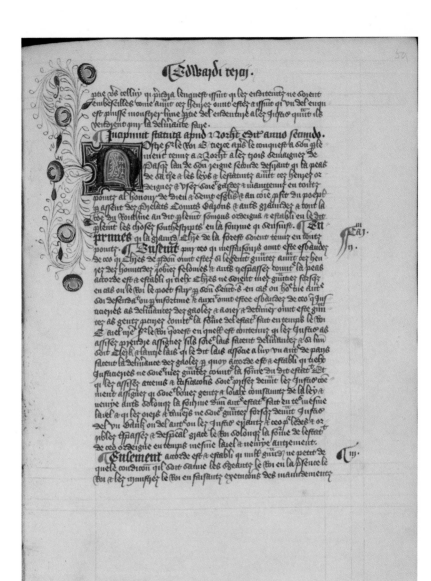

10. New Haven, Yale Law School, Goldman Library MssG +StII no.1, fol. 59r
Reproduced with the kind permission of the Lillian Goldman Law Library, Yale Law School

¶ tercius

meisme la ligeance et qi tout3 le3 enfaunt3 henter3 qi sount nee3 deuore
hor3 de la ligeance le roi de3 queux enfaunt3 le3 piere3 et mier3 au te~
de uestre conceit et sount a la fey et de la ligeance dir roi deng3 eient et
enioient meismes le3 buisti3 et auutage3 danoy et porter heritage
deng3 la dir ligeance come le3 aut3 heyte3 auuedit3 en te aueign
issuit tout3 soit3 qi le3 mier3 de3 tiel3 enfaunt3 passent la mer en
counge et volunte de3 roi3 baion3 Et si allegge soit countie iusti
tiel nee ideit qil est baptiz3 en cas la ou seneit3 soit auoy com
paunie de baptiz3le soit manifie al enes3 del lien sa ou la the
demaunde est de cesier la comp le roi ou le plee est pende si co~
me auuenement a3 enfee ysee en cas de baptiz3le allegge countie te
up qi nasquiyent en Engletre.

¶ Incipiunt statuta de deio apud Westm citra eodem
anno vicesimo quinto rege.

LO siir prele roi veiller3 et examiner3 y bon deliberacion
le3 peticion3 et queule3 a luy bailife3 en son gleme te
mi3 a Westm en la sert de seint hillari sain de son per3
ne deng3 puch et de manner goy y le3 honorable3
peire3 en dieu simon3 Eschenecz3 de Caunterb
et aut3 enesses3 de ca mauuce siir teo et de3 greinuo3 queles3
ils disoient estre sait3 a sount esglise et a la clergie encountre le3
priuileges de seint esglise et a3 onde3 ils piegent qi conuenable re
meisre eut soit ordeigne al iesteue de dieu et de seinte esglise et
del assent de son gleme qui liu3 et se3 heye3 voet et guide le3 po
int3 southescript3. ¶ Prouement qi tout3 le3 sinchise3
et a3 muilege3 graunter3 graunter y seint al dir clergie soie oursepule3
et tenu3 en tout3 point3. Et quint a3 psentent3 say qi nie dit
prele roy ou null de3 se3 heye3 au buste de seint esglise en aut
dort y amutem title iise prele roi al hond de dieu et de seinte es
glise voet et guite del assent du dit gleme qi deuore il ne uult
de se3 heye3 ne dreza title de psenter a mult busine en aut dort
de iuult temp3 de3 se3 purgentes ne qi iuult prelat de son roialme
soit tenu3 de icedimpe iuult tiel psentent assay ne say eut ex
ention ne iuult iusta del un place ne dauge am ie ne gmise
ne deme siir iuult tiel psentent assay plee tenu ou uigent3
doney mie3 qi le dir roi et se3 heye3 dieut de to iuche psentent3
fortbauez a3 tout3 ioun3 saunaut au dir roi et se3 heye3 to3
tiel3 psentent3 en aut dort de to son te et de te aueigny.

¶ tercius

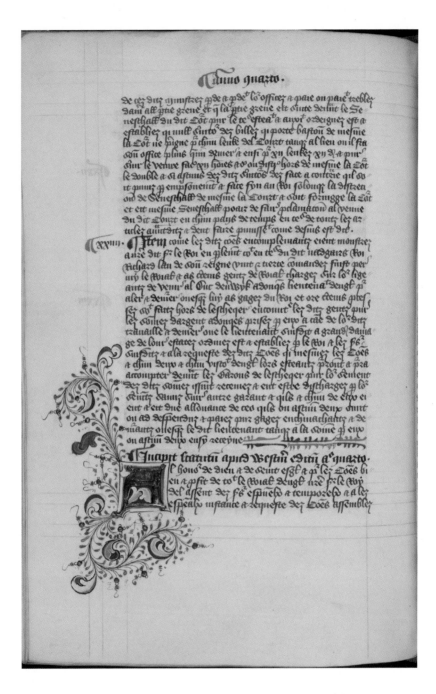

12. New Haven, Yale Law School, Goldman Library MssG +St11 no.1, fol. 211v
Reproduced with the kind permission of the Lillian Goldman Law Library, Yale Law School

13. New Haven, Yale Law School, Goldman Library MssG +Stii no.1, fol. 323ᵥ

Reproduced with the kind permission of the Lillian Goldman Law Library, Yale Law School

14. New Haven, Yale Law School, Goldman Library MssG +StII no.1, fol. 343ν
Reproduced with the kind permission of the Lillian Goldman Law Library, Yale Law School

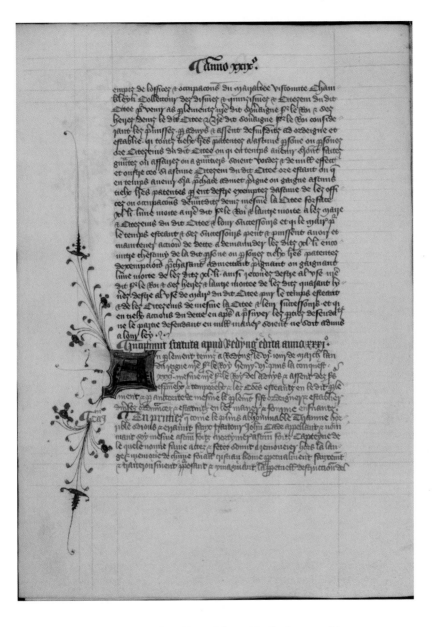

15. New Haven, Yale Law School, Goldman Library MssG +St11 no.1, fol. 344*v*
Reproduced with the kind permission of the Lillian Goldman Law Library, Yale Law School

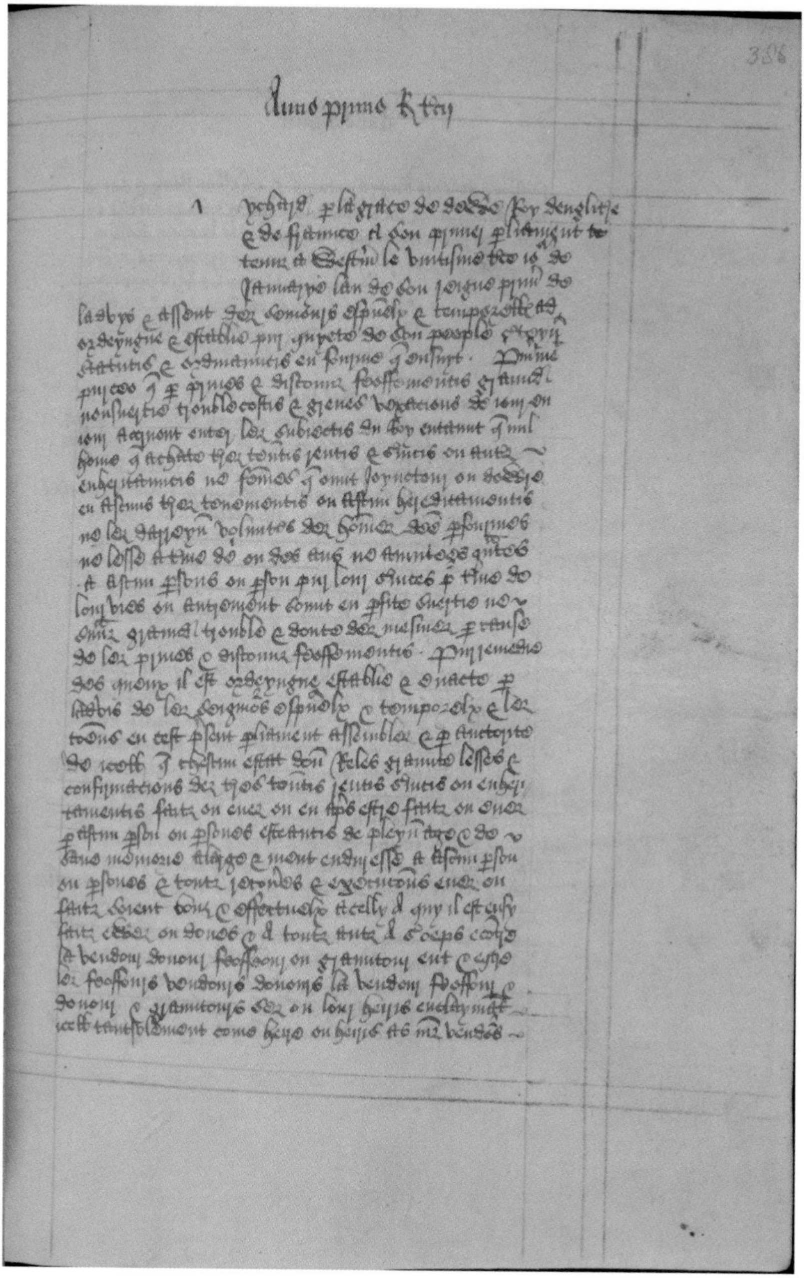

17. New Haven, Yale Law School, Goldman Library MssG +St11 no.1, fol. 386*r*
Reproduced with the kind permission of the Lillian Goldman Law Library, Yale Law School

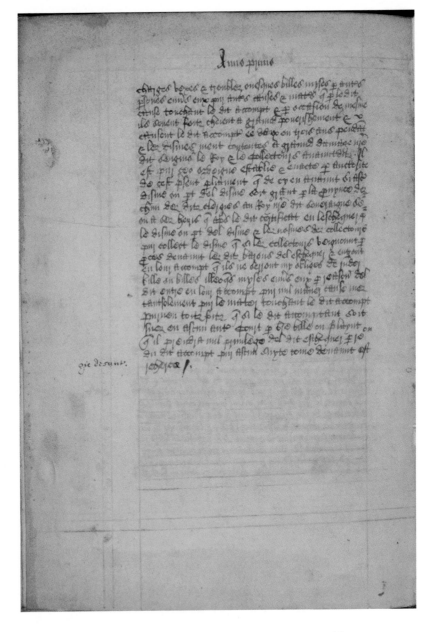

18. New Haven, Yale Law School, Goldman Library MssG +St11 no.1, fol. 389v
Reproduced with the kind permission of the Lillian Goldman Law Library, Yale Law School

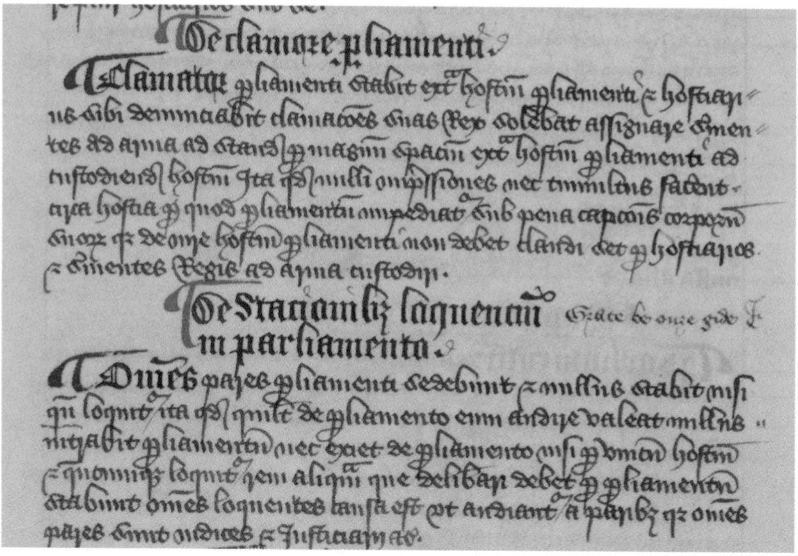

19. New Haven, Yale Law School, Goldman Library MssG +St11 no.1, fol. 6*r* (detail)
Reproduced with the kind permission of the Lillian Goldman Law Library, Yale Law School

20. New Haven, Yale Law School, Goldman Library MssG +StII no.1, fol. 235r (detail)
Reproduced with the kind permission of the Lillian Goldman Law Library, Yale Law School

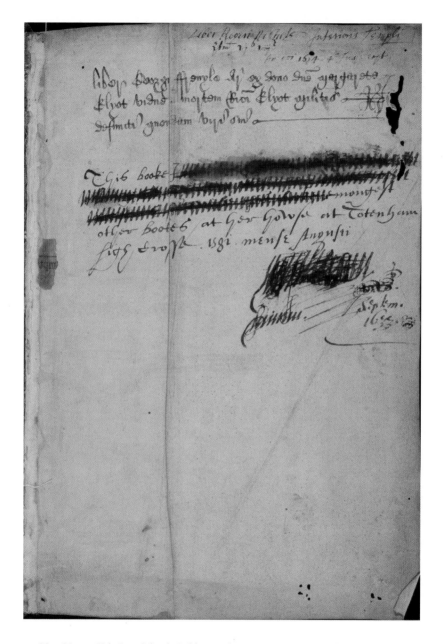

21. New Haven, Yale Law School, Goldman Library MssG +Stii no.i, fol. 1r

Reproduced with the kind permission of the Lillian Goldman Law Library, Yale Law School

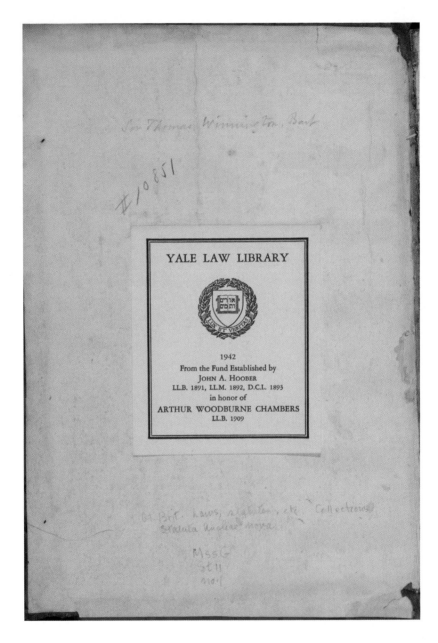

22. New Haven, Yale Law School, Goldman Library MssG +StII no.1, front pastedown
Reproduced with the kind permission of the Lillian Goldman Law Library, Yale Law School

23. New Haven, Yale Law School, Goldman Library MssG +St11 no.1, binding front
Reproduced with the kind permission of the Lillian Goldman Law Library, Yale Law School

24. New Haven, Yale Law School, Goldman Library MssG +St11 no.1, binding back
Reproduced with the kind permission of the Lillian Goldman Law Library, Yale Law School

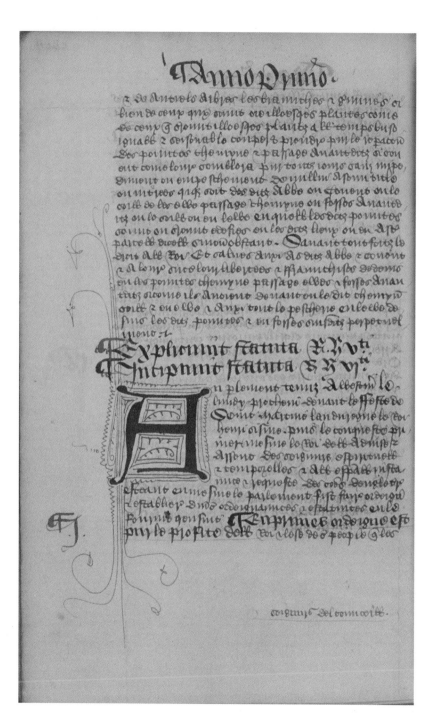

25. New York, Columbia University, Rare Book and Manuscript Library Plimpton
MS 273, fol. 304v *Reproduced with the kind permission of Columbia University Libraries*

26. Philadelphia, Free Library MS Carson LC 14. 10, fol. 314r
Used by permission of the Rare Book Department, Free Library of Philadelphia

27. London, British Library MS Arundel 331, fol. 22r
© The British Library Board

28. Cambridge (UK), St. John's College Library MS A. 7, fol. 133r (detail)
Reproduced by permission of the Fellows of St. John's College, Cambridge

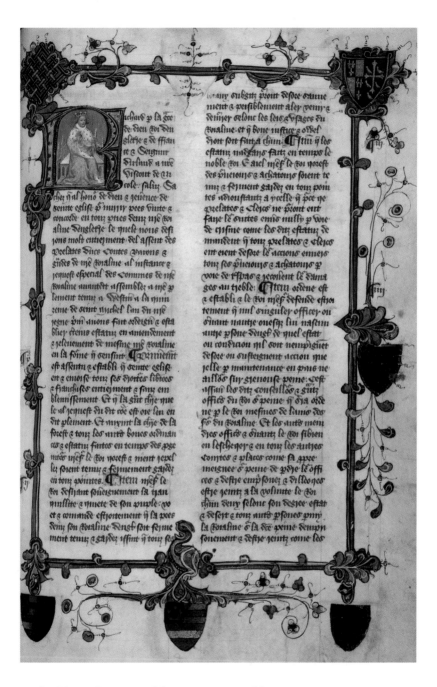

29. San Marino, Huntington Library MS HM 19920, fol. 173r
Reproduced by permission of the Huntington Library, San Marino, California

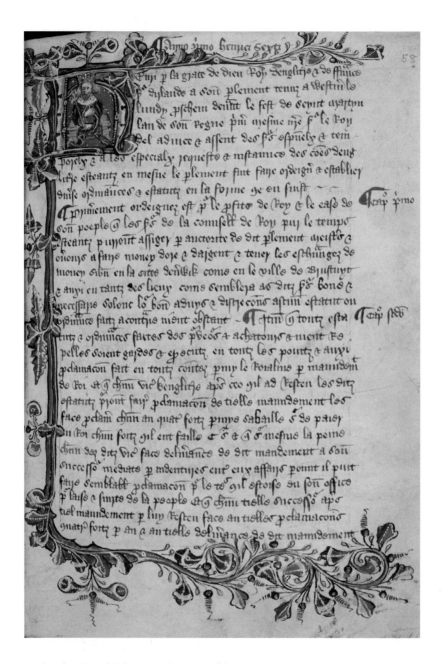

58

30. London, British Library MS Stowe 389, fol. 58r
© *The British Library Board*

31. London, Lincoln's Inn Library MS Hale 194, fol. 34r *Reproduced by permission of the Treasurer and Benchers of the Honourable Society of Lincoln's Inn.* © *The Honourable Society of Lincoln's Inn*

32. London, British Library MS Yates Thompson 48, fol. 41r
© *The British Library Board*

33. Philadelphia, Free Library MS Carson LC 14. 9.5, fol. 245r
Used by permission of the Rare Book Department, Free Library of Philadelphia

34. Kew, National Archives of the UK MS E 164/11, fol. 41r
Reproduced by permission of the National Archives of the UK

35. London, British Library MS Hargrave 274, fol. 328v
© *The British Library Board*

36. Oxford, St. John's College MS 257, fol. 86r *Reproduced by permission of the President and Scholars of Saint John Baptist College in the University of Oxford*

37. London, London Metropolitan Archives MS COL/CS/01/007, fol. 37r
Reproduced by permission of the City of London Corporation, London Metropolitan Archives

38. Oxford, Bodleian Library MS Jesus College 124 (detail) *Reproduced by the kind permission of the Principal, Fellows, and Scholars of Jesus College, Oxford*

39. Cambridge (UK), Fitzwilliam Museum MS 38-1950, fol. 1r
Reproduced by permission of the Syndics of the Fitzwilliam Museum, Cambridge

40. London, British Library MS Royal 15 E vi, fol. 2v
© The British Library Board

41. London, British Library MS Royal 15 E vi, fol. 3r
© The British Library Board

42. London, British Library MS Royal 18 D ii, fol. 95r (detail)
© *The British Library Board*

43. London, British Library MS Royal 20 C vii, fol. 192r (detail)
© *The British Library Board*

44. London, British Library MS Cotton Nero D vi, fol. 72r (detail)
© The British Library Board

45. Paris, Bibliothèque nationale de France MS lat. 18014, fol. 22r (detail)
Reproduced by permission of the Bibliothèque nationale de France

46. New York, Metropolitan
Museum of Art, The Cloisters
Museum, Acc. No. 54.1.1, fol. 91r
(detail) (© The Metropolitan
Museum of Art / Art Resource, NY)
*Reproduced by permission of the
Metropolitan Museum of Art,
New York*

47. New York, Metropolitan Museum of Art, The Cloisters Museum, Acc. No. 54.1.1,
fol. 91v (detail) (© The Metropolitan Museum of Art / Art Resource, NY)
Reproduced by permission of the Metropolitan Museum of Art, New York

48. Paris, Bibliothèque nationale de France MS lat. 17294, fol. 432v (detail)
Reproduced by permission of the Bibliothèque nationale de France

49. New York, Pierpont Morgan Library MS M102, fol. 2r (detail)
(Photographic credit: The Pierpont Morgan Library, New York)
Reproduced by permission of the Pierpont Morgan Library

50. Second Great Seal of Henry III (obverse), Durham, Durham Cathedral Library
MS I. 2. Reg. 6a *Reproduced by permission of Durham Cathedral*

51. Second Great Seal of Henry III (reverse), Durham, Durham Cathedral Library
MS I. 2. Reg. 6a *Reproduced by permission of Durham Cathedral*

52. Great Seal of Edward III (1364) (obverse) (London, British Library
MS Egerton Charter 2132) © *The British Library Board*

53. Great Seal of Edward III (1364) (reverse) (London, British Library
MS Egerton Charter 2132) © *The British Library Board*

54. Great Seal of Henry VI (1471) (obverse) (London, British Library
MS Egerton Charter 2129) © *The British Library Board*

55. Great Seal of Henry VI (1471) (reverse) (London, British Library
MS Egerton Charter 2129) © *The British Library Board*

56. London, British Library MS Arundel 109, fol. 8r (detail)
© *The British Library Board*

57. Austin, University of Texas, Harry Ransom Humanities Research Center
MS HRC 5, fol. 96r (detail) *Reproduced by permission of the Harry Ransom
Humanities Research Center, University of Texas at Austin*

58. Oxford, Bodleian Library MS Don. d. 85, fol. 21*v* (detail)
Reproduced by permission of the Bodleian Library, University of Oxford

59. New York, Pierpont Morgan Library MS M456, fol. 1r (detail)
(Photographic credit: The Pierpont Morgan Library, New York)
Reproduced by permission of the Pierpont Morgan Library

60. Paris, Bibliothèque nationale de France MS lat. 18014, fol. 121ᵥ (detail)
Reproduced by permission of the Bibliothèque nationale de France

61. Cambridge (UK), King's College Library MS KC/18 (detail)
Reproduced by permission of King's College Library, Cambridge

62. Windsor, Eton College Archives MS 39/57 (detail)
Reproduced by permission of the Provost and Fellows of Eton College

63. 1444 Charter (London, the Leathersellers' Company) (detail)
Reproduced by the kind permission of the Leathersellers' Company

64. London, British Library MS Hargrave 274, fol. 204v (detail)
© The British Library Board

65. London, British Library MS Cotton Domitian A xvii, fol. 50r
© *The British Library Board*

66. London, British Library MS Cotton Domitian A xvii, fol. 13r
© *The British Library Board*

67. London, British Library MS Cotton Domitian A xvii, fol. 206v
© The British Library Board

68. London, British Library MS Cotton Domitian A xvii, fol. 207r
© *The British Library Board*

69. London, British Library MS Cotton Domitian A xvii, fol. 178r
© *The British Library Board*

70. London, British Library MS Cotton Domitian A xvii, fol. 75r
© *The British Library Board*

71. London, British Library MS Cotton Domitian A xvii, fol. 74v
© The British Library Board

72. Kew, National Archives of the UK MS KB 27/796 (detail)
Reproduced by permission of the National Archives of the UK

73. Kew, National Archives of the UK MS KB 27/798 (detail)
Reproduced by permission of the National Archives of the UK

74. Kew, National Archives of the UK MS KB 27/819 (detail)
Reproduced by permission of the National Archives of the UK

75. Kew, National Archives of the UK MS KB 27/820 (detail)
Reproduced by permission of the National Archives of the UK

The Queen Margarete sithe ne wyff and spowse to kyng mary the ferthe.

76. London, London Metropolitan Archives, Guildhall Library MS 31692, fol. 34v (detail) *Reproduced by kind permission of the Skinners' Company and the City of London Corporation, London Metropolitan Archives*

77. Portrait of Sir Thomas Elyot by Hans Holbein the Younger
(1532–33) (Windsor Castle, Royal Collection)
The Royal Collection © 2010, Her Majesty Queen Elizabeth II

The Lady Eliot.

78. Portrait of Lady Margaret Elyot by Hans Holbein the Younger
(1532–33) (Windsor Castle, Royal Collection)
The Royal Collection © 2010, Her Majesty Queen Elizabeth II

79. Portrait of Sir Francis Winnington, artist unknown
(London, National Portrait Gallery) © *National Portrait Gallery, London*

80. Portrait of Sir Thomas Winnington by Christian Friedrich Zincke
(London, National Portrait Gallery) © *National Portrait Gallery, London*

England in the fifteenth century was "in charge of drawing up, sealing, issuing, and enrolling such documents as charters, letters patent, and letters close,
while exercising certain equitable jurisdiction."[8] By expressing the hope that
Margaret will herself be guided by the grace of God throughout her reign,
the pageant sets her in parallel with the Four Daughters of God, who are sent
by God's chancellor to make God's will known to the people of the realm, in
order to teach them what they must do to achieve peace.

The depiction of Grace in this pageant as the administrative representative of the heavenly king and the guide to human beings also inscribes a link
between this pageant and another fifteenth-century Middle English text that
was well known to city and courtly readers: *The Pilgrimage of the Soul*. Written
in 1413, *The Pilgrimage of the Soul* is an anonymous adaptation of a fourteenth-
century French poem by Guillaume de Deguileville.[9] *The Pilgrimage of the Soul*
differs from its French source in also circulating under the title *The Book of
Grace Dieu*. Book 1 of *The Pilgrimage of the Soul* includes an account of the
soul's earlier guidance by Grace Dieu and then presents a letter from Grace
Dieu to the soul, in which she describes herself as deputized by God to act as
guide to human beings (McGerr 1990, 32–36). *The Pilgrimage of the Soul* not
only borrows the discourse of a legal proceeding to depict the human soul's
judgment after death, but also highlights the role of written documents in the
determination of justice (Steiner 2003, 32–34): in addition to the letter from
Grace Dieu, the text presents a petition submitted to the court by Satan and
a charter granted by Christ. The scene of the soul's judgment, like the London
pageant for Margaret of Anjou, also makes use of the alliance of the Four
Daughters of God from the Book of Psalms. In this case, Mercy and Justice
are finally accorded in the judgment of the soul, because Mercy presents to
the court the charter of grace that she has received from the heavenly king.

Depicting Grace Dieu, God's chancellor, as Margaret's guide clearly associates the new queen with both grace and justice. Nevertheless, this pageant
does not present Dame Grace, or by extension Queen Margaret, as having
the only voice in the process of establishing a just peace. Laynesmith suggests
that the pageant depicts Margaret in the role of assistant to the king in his
role as judge of his subjects (Laynesmith 2004, 83–84). The final stanza of
the pageant also depicts the three "estates" of medieval society – "Clergie,
Knyghthode, the Lawes commendable" ("Clergy, Knights, the commendable
Common People") – in the role of "assentyng" to ratify the counsels of Grace
(lines 49–51), as if these counsels were documents sent for Parliament's approval by an earthly king.[10] Here, the legal discourse widens beyond the role

of the Daughters of God and Margaret as emissaries of Divine Grace: the third stanza describes a process in which the diverse parts of the English community come together to find a unified voice inspired by Grace, just as late medieval English writers compared Parliament to Christ's disciples, who were inspired by divine grace at Pentecost (Giancarlo 2007, 50–52). Though the pageant depicts Margaret as one who is guided by divine grace, this stanza reminds the queen of the important role played by Parliament in providing counsel and assent to the monarchy, just as the account of Edward III and Queen Isabelle in the *Nova statuta* stresses the importance of Parliament's counsel and assent. The unity inspired by divine grace takes on an international dimension when the third stanza depicts the patron saints of England and France, St. George and St. Denis, asking the divine king that "alle schall iustefie / This tyme of Grace" ("all shall make just / this time of Grace") (lines 53–54). These lines suggest that the French, as well as the English, should join together to make this an era of Grace, reminding Margaret that her marriage is meant to build another bridge between the two peoples.

It is also notable that the end of the last stanza in this pageant reinforces its own documentary discourse. Grace asserts, "Thus wolde the storie seyne" ("Thus will the account say") (line 54). This time of grace is what the English welcoming pageant both represents and performs by offering the prayer that Margaret will follow the guidance of divine grace and by "trustyng that pees schall floure and fructyfye" ("trusting that peace will flower and bear fruit") (line 55) through the new queen – another possible reference to the son that Margaret was expected to bear and prepare for kingship. Here, the pageant seems to depict itself as a first draft of later inscriptions of the just peace it describes as the goal of divine and human law. Medieval discourses of queenship often associate queens with peace, prosperity, mercy, and fertility; but this pageant also depicts Margaret's new role in terms of earthly processes of ratifying laws, encouraging dialogue between representatives of royal authority and others in the community, and documenting legal agreements, as if to suggest that divine grace should lead Margaret in earthly negotiations of power, as much as in spiritual matters.

At the same time, the pageant's depiction of Margaret's relationship to divine grace suggests the need for the queen's grace to be inclusive, establishing concord among diverse groups, just as the four Daughters of God are accorded by Grace. The performative dimension of this pageant also suggests that creating unity out of diversity is one of its major themes. Dame Grace, the chancellor of God, welcomes Margaret of Anjou at Leadenhall Market, after the French princess has crossed over the Thames River and entered into the city of London. This market had grown up behind the grand lead-roofed manor house called Leadenhall in the fourteenth century, as the knight who owned it leased portions of his land to merchants.[11] In the early fifteenth century, the entire manor was purchased by the mayor of London for the city's use as a general market, as well as storage space for the equipment used in civic pageants and processions. It was also a place of international exchange, since foreign merchants could sell their wares at Leadenhall Market on two days each week. The Leadenhall Market setting for Grace's words of welcome to Margaret constructs an expanded frame of reference for the pageant's presentation of royal guidance, parliamentary legislation, and international peace: through its setting, the pageant includes commercial interests that might seem marginal to the traditional political order, but played an increasingly larger role in the negotiations of justice and peace that Margaret entered when she became queen.

Margaret of Anjou's associations with divine grace and justice also play a prominent role in another set of pageants that have survived, this time welcoming Margaret to the city of Coventry in September 1456. The unique copy of these pageants in the record book of the Coventry mayors only once refers explicitly to the grace of God: in the concluding pageant of the sequence, the queen's namesake, St. Margaret, tells the queen that she will pray to Christ "To socour you with solas of his high grace" ("To comfort you with the solace of his high grace") (Harris 1907, 292). Despite the small role given to explicit references to grace, however, several of the pageants suggest Margaret's association with divine grace by comparing her to the Virgin Mary and comparing Margaret's young son, Edward of Lancaster, to Christ. In the first of these pageants, the speeches take place near a visual representation of the Tree of Jesse, a traditional image of the descent of Mary and Christ from the lineage of Jesse, which also linked them to King David. The first speaker of the pageant, the prophet Isaiah, often depicted as foretelling the Virgin Mary's role as bearer of the son of God, tells Margaret,

> Like as mankynde was gladdid by the birght of Jhesus,
> So shall þis empire ioy the birthe of your bodye;
> The knightly curage of prince Edward all men shall ioy to se.

> (Just as mankind was made glad by the birth of Jesus,
> So shall this empire rejoice at the birth from your body;
> The knightly courage of Prince Edward shall all men rejoice to see.)
>   (Harris 1907, 287)

In the second stanza of the opening pageant, the prophet Jeremiah echoes Isaiah in depicting Margaret and Prince Edward in parallel with the Virgin and Christ:

> Vn-to the rote of Jesse rote likken you well I may;
> The fragrante floure sprongon of you shall so encrece & spredde,
> That all the world yn ich party shall cherisshe hym, love & drede.

> (To the descendant of Jesse's lineage well may I compare you;
> The fragrant flower sprung from you shall so grow and flourish,
> That all the world in each part shall cherish, love, and fear him.)
>   (Harris 1907, 287)

As in the London pageants, Margaret here is depicted as bringing divine grace to her people through her fertility and her virtue; but in this case her son has been born, and the recognition of his virtue reflects back onto her as well. In the next pageant, St. Edward and St. John the Evangelist declare heaven's approval of Queen Margaret and her son. St. John tells the queen, "I knowe your lyf so vertuus þat God is plesyd therby" ("I know your life [to be] so virtuous that God is pleased by it"), and continues, "The vertuus voyce of prince Edward shall dayly well encrese; / Seynt Edward, his godfader, & I shall pray þerfore dowtelesse" ("The virtuous reputation of Prince Edward shall daily well increase; / St. Edward, his godfather, and I shall pray for this, without a doubt") (Harris 1907, 288).

Like the London pageants, the Coventry pageants associate Margaret with both grace and justice. After the welcome by two Jewish prophets and two Christian saints, the four cardinal virtues, rather than the Four Daughters of God, welcome the queen. One of the cardinal virtues is Righteousness or Justice, who claims to be both the source of truth and Margaret's constant companion: "I, Rigthwesnes, that causeth treuth to be had / . . . / With you wyll I be dwelling & neuer you forsake" ("I, Righteousness, who cause truth to be found / . . . / With you will I be dwelling and never forsake you") (Harris 1907, 288). Another of the cardinal virtues, Prudence, depicts Margaret's child as the blessed source of peace for England: "The blessyd babe þat ye haue born, prynce Edward is he, / Thurrowe whom pece & tranquilite shall take þis reme on hand" ("The blessed baby that you have borne, he is Prince Edward, / Through whom peace and tranquility shall take this realm in hand") (Harris 1907, 289). Prudence goes on to explain that the cardinal virtues will endow Margaret and her son with clear understanding and protect them both forever.

The pageants next present speeches by each of the Nine Worthies that continue the depiction of Margaret's son as a child of divine blessing, who will bring peace and prosperity; but these speeches also celebrate Henry VI. Alexander the Great tells Margaret, "The nobilest prince þat is born, whome fortune hath famyd, / Is your souereyn lorde Herry, emperor & kyng" ("The most noble prince alive, whom fortune has made famous, / Is your sovereign lord, Harry, emperor and king") (Harris 1907, 289). The speech by Judas Maccabeus also praises Henry VI and reveals that the king is also present: "Your own souerayn lorde & kynge is present here, / Whome God for his godenes preserve in good helthe" ("Your own sovereign lord and king is present here, / Whom God, for his goodness, preserve in good health") (Harris 1907, 290). Though this prayer for the king's health is traditional, in 1456 it might also remind the audience of Henry's recent illness and the political instability it generated. Tensions between royal presence and absence, centrality and marginality thus come into play most explicitly in this final set of speeches. Though the Nine Worthies declare their loyal service to the royal family, Margaret is the only person they address directly. The queen is at the center of this performance, since neither her husband nor her son is able in September 1456 to perform the role of ideal leader ascribed to them in the pageants, and the Coventry pageants allude to several kinds of authority – religious, legal, and military – that Margaret will need to marshal in order to protect both the king and the prince.

When Margaret became queen, she did take a greater interest in legal matters than had her immediate predecessors. Though Margaret's activities aroused suspicion and criticism in some quarters, Henry VI seems to have supported her efforts, designating space in a new tower at Westminster Palace in 1452 for the meetings of her council and the safe-keeping of her books and documents (Myers 1957–58, 95, 417). Margaret also differed from her predecessors in the large number of lawyers she retained in her service.[12] For several years following her wedding, much of Margaret's need for legal counsel stemmed from difficulties in collecting the income due to her, difficulties that often had to be resolved by Parliament.[13] Margaret probably learned about legal texts like the *Nova statuta Angliae* from the lawyers in her service, at least one of whom owned his own manuscript copy: three inscriptions in London, British Library MS Additional 81292, one of the few surviving manuscript copies of the statutes in English, attest to its ownership by Sir William Coote of Coningsby, Lincolnshire, who served as the queen's attorney general.[14] Graver legal and political issues arose in the 1450s, increasing Margaret's need for legal advice and knowledge. She began to take an active role in legal measures to maintain Henry VI's authority during his incapacity from August 1453 until December 1454.[15] Although the king's supporters attempted to seclude the king in order to minimize knowledge of his condition, when he was unable to participate in the November 1453 preparations for the next session of Parliament, competition for the authority to speak for him began. The Duke of York's party was successful in removing a strong candidate for that role, Henry's chancellor, the Duke of Somerset, by having him arrested for treason and imprisoned without ever being formally charged or brought to trial.[16] With the Lancastrian political leadership in disarray, in January 1454 Margaret submitted a petition to Parliament requesting appointment as Henry's regent. A major factor in the queen's emergence as the leader in defense of the king and the Lancastrian monarchy at this time was the birth of Margaret and Henry's son on 13 October 1453, for the prince's security depended on the security of his father. After her petition to be appointed regent failed in March 1454, Margaret's construction of her role as mother of Henry's heir was one of the few options she had for exercising authority on behalf of her husband (Laynesmith 2004, 160–62). Although Parliament appointed the Duke of York as Protector and Defender of the Realm, the declaration specified that Prince Edward would remain heir apparent. Deprived of most means to help the king directly, Margaret highlighted the laws of succession on public occasions and followed Lancastrian tradition in using different types of iconography in order to depict Henry and Prince Edward as members of a glorious and unbroken line of English kings, who represent divine justice on earth.

Edward of Lancaster's claim to be Henry's VI's heir was indeed one that needed demonstrations of support, since even before his birth the Yorkists spread rumors denying his legitimacy.[17] With Henry VI's bouts of illness preventing him from leading public celebrations of the young prince or participating in plans for Edward's education, Margaret took an active role in protecting her son's rights and preparing him to take on the responsibilities of kingship. Margaret's considerable skill in performing royal authority can be seen, for instance, in the christening ceremony at Westminster Abbey that she arranged for Prince Edward. The splendor of the infant prince's christening robe, which cost more than five hundred pounds, and his attendance by ten duchesses and eight countesses suggest an attempt to deflect attention from the absence of Prince Edward's father from the ceremony (Jones and Underwood 1993, 254; Laynesmith 2004, 140n; Yonge 1877, 95). Margaret continued to find ways in which to secure public recognition of Prince Edward's claim as legitimate heir to the throne. Though it had more symbolic than practical significance, since he was barely five months old at the time, Edward of Lancaster was formally invested as Prince of Wales and Earl of Chester in March 1454 (Roskell 2005, 2:217). Margaret's attempts to exert influence at court through the household of her son were challenged by York, who, in his role as Protector of the Realm, ordered the household staff of the prince reduced to thirty-eight (Orme 1984, 14). Nevertheless, at the end of York's protectorate in December 1454, Margaret succeeded in taking control of the prince's affairs and resources through the appointment of his officers.[18] To shape public perception of the prince, the queen continued to encourage public events that highlighted her young son's role as heir to the throne. As we have seen, the pageants that welcomed Margaret to Coventry in September 1456 echo the public role that Margaret created for her son and serve to "construct the new prince as a potential exemplar of kingship" in order to "emphasize the potential and legitimacy of Lancastrian kingship."[19] In the summer of 1459, Margaret also arranged for Prince Edward to distribute swan badges – an emblem used by Edward III, Henry IV, and Henry V – as gifts to knights in the midlands, allowing them an opportunity to display their Lancastrian loyalty in a visual form (Palliser 1870, 360–69; Dockray 2000, 81). In December 1459, the Lancastrians successfully worked through Parliament to strengthen legal support for Prince Edward as Henry's rightful heir: at the Coventry session of Parliament, after the declaration of attainder against the Yorkist lords, sixty-six peers of England swore life-long allegiance to King Henry and also loyalty to Prince Edward, accepting his succession as heir to the throne and the succession of his legal heirs (Watts 1996, 353; Maurer 2003, 173).

Margaret may have been inspired to take an active role in defending the Lancastrian monarchy by her knowledge of the role played by Edward III's French mother, Queen Isabelle, in bringing him to the throne. At the same time, Margaret probably also saw parallels between Henry VI's illness and the periods of mental illness suffered by his maternal grandfather, Charles VI of France. As a result, Margaret would have recognized the parallel between her situation and that of Charles VI's queen, Isabelle of Bavaria.[20] It was Isabelle who in 1420 helped arrange the treaty whereby her daughter Katherine married Henry V of England and Henry VI was then crowned king of France after Charles VI's death in 1422, because Henry V had already died. Margaret would also have been familiar with the accounts of Charles VI's illness and Isabelle's actions on behalf of her children because of the important role played at that time and subsequently by Margaret's grandmother, Yolande of Aragon, Duchess of Anjou, with whom Margaret lived for eight years as a child. Yolande arranged for the engagement of her daughter Marie, Margaret's aunt, to Isabelle's younger son, Charles, who came to live at the court of Anjou. After his father and older brothers died, Charles claimed the throne of France as Charles VII, thanks in part to Yolande and Margaret's mother, Isabelle of Lorraine, who introduced him to Joan of Arc and supported him during the round of battles with the English that Margaret's marriage to Henry VI in 1445 was supposed to resolve.

With Margaret's attempt to be appointed regent for Henry VI denied, an alternative plan for thwarting the efforts of the Duke of York to gain royal power was for Margaret to prepare her son to rule as soon as possible. Just as Charles VI's eldest son, Louis of Guyenne, represented his father in the government during Charles's periods of mental illness (Hedeman 2001, 47–48), Parliament could allow Edward of Lancaster to take on a similar role when Edward reached a suitable age – or, if Henry VI's illness worsened, Prince Edward could be prepared to replace his father entirely, as Edward III replaced Edward II. Queens sometimes supervised the early education of princes; but the unusual circumstances in which Margaret began to provide for her son's education combined opportunity with urgency. One of her resources would have been the literature of advice to princes. To help Isabelle of Bavaria educate her oldest son during Charles VI's incapacity, John of Burgundy asked Christine de Pizan to make a French translation of Vegetius's *De re militari*, the same Latin text that would be translated into English verse in the late 1450s as *Knyghthode and Bataile* (*Knighthood and Battle*).[21] Margaret of Anjou owned a copy of Christine's translation, *Le livre des fais d'armes et de chevalerie* (*The Book about Feats of Arms and about Chivalry*), in the anthology she had received as a wedding present from Sir John Talbot.[22] As Bossy suggests (1998, 246), Talbot may have intended the anthology not only as a gift for Margaret's enjoyment and education, but also as a resource for educating a royal heir on the ideals and models of kingship. Christine's *Fais d'armes* would certainly have been a logical choice for Margaret to use in educating Prince Edward, for its content as well as its history.

From the title of Christine's work, we can see that her treatise constructs chivalry as more than the use of arms. The invocation of Minerva, rather than Mars, in the preface also signals the treatise's emphasis on the contributions of wisdom and justice to chivalric ideals: the narrator describes Minerva as "la saige dame . . . que les anciens pour son grant sçavoir repputerent deesse" ("the wise lady . . . whom the ancients considered a goddess for her great knowledge") and goes on to address her as "deesse d'armes et de chevallerie" ("goddess of arms and chivalry") (Laennec 1988, 22). As Le Saux argues, in this treatise, chivalry "takes on marked ethical connotations" (Le Saux 2004, 100).[23] Indeed, the opening chapters of the *Fais d'armes*, which are Christine's addition to Vegetius's treatise, make clear that the focus of Christine's work will be the relationship between chivalry and justice. For example, the narrator explains that the first concern of the treatise will be "assavoir se guerras et batailles, chevalerie et faiz d'armes, de laquelle chose esperons parler, est ou non chose juste" ("to learn whether wars and battles, chivalry and deeds of arms, of which thing we hope to speak, is or [is] not a just thing"). The same chapter ends by indicating that the treatise will discuss the proper use of arms as defined by secular law and canon law ("limitees selon les loix et droit canon") (Laennec 1988, 24).

The *Fais d'armes* describes the ancient practice of beginning military education for noble sons at age thirteen (Laennec 1988, 44).[24] Nevertheless, because Christine's treatise emphasizes the need for the king to be educated in the principles of good government and law in order to engage in the just use of arms, it suggests that this part of a prince's education could begin even earlier. Especially in the opening chapters, the *Fais d'armes* discusses the king's responsibility to pursue justice through wars that follow divine and earthly law.[25] For example, Christine's narrator argues that "bataille qui est faitte a juste querelle" ("battle that is waged for a just cause") is "la droitte excecucion de justice" ("the correct execution of justice") and that such wars follow the laws established by God and human beings: "Et ce accorde meesmes le droit divin, et semblablement les loys ordonnees des gens pour contrester aux arrogans et malfaiteurs" ("And this accords both with divine law and similarly with laws ordained by people to punish the arrogant and evildoers") (Laennec 1988, 24). Since justice should be the goal of battle and chivalry, Christine's treatise argues that the king should seek wise counsel before deciding to engage in battle, including the advice of those who are learned in law ("clercs legistes") (Laennec 1988, 31). When the king determines that the use of arms in a situation accords with the law, the treatise argues, the war should be considered "pure excecucion de droitturiere justice" ("pure execution of lawful justice") (Laennec 1988, 28). This focus on just use of arms as the king's right and responsibility puts Christine's mirror for princes in parallel with the themes of the opening of the *Nova statuta*, as well as the pageants that welcomed Margaret to London and Coventry.

One must not underestimate the authority that Christine de Pizan's texts had for readers in England, as well as France, in the fifteenth century. Among the members of the French royal and ducal families who owned at least one of Christine's works between 1405 and 1425 were Charles VI, Charles VII, Isabelle of Bavaria, Louis of Guyenne, Louis of Orléans, Philip of Burgundy, Marguerite of Burgundy, John of Berry, and Marie of Berry, while John of Burgundy, Philip's son, owned seven volumes of Christine's works.[26] French copies of Christine's works also circulated in England. For example, the volume of thirty texts by Christine (London, British Library MS Harley 4431) that was made for Charles VI's queen, Isabelle of Bavaria, came to England when John of Lancaster, Duke of Bedford, purchased the French royal library in 1425. The book passed to John of Lancaster's second wife, Jacquetta of Luxemburg, and then to her son, Anthony Woodville (or Wydville), Baron Scales and second Earl Rivers, who translated Christine's *Morales proverbs* and probably her *Livre du corps de policie* into English (Mahoney 1996, 405; Chance 1998, 165). In addition to owning a copy of *Le livre des fais d'armes et de chevalerie*, Margaret of Anjou probably had knowledge of and access to several of Christine's other works. It is very likely that Margaret knew Christine's *Livre de la cité des dames*, *Le livre des fais et bonnes meurs du sage roi Charles V*, and *Le livre du corps de policie*, as well as *Le livre des fais d'armes et de chevalerie*. In France, Margaret's family had close relationships with many of Christine's original patrons, so that Margaret could have read or listened to many of Christine's works when she visited other courts, if her family had no copies of these in its own collection. In England, Margaret became close friends with Alice Chaucer, Duchess of Suffolk, who owned a copy of Christine's *Livre de la cité des dames*.[27] Helen Maurer (2003, 5–9, 151) maintains that Margaret followed Christine's ideals of queenship in seeking reconciliation between Henry VI and his opponents before 1459, while Frances Teague (1991, 31) suggests that Margaret followed Christine's ideals of kingship in rallying the Lancastrian forces against Henry's foes. As a mirror for princes that Christine composed for the son of Charles VI of France, *Le livre des fais d'armes et de chevalerie* would have held special significance for Margaret of Anjou when she sought education in kingship for her own son. With its emphasis on the king's need to understand religious and secular laws in order to use the force of arms justly, Christine's treatise offered Margaret a model for encouraging her own son to study English law; but, for this part of his education, Prince Edward would need another book, a copy of the *Nova statuta Angliae*.

Although any of the events highlighting the prince's authority might have been an appropriate context for a gift like the Yale *Nova statuta*, Margaret's concern for the prince's formal education might also have led her to consider Edward's need for books about English law as soon as he was old enough to listen, if not yet read. In January 1457, when Prince Edward was three years old, a council was appointed to advise the prince and guide his education, though the appointment stipulated that the council would require the queen's approval for its actions.[28] One of the members appointed to this council was Lawrence Booth. Though Margaret's chancellor at the time, Booth was also master of Pembroke College in Cambridge and chancellor of Cambridge University; as a student, he had taken degrees in civil and canon law at Pembroke.[29] Booth had also taken orders as a priest in 1446 and had served as dean of St. Paul's Cathedral. In 1457, after joining the prince's council, Booth became bishop of Durham, which carried civil as well as ecclesiastical responsibilities. Appointing Booth to Prince Edward's council may have been a way for the Lancastrians to signal that the prince would receive a substantial education.

In March 1460, the complete supervision of Prince Edward's education was officially transferred from women to men (Maurer 2003, 177; Laynesmith 2004, 147–52; *Calendar* 1891–1916, 49:567). Although this transition traditionally occurred when a noble son reached the age of seven, Margaret appears to have found it important to announce the prince's formal education six months early, perhaps because of increased political tensions with the Yorkists.[30] Given Margaret's concerns about establishing her son's authority in the face of Yorkist challenges, she might have commissioned a book that highlighted his ancestry, such as the Yale Law School *Nova statuta*, as a gift to celebrate this transition in the prince's education. An even more appropriate event for such a gift, however, would have been Prince Edward's knighting ceremony, which Margaret probably planned for October 1460, when he would reach the age of seven. No grand celebration of the prince's seventh birthday took place that October, however, because in July the Duke of York's forces captured the king, and Margaret and the prince took refuge in Scotland. Instead of celebrating his son's seventh birthday in October, the imprisoned Henry accepted an agreement that allowed him to remain king if he designated the Duke of York as his heir and disinherited Prince Edward. Margaret responded by sending the Lancastrian army in the livery of Prince Edward to meet York's forces, and the Lancastrians captured and executed York in December. After another Lancastrian military victory in February

1461 brought Henry VI's release, he celebrated his reunion with his family by knighting his son (Maurer 2003, 191–96).[31] The ceremony must have been considerably less elaborate than the one Margaret and the Lancastrians would have preferred, however, since any plans that may have been in the works for gifts and public spectacles had been interrupted by eight months of exile and warfare. If the Yale Law School *Nova statuta* was commissioned as a gift in honor of the prince's knighting, the political and geographic dislocations of the time might help explain the unfinished qualities of the manuscript – the lack of presentation miniature and inscriptions of the gift – as well as the continuation of the manuscript into the reign of Edward IV, but with a change of iconography. The Lancastrians' celebration of their victory did not last long, for less than a month later York's son Edward persuaded Parliament to declare him king. Henry, Margaret, and their son first took refuge in Scotland; then in July 1463 Margaret took Prince Edward and a group of about fifty supporters into France, where they set up a Lancastrian court in exile at St. Mihiel-en-Barre and worked to find a way to restore Henry VI to the throne. At the same time, as we will see in the next chapter, Margaret and her supporters continued to prepare Edward of Lancaster to fulfill his role as Henry VI's heir.

Margaret's attempts to use English law to defend her husband and son, her possession of the *Fais d'armes*, and her probable knowledge of the commissioning of that text to prepare the French dauphin to represent his ailing father all suggest that Margaret could well have been responsible for including law in Prince Edward's studies and commissioning a statute book for her son that would also serve as a mirror for princes highlighting the integral connection between law and good kingship. If such a book also presented Henry VI as an embodiment of good kingship, as the Yale Law School manuscript of the *Nova statuta* does, this would certainly have served Margaret's purposes even better. The intertwining of discourses in the Yale Law School manuscript has important connections to Lancastrian textual traditions; but it also has links with texts and iconographic traditions found in manuscripts and works of art closely associated with Margaret of Anjou and her family in France. For example, Margaret certainly knew about the representation of King David as one of the Nine Worthies by September 1456, when she was welcomed to Coventry with the pageant depicting these noble heroes. She was probably already familiar with the tradition of presenting King David as one of the Nine Worthies before she arrived in England, thanks to the widespread influence of this theme in French literature and art. In the early fifteenth century, for example, the Duke of Berry commissioned tapestries that depict the Nine Worthies and use his own coat of arms in the background of the images of the three biblical heroes (Joshua, David, and Judas Maccabeus).[32] If Margaret sought additional images that linked a contemporary prince with King David, she could have found these in the Duke of Berry's own prayer books, which use the King David iconography from psalters and books of hours as models for depictions of the duke at prayer.[33] Growing up at the court of her grandmother Yolande of Aragon, a collector and commissioner of illustrated manuscripts, Margaret would have had knowledge of the Duke of Berry's famous collection of devotional books and almost certainly would have seen at least one of these in her grandmother's collection: after the duke's death, Yolande purchased his *Belles heures,* which she gave to the master of the *Rohan Hours* to use as a model for the four prayer books she commissioned for members of her own family (Porcher 1945, Meiss 1973). In her father, Duke René of Anjou, and her uncle, Charles VII of France, Margaret had two more models to reinforce the family tradition of commissioning deluxe manuscripts and participating actively in their design.[34]

Margaret's own interest in collecting and commissioning books can be seen in the manuscripts associated with her.[35] In addition to the anthology of French texts that she received as a wedding present from Sir John Talbot, Margaret is thought to have owned Oxford, Bodleian Library MS Hatton 73, which contains Lydgate's *Life of Our Lady* and lyrics by Lydgate, Chaucer, and others.[36] A manuscript made expressly for her (Oxford, Bodleian Library MS Jesus College 124) contains a set of Latin prayers to the Virgin accompanied by an image of Margaret kneeling before a *prie-dieu* and her coat of arms (her father's arms impaled with Henry VI's) (plate 38).[37] Margaret seems to have come into possession of the psalter made for Henry IV on his marriage to Mary de Bohun (Cambridge [UK], Fitzwilliam Museum MS 38-1950), which has Margaret's arms added on fol. 1r (plate 39). Other devotional manuscripts owned by Margaret of Anjou include Oxford, Bodleian Library MS Digby 36 (a Latin life of Gilbert of Sempringham made in England in the fifteenth century, with a version of Margaret's arms on fol. 7r); New York, Pierpont Morgan Library MS M253 (a late fifteenth-century book of hours with Margaret's arms on fol. 249v); and New York, New York Public Library MS 32 (a fifteenth-century book of hours).[38] Among the secular books in her collection, Margaret owned an ordinary of arms, which suggests that she had contact with the newly established College of Arms, a possible source, according to some legal historians, for the standardized copies of the *Nova statuta*

Angliae.[39] London, British Library MS Harley 937 is a perpetual calendar that seems to have been made for Margaret of Anjou.[40] Margaret probably also owned a manuscript copy of Georges Chastellain's *Temple de Boccace*, a work the author dedicated to her, possibly composed in the mid-1460s during her exile in France: Vatican City, Vatican Library MS Reginense latino 1520 has what appears to be the only surviving presentation miniature, yet this copy must have been made after 1471, because it includes references to events that took place during that year.[41] Margaret's appreciation for the power of visual images in manuscript books can be surmised from the manuscripts in her own collection. In particular, the anthology she received from Sir John Talbot offered a splendid example of the ways in which texts that had no original links to each other or to a particular political context could be shaped by their arrangement and decoration in a new manuscript to have new meanings in a new context: the genealogy, the coats of arms, and the images of Margaret, Henry, and Talbot himself resonate with the other illustrations and texts included in the manuscript (plates 40, 41). Given her family's history of commissioning books, it is likely that Margaret took an active interest in the design of the books she commissioned and would have understood the potential for expressing political views through artistic means. As Sharon Michalove argues, Margaret's collection of books illustrates "the connectivity between books and politics in the fifteenth century" (Michalove 2004, 68). Deprived of independent authority to protest the actions of those who sought to undermine the legitimacy of her husband and son, she may well have commissioned a manuscript copy of the *Nova statuta Angliae* for her son that would express her views about the Lancastrian monarchy in a symbolic fashion.

The role of medieval women in commissioning works on statecraft is one that has only begun to receive full investigation. Anne Clark Bartlett argues,

> although women have long been identified as readers of medieval romance and occasionally – as in the case of Christine de Pizan – as translators of handbooks on war and governance, female readers have rarely been seen as important audiences for this material on secular governance. Yet records of book ownership and patronage indicate that royal, noble, and gentry women owned, commissioned, and bequeathed works such as Vegetius's *The Epitome of Military Science*, the *De regimine principum*, and the pseudo-Aristotelian *Secretum Secretorum*, all guides for the education of princes that circulated widely in various redactions, adaptations, and translations, throughout and beyond the Middle Ages and achieved their most celebrated expression as

Machiavelli's *The Prince*. Medieval women read, commissioned, and taught their children from this material: manuals of knighthood, chivalric romances, and numerous versions of the Troy histories, which were widely used as a reference point for contemporary political events. (Bartlett 2005, 53–54)

Bartlett's argument suggests that, if Margaret of Anjou commissioned the Yale manuscript of the *New Statutes of England* for Prince Edward, she followed a strong tradition of medieval women who sought out a variety of texts to educate their children, including transforming older texts for new purposes. Just as Edward III's mother commissioned a copy of the older English statutes to help prepare her son to restore peace and justice to his land, Margaret may have hoped that a statutes book that begins with the story of Edward III would prepare her son to do the same.

FOUR

Educating the Prince

THE YALE *NEW STATUTES* MANUSCRIPT AND
LANCASTRIAN MIRRORS FOR PRINCES

Decorated with the arms of both of Edward of Lancaster's parents, offering portraits of his royal English forebears, and including the introductory treatises and index to the statutes, the Yale *Nova statuta Angliae* would have been a particularly appropriate copy of the Statutes of the Realm for the young prince. There is also evidence to suggest that members of the Lancastrian court close to Prince Edward expected he would have access to a copy of the *Nova statuta Angliae* for study. To begin with, the texts that we know were written to advise the prince suggest that learning about the laws of England is central to good kingship. Some of these mirrors for princes make reference to specific statutes, which the prince could consult if he had a copy of the *Nova statuta* in his possession. Even more important is the fact that one of the works of advice written for Prince Edward makes direct reference to the prince's need to own a personal copy of the statutes for study, in order to become the kind of king who carries out the ideals of kingship inscribed in the Bible. According to this argument, one might well consider the *Nova statuta* itself a mirror for princes – especially in the form found in the Yale Law School manuscript, with its portraits of English kings and support texts. Reading the Yale *Nova statuta Angliae* in the context of Lancastrian mirrors for princes makes clear that this manuscript indeed has much in common with other forms of instruction in kingship associated with the Lancastrian court in the middle of the fifteenth century.

Public references to the education of the heir to the throne had become an important part of upholding the Lancastrian monarchy earlier in the century, when Henry VI's father was Prince of Wales. Before he became king, recognizing the questions surrounding the legitimacy of his father's kingship and his own performance as heir to the throne, Henry V commissioned *The Regiment of Princes* from Thomas Hoccleve and *The Troy Book* from John Lydgate to demonstrate his interest in learning about good kingship: the commissioning of these works was itself depicted as verification of his potential to become an ideal king.[1] Presumably, Henry V would have passed these works on to his son and perhaps also commissioned a new set of mirrors for princes to demonstrate the care with which the new heir apparent received his education in kingship. Unfortunately, Henry V's early death in August 1422 prevented him from overseeing the education of his son in person; but, in a codicil to his will made shortly before he died, Henry V assigned guardianship of his son to his uncle, Thomas Beaufort, Duke of Exeter (Strong 1981, 99; R. Griffiths 1981, 51; and Wolffe 1981, 29). Exeter seems to have provided formal supervision of the trusted knights and nurses he appointed for the infant king's personal protection and care. When Exeter died at the end of 1426, the young king's education in proper conduct was in the hands of Dame Alice Botiller (R. Griffiths 1981, 52–53). Henry VI's formal education began in the spring of 1428, when he was six years old: on the advice of his Privy Council, he appointed Richard Beauchamp, Earl of Warwick, as his tutor, and the records of the Privy Council indicate that Warwick was instructed to use examples of good and bad kings from history to teach his young student (Nicolas 1834–37, 3:299; R. Griffiths 1981, 52). Several new texts on kingship date from the early decades of Henry VI's reign. One example, Lydgate's *Fall of Princes*, is thought to be a text commissioned by Henry VI's uncle Humphrey, Duke of Gloucester, in 1431 to aid in the young king's education.[2] In addition, in the late 1430s an anonymous author composed the *Tractatus de regimine principum ad Regem Henricum Sextum* (*Treatise on the Government of Princes for Henry the Sixth*) based on the *De regimine principum* of Giles (Egidius) of Rome: the unique copy of the *Tractatus* that survives in London, British Library MS Cotton Cleopatra A xiii, has an opening eight-line initial containing the royal coat of arms and is thought to be the presentation copy.[3]

With the birth of Henry VI's own son in 1453, the issue of educating the heir apparent arose again, and the context was one of even greater crisis. Henry VI's hold on the throne grew more and more tenuous between 1453 and 1460, and discussions of Prince Edward's education became a strategic part of Lancastrian discourse in response to Yorkist challenges to his father's rule. Even after Henry VI's deposition in 1461, authors continued to compose works for Prince Edward's education. For Lancastrian loyalists in the 1450s and 1460s, including Sir George Ashby and Sir John Fortescue, educating the prince and defending the king became complementary parts of the same process.[4]

Lancastrian authors during this period used a variety of genres to defend the Lancastrian claim to the throne, in part to counter Yorkist polemics and in part "to assure those internal to the regime of the validity of their cause" (Gross 1996, 36). A theme that links many of the Lancastrian polemical works, despite differences in genre, is the importance of upholding the law: they repeatedly depict the Lancastrian kings as using the law to govern justly and the Yorkists as subverting the laws of the land. For example, the anonymous Lancastrian tract that has come to be called *Somnium vigilantis* (*The Dream of the Vigilant One*) includes several passages that describe Richard of York and his supporters as undermining the fundamental laws and processes of justice that secure the order of the realm.[5] The speaker in the text who calls for the attainder of York and his supporters argues that they have broken the laws of the land both by taking up arms against the king and his faithful subjects and by not taking their grievances to the king or his courts: "alle controversies and debates civile or criminalle, realle or personale, ben decided by the kynges lawes withoute mayntenance or wylfull interruption of the cours of justice" ("all controversies and debates, civil or criminal, relating to property or a person, are decided by the king's laws, without wrongful aiding of litigation or intentional interruption of the course of justice") (Gilson 1911, 518). The Lancastrian speaker argues in a later passage that the true goal of the Yorkists has been "the fynal subversion of þe kynge, of his lawes and of his tru peple" ("the final subversion of the king, of his laws, and of his loyal subjects"). The speaker goes on to assert that York and his men acted "ayenst all maner laws" ("against all forms of law") (Gilson 1911, 520). If, as Margaret Kekewich argues, this tract was composed in order to support the petition of attainder against York and his followers that was presented to the Coventry Parliament in November 1459, the depiction of the Yorkists as undermining the rule of law suggests that they also attempted to usurp the legal power invested in the members of Parliament, who serve, according to the *Modus tenendi Parliamentum*, as "iudices et iusticiarii" ("judges and justices") (Pronay and Taylor 1980, 77, 89).[6] In the construction of the issues offered by this text, to allow York and his supporters to go unpunished would endanger the rule of law, which unites the English king and his subjects in the pursuit of justice.

In addition to dream visions, treatises on royal succession, and satirical attacks on Yorkist claims against Henry VI, Lancastrian writers composed works in the *speculum regis* tradition that associate both Henry and Prince Edward with ideals of kingship. One of these Lancastrian mirrors for princes, this one addressed to Henry VI, is *Knyghthode and Bataile*, an anonymous English verse translation of Vegetius's *De re militari*, thought to have been composed in early 1460 and perhaps commissioned by John, Viscount Beaumont.[7] The narrator refers to himself in the prologue as a priest (lines 47 and 53) from Calais (line 33) who gave his poem to Beaumont so that he could present it to the king (lines 47–64). Beaumont had served as constable of England and as steward of Queen Margaret's lands before being appointed chief steward of Prince Edward's lands in 1456 (R. Griffiths 1981, 782). Whether commissioned by Beaumont or merely delivered by him, the gift appears to have come to Henry soon after the attainder of the Yorkists – a time when the Lancastrians were concerned to maintain sympathy for Henry VI and his son. It is therefore significant that, despite using a fourth-century Latin military treatise as its source, the English poem discusses knighthood in terms of obedience to divine law. The poem's narrator compares the king to "Goddes sone" ("God's son") (line 17) and refers to the rebels as those who "fordoon Goddes forbode" ("act counter to God's prohibition") (line 29). The poem goes on to describe obedience to God's law as knighthood's first ideal:

> Knyghthode an ordir is, the premynent;
> Obeysaunt in God, and rather deye
> Then disobeye; and as magnificent
> As can be thought; exiled al envye;
> As confident the right to magnifie
> As wil the lawe of Goddis mandement,
> And as perseueraunt and patient. (lines 131–37)

> (Knighthood is an order, the preeminent one;
> Obedient to God, and [would] rather die
> Than disobey; and as magnificent
> As can be thought; [with] all envy exiled;
> As confident to praise what is right
> As the law of God's commandment allows,
> And as perseverant and patient.)

The narrator reminds the king (and by extension other readers) that all earthly lords are subject to God's authority, and the narrator ascribes discord among lords to the influence of Satan:

> The premynent is first thalmyghti Lord,
> Emanuel, that euery lord is vndir
> And good lyver; but bataile and discord
> With him hath Sathanas. . . . (lines 138–41)
>
> (The preeminent [knight] is first the almighty Lord,
> Emanuel, under whom is every lord
> And person who lives righteously; but Satan has
> Battle and discord with him. . . .)

The passage's play on "lord" and association of battle and discord with Satan suggest that the type of battle here linked to evil is battle against one's sovereign lord, which was one of the charges against York and his supporters in the 1459 parliamentary petition for their attainder. Since the poem earlier associates Henry VI with God's son, the reference to Emanuel as Satan's opponent in this last passage again suggests that those knights who fail to obey the king's laws and take up arms against him ally themselves with Satan, rather than with Christ.

The Lancastrian focus on the importance of upholding divine and earthly law can also be found in the mirrors for princes addressed to Prince Edward, which offer the prince instruction but also defend Henry VI's right to rule by presenting kings as the earthly representatives of "universal justice and the divine order" (Gross 1996, 37).[8] At the same time, like Christine de Pizan's *Fais d'armes*, the works of instruction composed for Prince Edward by members of the Lancastrian court highlight the link between good kingship and just laws and instruct the prince to take an active role in creating and enforcing just laws for his people. This is one of the central themes, for example, in *On the Active Policy of a Prince* (*De actiua pollecia principis*) by Sir George Ashby (or Assheby). Ashby's poem advises Prince Edward to enforce the statutes authorized by the kings who preceded him:

> Prouide that lawe may be excercised,
> And executed in his formal cours,
> Aftur the statutes autorised
> By noble Kynges youre progenitours. . . . (lines 520–24)
>
> (Provide that the law may be implemented
> And executed in its formal course,

According to the statutes authorized
By noble kings, your progenitors. . . .)⁹

Ashby's narrator goes on to suggest specific statutes that Prince Edward should enforce, including a law restricting extravagant clothing (lines 534–40) and a law restricting the carrying of weapons (lines 541–47). Earlier in the poem, the narrator exhorts the prince to use the laws against treason to root out conspiracies against the Crown:

> Be wele ware by discrete prouision
> For to suppresse youre false conspiratours,
> Aftur the lawe & constitucion,
> Established ayenst opyn traiterous. . . . (lines 380–83)

> (Be very careful, by wise preparation,
> To prevail over false conspirators against you,
> According to the law and statute,
> Established against known traitors. . . .)

If the prince had a copy of the *Nova statuta Angliae,* like the Yale Law School manuscript, in his possession, he could find all of these statutes easily by using the index that appears before the statutes text itself begins (fols. 10r–53v) (see, for example, plate 9).

Ashby's poem also argues more generally for the importance of upholding the law to preserve the well-being of the individual and the kingdom: "Euery man ought to lyve vnder a lawe, / And namly cristenmen that wold god please" ("Every man should live according to laws, / And especially Christians who wish to please God") (lines 555–56). Just as the first five royal portraits in the Yale *Nova statuta* frame the text of England's laws with an image of royal humility before divine law, Ashby's treatise reminds the prince that kings are subject to God's laws:

> And for most especial Remembrance
> Thinketh that men be erthly & mortal,
> Nor there is worldly Ioy ne assurance
> But in almyghti Ihesu eternal,
> Bi whos myght & power especial,
> Reignen kynges, and be to hym soubget,
> And hym to obey is thaire deutee & dette. (lines 597–603)

> (And, as the most important thing to remember,
> Consider that men are earthly and mortal,
> Nor is there joy or assurance in the world,

But [there is] in almighty, eternal Jesus,
By whose might and special power
Kings reign and are subject to him,
And to obey him is their duty and obligation.)

Like the Yale *Nova statuta* manuscript, Ashby's advice to Prince Edward combines instruction on English statutes with instruction on the role of the king as both representative of divine justice on earth and leader of his subjects in humble obedience to God's law. At the same time, by presenting Prince Edward's predecessors as kings who fulfilled these roles, both the Yale manuscript and Ashby's poem help to defend the Lancastrians' claims to royal legitimacy against those of the House of York.

By highlighting Prince Edward's descent from both the royal houses of England and France through his father and mother, Ashby's poem also offers a parallel with the use of Henry VI's and Margaret of Anjou's coats of arms in the Yale *Nova statuta* manuscript. In the opening address to the prince, the speaker describes him as "Linially comyn of blode royale, / Bothe of Faders & moders") ("Directly descended from royal blood, / Both father's and mother's") (lines 86–87) and "Trewe sone & heire to the high maiestie / Of oure liege lorde Kynge Henry & dame / Margarete, the Quene" ("True son and heir to the high majesty / Of our liege lord King Henry and Dame / Margaret, the Queen") (lines 93–95). The narrator depicts both of the prince's parents as authorized to rule by divine grace: "Occupying by grace celestial / Thaier Roiaulmes" ("Governing their realms / By heavenly grace") (lines 88–89). The narrator exhorts the prince to follow his English and French ancestors in their devotion to God and in their just rulership:

Seintes of youre noble blode ye may knowe,
Diuers many that lyued blessedly,
Bothe of this England and of Fraunce ynowe,
That yave theire hertes to god Inwardly,
Abydyd in goddess feith stedfastly,
Whos pathes ye may beholde & eke see,
And theim folowe in theire benignitee.

Beholde eke youre noble progenitours,
Howe victorious thei were in corage,
How Iuste, how sad & eke wise at al houres. . . . (lines 141–50)

(Saints of your noble blood you may know,
Many different ones who lived blessedly,

Enough both of England and of France,
Who inwardly gave their hearts to God,
Continued in God's faith steadfastly,
Whose paths you may behold and see as well,
And follow them in their blessedness.

Behold also your noble progenitors,
How victorious they were through courage,
How just, how steadfast and also wise at all times. . . .)

Like the visual and verbal texts in the Yale *Nova statuta* manuscript, then, Ashby's poem serves to remind the prince (and, by extension, other readers) of his role as rightful heir to the throne of England and as future upholder of faith and just laws for his subjects.

Since Ashby's poem suggests that Prince Edward's education should include study of the Statutes of the Realm, knowing when Ashby wrote *On the Active Policy of a Prince* might help with dating the Yale Law School manuscript of the *New Statutes*. While we know a fair amount about Ashby himself, scholars continue to debate the date of this poem. Ashby spent most of his career in service to the Lancastrian court, beginning long before Prince Edward was born. He began as an assistant to Thomas Bekynton, secretary to Humphrey, Duke of Gloucester. After appointment as a clerk in the royal signet office in 1437, when Bekynton became Henry VI's secretary, Ashby rose to receive additional diplomatic and administrative offices.[10] He was appointed as a royal clerk in Calais in 1439, participated in the embassy that brought Margaret of Anjou to England in 1444–45, and became clerk of the queen's signet in 1446, a post he retained until Henry VI was deposed. References to Ashby as a king's serjeant in 1441 reveal that he was a lawyer by training and had the authority to represent the Crown in Parliament.[11] Ashby also received an appointment as steward of Warwick in 1446 and represented Warwickshire in the 1459 Parliament that attainted the Yorkists. After Henry VI was deposed in 1461, Ashby was captured by the Yorkists and sent to Fleet Prison in London, where he wrote *A Prisoner's Reflections* in 1463. There are no records that indicate when Ashby was released from prison; but his death at his estate of Breakspear in Harefield, Middlesex, is recorded in January 1475. A brass memorial to Ashby and his wife, Margaret, remains in the Breakspear Chapel at St. Mary's Church, Harefield.

While Ashby includes reference to the year of composition in *A Prisoner's Reflections* (1463), he does not include reference to the year of composition in

On the Active Policy of a Prince. Though the poem addresses itself to Prince Edward, no presentation copy of it survives. The only known copy of the poem is found in Cambridge (UK), Cambridge University Library MS Mm. iv. 42, a collection of texts that is thought to date from the third quarter of the fifteenth century. The manuscript could therefore have been made during Ashby's lifetime, but scholars differ significantly on whether Ashby composed the poem before, during, or after his imprisonment. Because the speaker of the poem assumes that Prince Edward will have the opportunity to inherit the throne, Bateson suggests that Ashby's poem could have been written at any point between Edward's birth in 1453 and 1461, when Edward of York became king; but Bateson argues that Ashby probably wrote the poem between October 1470, when Henry VI was briefly restored to the throne, and May 1471, when both Henry VI and Edward of Lancaster were killed (Bateson 1899, vi). Margaret Kekewich concurs with the latter assessment (Kekewich 1990, 533), as does David Lawton (Lawton 1987, 772). Nevertheless, Paul Strohm dates Ashby's treatise to the 1450s, prior to the Yorkists' overthrow of Henry VI (Strohm 2005, 125). For his part, John Scattergood argues that the poem was written shortly after 1463, when Ashby was in prison, because the comments in the poem about cloth-making and sumptuary laws echo language found in two petitions that were presented in Parliament during that year (Scattergood 1996, 259–62). However, Ashby is unlikely to have composed the passages in the poem that call for Prince Edward to punish those who dispute his legitimacy as heir while Ashby was in Yorkist custody. The poem's advice to Edward to suppress every person who claims the right to the throne in his place (lines 415–21) would have had most relevance either during Henry VI's readeption in 1470–71 or in July–October 1460, when Richard of York captured Henry VI and persuaded the king to name him heir to the throne, instead of Prince Edward. The poem's advice to Prince Edward to punish conspirators according to the laws against treason (lines 380–83) would fit well with the attainder of the Yorkists by the 1459 Parliament in which Ashby participated, but would have become relevant again in 1470–71, during Henry VI's restoration. As a result, internal evidence does not resolve the question of composition date.

Robert Meyer-Lee has recently argued for dating *On the Active Policy of a Prince* to 1468 and for locating its place of composition in France (Meyer-Lee 2004, 710–12; Meyer-Lee 2007, 152–54). Though he offers no documentary evidence to support his view, he argues that Ashby was probably released from prison in the mid-1460s and joined the Lancastrian exiles in St. Mihiel-en-Bar in France.[12] Having served as one of Margaret of Anjou's administrators since she became queen, as well as being well acquainted with English law and Parliament, Ashby would have been an important assistant for Margaret in her attempts to undermine Edward IV's hold on the English throne. In Meyer-Lee's view, Ashby wrote *On the Active Policy of a Prince* in 1468 to help Margaret garner support for an invasion of England after Richard Neville, Earl of Warwick, fell out with Edward IV and came to France to seek assistance from Louis XI and negotiate an alliance with Margaret of Anjou. While Ashby's *Active Policy of a Prince* is like many works of advice to princes in the ways that it interweaves literary traditions with history and politics, Meyer-Lee argues that Ashby's poem was written for the specific political purpose of furthering Margaret's new project, beginning in late 1468, to restore the Lancastrian line to the throne with the help of Warwick. Negotiations between Warwick and Margaret were not formally concluded until the summer of 1470. In July, Warwick made a public apology to the queen; but much of the public representation of Warwick's relationship with the Lancastrians focused on the prince. By "making the prince appear as the authentic and fully capable heir to the throne" (Meyer-Lee 2007, 153), Ashby's poem helps lend authority to the idea that Warwick's new alliance was with Prince Edward, rather than with Queen Margaret, whose involvement in English politics remained controversial. Meyer-Lee's reading allows us to situate Ashby's poem in parallel with the other steps taken by Margaret and her supporters to highlight the prince's close relationship with Warwick in 1470. Edward's betrothal to Warwick's daughter Anne Neville took place soon after Warwick's formal apology to the queen, and the marriage took place shortly after Warwick's success in liberating Henry VI from the Tower. The strategy of presenting Prince Edward as sovereign-in-training can also be seen in the set of seven principles for England's government sent to Warwick by the prince, but drafted by John Fortescue, for implementation in the restored Lancastrian monarchy.[13] Ashby's poem likewise associates Prince Edward with the restoration of justice in England, an ideal through which the poem links the prince to a long line of royal forebears, not just his father: thus the poem refers in lines 523–24 to the statutes authorized by the noble kings who are the prince's progenitors. Indeed, Meyer-Lee argues that Ashby's poem borrows from Hoccleve's *Regement of Princes* "in a bold attempt to depict Edward as the second coming of the ultimate Lancastrian hero" – his grandfather, Henry V (Meyer-Lee 2007, 154).

Meyer-Lee thus reads Ashby's poem as part of a conscious effort by the Lancastrians, led by Margaret of Anjou, to use traditional genres of literature as vehicles to present arguments against the Yorkists and in support of restoring the Lancastrian line to the throne. He describes Ashby's poem as "a sophisticated piece of propaganda, encouraged or perhaps even commissioned by Margaret," who "understood the value of such literary propaganda" (Meyer-Lee 2007, 153). Like devotional and legal texts, literary works of the past could also be harnessed to a new purpose. For example, in addition to opening his poem by naming Gower, Chaucer, and Lydgate as the "Primier poetes of this nacion" ("Leading poets of this nation") (lines 1–2), Ashby self-consciously links *On the Active Policy of a Prince* to earlier English works in order to create the impression of a continuous English poetic tradition that parallels the royal heritage Prince Edward will continue: "Ashby's entire poem is steeped in Hoccleve and Lydgate, with other open debts to Gower (book 7 of the *Confessio Amantis*), Chaucer (*Melibeus*, but this may be by way of Hoccleve's versification of portions in the *Regement*), and the *Court of Sapience*, from which a whole stanza is borrowed" (Lawton 1987, 772). In 1468, with Prince Edward turning fifteen, Margaret and her advisors would have found it useful to present him to potential supporters in England and on the Continent as the true heir to England's throne, who was now ready to assist his father in reestablishing just rule and who symbolized even greater glory to come.

Meyer-Lee suggests that Ashby's poem should therefore be read as a companion piece to Sir John Fortescue's *De laudibus legum Angliae* (*In Praise of the Laws of England*), which Meyer-Lee describes as combining a celebration of the ideals of English law, a mirror for princes, and sophisticated propaganda (Meyer-Lee 2007, 153).[14] Though the precise date of Fortescue's text is not known, internal evidence indicates that he wrote it between 1463 and 1471, while serving as Henry VI's chancellor-in-exile in St. Mihiel, liaison to the French royal court, and tutor to Prince Edward. Fortescue's role in the vanguard of the textual war to defend the Lancastrian monarchy is clear. He served as a leader in England's legal profession, as well as in both elected and appointed government roles, before taking a major role in the Lancastrians' attempts to retain and then regain the throne. Born in about 1397 to a Devonshire family that claimed descent from a knight who fought beside William the Conqueror, Fortescue was one of three sons who had careers as lawyers and servants of the Crown.[15] Records show he was a member of Lincoln's Inn by 1420 and served as governor of the inn for three terms before being appointed serjeant-at-law in 1438. From 1421 until 1437, he also repeatedly served as a member of Parliament, representing a series of communities in Devonshire and Wiltshire. After serving as legal counsel to a variety of high-profile clients, including the Corporation of Canterbury, the Duchy of Lancaster, and the treasurer of the Exchequer, Fortescue became king's serjeant and circuit judge in 1441. In 1442, he was appointed chief justice of the King's Bench and knighted. When the Yorkists challenged Henry VI's rule beginning in the 1450s, Fortescue and his family remained loyal to the king: Fortescue's younger brother lost his life in the Yorkist assault on Henry VI and his escort at St. Alban's in 1455, and Fortescue's only son seems to have died fighting for the Lancastrians in 1471. Fortescue probably played a leading role in the unsuccessful attempt to have the queen designated regent for Henry VI during his illness in 1453–54, as well as in the successful attainder of the duke of York and his supporters in the Parliament of 1459. Even after York captured the king in July 1460, Fortescue continued to preside over the King's Bench, only joining the queen and prince in Scotland in January 1461. When the Lancastrian forces rescued Henry the following month, he appointed Fortescue as his chancellor; but the Yorkist military defeat of the Lancastrians soon after meant that Fortescue would serve his king in exile, traveling to France with the queen and prince in 1463 and remaining with them until their return to England in March 1471.

Though some of his written works are lost, enough survive to illustrate why Fortescue earned a reputation during his lifetime and after as a gifted writer in Latin, French, and English. Many of his shorter works are explicitly anti-Yorkist tracts; but his skills as a polemicist saved his life when he was captured after the final defeat of the Lancastrians and Edward IV gave him the opportunity to refute his own arguments against the Yorkists in exchange for a pardon.[16] Fortescue's treatises on law, which later generations considered important philosophical discussions of the legal powers of the English monarchy, have received more commentary in modern scholarship for their political content. For example, Arthur Ferguson and Anthony Gross have demonstrated that Fortescue's *De natura legis naturae* (*On the Nature of the Law of Nature*) and *De laudibus legum Angliae* address issues of law and kingship in such a way as to respond to Yorkist criticism of the Lancastrian monarchy (Ferguson 1959, 179, 181; Gross 1996, 70–90). Most critics do not go as far as Meyer-Lee, however, in declaring Fortescue's treatises propaganda. Ferguson considers Fortescue, not as a legal theorist or royal propagandist, but as an author of political commentary and social criticism, someone "whose concern was for the body politic as a functioning organism rather than as the object of theoretical analysis, whose purpose was to lay bare the sores of that body and to prescribe some kind of remedy" (Ferguson 1959, 177). Strohm finds Fortescue's works on law "less serviceable to the interests of any one sponsoring regime . . . than the word 'propaganda' would seem to imply" (Strohm 2005, 147). In the case of *De laudibus*, Strohm points out that the text's discussion of English law and its role in the prince's education is framed by an introduction that highlights the Lancastrians' loss of power, at the same time that it encourages sympathy for the exiles (Strohm 2005, 142–43). Fortescue's work is thus "Lancastrian," not just because it presents views sympathetic to the Lancastrian monarch, but because it embodies the anxiety inherent in the Lancastrian monarchy from its beginnings.

Fortescue's *De laudibus legum Angliae* presents itself explicitly as a work of instruction for Prince Edward of Lancaster, in the form of a dialogue in which Fortescue (as chancellor) advises the prince in order to prepare him for good kingship. As Ferguson notes, however, Fortescue's text differs from some other examples of the *Fürstenspiegel* in its focus on just laws as the central measure and responsibility of good kingship (Ferguson 1959, 182–83). In addition, though other works on good kingship addressed to Henry VI or Edward of Lancaster discuss the importance of instituting and upholding good laws, Fortescue's *De laudibus* directly addresses the prince's need to study the laws of England. In the opening chapters of this prose treatise, the chancellor cites classical and biblical authorities to support his argument that the prince should add the study of law to his other preparations for kingship:

> *Regis namque officium pugnare est bella populi sui, et eos rectissime iudicare*, ut in primo Regum, viij° capitulo, clarissime tu doceris. Quare, ut armorum utinam et legum studiis simili zelo te deditum contemplarer, cum ut armis bella, ita legibus iudicia peragantur.
>
> (*For the office of a king is to fight the battles of his people and to judge them rightfully*, as you may very clearly learn in I Kings, chapter viii. For that reason, I wish that I observed you to be devoted to the study of the laws with the same zeal as you are to that of arms, since, as battles are determined by arms, so judgements are by laws.) (*De laudibus*, chapter I [Chrimes 1942, 2–5])

Like Glanville's treatise, Fortescue's text argues that the good king rules with laws as well as arms, an ideal Fortescue attributes to Justinian's *Institutes* (*De laudibus*, chapter I [Chrimes 1942, 4–5]). Fortescue's text also stresses the divine authority behind earthly justice:

> A Deo etiam sunt omnes leges edite, que ab homine promulgantur. . . . Ex quibus erudiris quod leges licet humanas addiscere leges sacras et ediciones Dei, quo earum studia non vacant a dulcitudine consolacionis sancte.

(Moreover, all laws that are promulgated by man are decreed by God. . . .
By this you are taught that to learn the laws, even though human ones, is to
learn laws that are sacred and decreed of God, the study of which does not
lack the blessing of divine encouragement.) (*De laudibus*, chapter 3 [Chrimes
1942, 8–9])

Like the narrator of Christine's *Fais d'armes*, Fortescue's chancellor argues
that a king is only able to fight just wars if he governs his realm justly, but he
goes further by making justice the primary goal of kingship: "Iusticia vero hec
subiectum est omnis regalis cure, quo sine illa rex iuste non iudicat nec recte
pugnare potest. Illa vero adepta perfecteque servata equissime peragitur omne
officium regis" ("This justice, indeed, is the object of all royal administration,
because without it a king judges unjustly and is unable to fight rightfully. But
this justice attained and truly observed, the whole office of king is fairly dis-
charged") (*De laudibus*, chapter 4 [Chrimes 1942, 12–13]). As Ferguson notes,
Fortescue's mirror for princes shifts its concern from the personal qualities
of the ruler and focuses instead on the law as the source of justice and peace
for the realm, providing protection and limit for both monarch and subject
(Ferguson 1959, 186, 191).

According to the chancellor in *De laudibus legum Angliae*, a king's education in recognizing and attaining justice requires reading the laws of his land.
To make his case, the chancellor cites Deuteronomy 17:18–19, which commands that the king of Israel have his own copy of the laws to keep with him
and read all the days of his life. The chancellor then argues that the command
in the Bible means that the prince should study the laws of his own country
as well as the laws of God, with the implicit suggestion that the prince should
have his own copy of the laws by which he will one day rule – that is, his own
copy of the *Nova statuta Angliae*. The chancellor first states, "Liber quippe
Deuteronomii est liber legum quibus reges Israel subditum sibi populum
regere tenebantur" ("The book of Deuteronomy, indeed, is the book of the
laws by which the kings of Israel were bound to rule the people subject to
them") (*De laudibus*, chapter 1 [Chrimes 1942, 4–5]). He then tells the prince,

Nec solum legibus quibus iusticiam consequeris, fili regis, imbui te iubet
sacra scriptura, sed et ipsam iusticiam diligere tibi alibi precipit, cum dicat,
Diligite iusticiam, qui iudicatis terram, Sapiente, capitulo primo.

(Nor does Holy Scripture command you only to be instructed, O king's son,
in the laws by which you shall pursue justice, but also, in another place, it
requires you to love justice itself, when it says, *Love justice, ye who judge the
earth* [Wisdom, chapter i].) (*De laudibus*, chapter 4 [Chrimes 1942, 14–15])

In citing the command in Deuteronomy 17:18–19 that the good king read the laws God established for the nation of Israel, Fortescue's text parallels book 4 of John of Salisbury's *Policraticus*.[17] Nevertheless, Fortescue's text goes beyond the *Policraticus* in depicting the laws that the prince must study as the laws of his own kingdom, which the chancellor argues are also sacred. After the prince argues that the Bible passage only applies to the kings of Israel, the chancellor adds, "Scire, igitur, te volo quod non solum Deuteronomii leges sed et omnes leges humane sacre sunt; quo lex sub hiis verbis diffinitur: *Lex est sanccio sancta iubens honesta et prohibiens contraria*" ("I want you, then, to know that not only the laws of Deuteronomy, but also all human laws, are sacred, inasmuch as law is defined by these words: *Law is a sacred sanction commanding what is honest and forbidding the contrary*") (*De laudibus*, chapter 3 [Chrimes 1942, 6–9]). This association of English law with divine law parallels the use of religious imagery in the illustrations of the Yale Law School *Nova statuta*, which differ so strikingly from those in other copies of the statutes that they seem to reflect customization for a particular owner.

Did Fortescue highlight Prince Edward's need for a personal copy of the statutes in order to encourage the commission of a manuscript copy for the prince or because he knew that such a gift was in preparation? The introduction to the dialogue between the prince and chancellor depicts the discussion taking place during the Lancastrian exile in France, but it would have been extremely difficult to have a copy of the statutes made for the prince there, since the resources for making a copy of the *Nova statuta* were not available. Commissioning a statutes manuscript for the prince from a shop in England while the Lancastrians were in France would also have been extremely difficult. Was this part of the treatise therefore a hidden message to the people in England who supervised construction of the Yale Law School *Nova statuta* that they should continue to work on the manuscript? Did Fortescue hope that a personal copy of the statutes could await the prince on his triumphant return to England? Knowing when Fortescue composed this treatise for Prince Edward would help in finding answers to these questions; but the evidence is not clear. The opening of the text depicts the dialogue between Fortescue and the prince taking place at an unspecified time during their exile in France, which began in 1463 when the prince was not quite ten years old; but the introduction to Fortescue's treatise presents Prince Edward as an engaged and mature student: "Princeps ille mox ut factus est adultus . . ." ("This prince, as soon as he became grown up . . .") (*De laudibus*, introduction [Chrimes 1942, 2–3]). This representation of the prince as an adult suggests that Fortescue completed the work toward the end of the exile, between 1468 and 1470, when the prince was at least fifteen and could be presented as ready to assume the role of regent for his father, as Charles VI's son had and as Parliament had originally authorized Edward to do, when he was of the age of discretion, in the appointment of York as protector (Maurer 2003, 122; Watts 1996, 309). In addition, by depicting the dialogue between chancellor and prince in the context of their unjust exile from England, Fortescue encourages his readers to understand the text's arguments about just kingship as an indictment of Edward IV. The critique of Edward IV and representation of Prince Edward as ready to bring about just rule in England suggest that the *De laudibus*, like Ashby's *Active Policy of a Prince*, could well have been or have become part of Margaret of Anjou's campaign to encourage the joint efforts of Warwick's supporters and the loyal Lancastrians remaining in England to assist the prince by restoring his father to the throne, as they did in the fall of 1470.

At the same time, a connection between the *De laudibus* and the negotiations with Warwick in 1468–70 need not indicate that Prince Edward's earlier education was devoid of instruction about English law. Though the version of the *De laudibus* that survives depicts the dialogue between chancellor and prince taking place during their exile in France, Fortescue may have prepared an earlier version of the *De laudibus* for the prince's personal guidance and later revised it for public circulation, as he seems to have done with several of his works. Fortescue also uses *De laudibus legum Angliae* to indicate that he began Prince Edward's instruction in law at an earlier time, for the chancellor and prince in *De laudibus* refer several times to another Latin treatise on the law, *De natura legis naturae* (*On the Nature of the Law of Nature*), that the chancellor wrote for the prince in the past. In chapter 9, the chancellor states, "Tamen quia de materia ista in Opusculo quod tui contemplacione De Natura Legis Nature exaravi, sufficienter puto me desceptasse, plus inde loqui iam desisto" ("But as I think I have discussed this matter sufficiently in a small work *Of the Nature of the Law of Nature* which I wrote for your consideration, I desist from saying more about it now") (Chrimes 1942, 26–27). In chapter 11, he refers to evidence he presented "in supradicto Opusculo" ("in the small work I have mentioned") (Chrimes 1942, 27–28). Then, in chapter 14, the prince recalls an argument that the chancellor made "in tractatu De Natura Legis Nature" ("in your treatise *Concerning the Nature of the Law of Nature*") (Chrimes 1942, 34–35), verifying that the treatise has been part of his earlier study. In chapter 34 the chancellor again refers to an argument he made "in predicto Tractatu de Natura Legis Nature" ("in the aforesaid *Treatise on the Nature of the Law of Nature*") (Chrimes 1942, 80–81), and in chapter 37 he claims that he made an argument clearly "in predicto Tractatu de Natura Legis Nature" ("in the *Treatise Concerning the Nature of the Law of Nature* before mentioned") (Chrimes 1942, 90–91). Since Fortescue wrote *De natura legis naturae* prior to *De laudibus legum Angliae*, he may have begun Prince Edward's education in law at an earlier time, perhaps when the chancellor first joined the queen and prince in Scotland in 1461, or perhaps even earlier, when the prince's formal education was just beginning in 1459 or 1460.[18] By including multiple references to Fortescue's earlier treatise for the prince, the text presents the prince as someone whose education has already included study of the philosophy of law, but who now focuses his study on the laws of his own realm.

If the Yale *Nova statuta Angliae* was commissioned as a gift for Prince Edward, work on it most probably began before the Lancastrian exile, though the statutes of Edward IV enacted during 1461–68 could not have been added until 1469. Since the discussion of the prince's reading of English statutes in *De laudibus* indicates that he did not yet possess his own copy of the *Nova statuta Angliae* while in exile in France, this suggests that even the earlier parts of the Yale manuscript remained in England when the royal family fled in July 1460. The references to the prince's need for his own copy of the statutes in *De laudibus* may suggest that Fortescue knew of plans to have such a manuscript made and may indeed have been involved in the planning. It is interesting to note several parallels between Fortescue's *De laudibus* and the imagery of the Yale Law School *Nova statuta*. For example, Fortescue's treatise makes a direct connection between the king's prayers to God and the king's implementation of justice through law. While encouraging Prince Edward to study the laws of England, the chancellor also argues that earthly kings should pray for divine guidance in their pursuit of justice: "Sed quia ista, sine gracia lex operari nequit tibi, illam super omnia implorare necesse est; legis quoque divine et sanctarum scripturarum indagare scienciam tibi congruit" ("But because this law cannot flourish in you without grace, it is necessary to pray for that above all things; also it is fitting for you to seek knowledge of the divine law and Holy Scripture") (*De laudibus*, chapter 6 [Chrimes 1942, 18–19]). Although the chancellor does not cite the Bible as the authority behind this argument, Fortescue may have expected readers to recognize an echo of Psalm 118 in the Vulgate Bible, in which the speaker appeals for divine guidance in learning about true justice and law, often depicted as God's statutes: "Doce me statuta tua" ("Teach me thy statutes"), "Ostende mihi, Domine, viam statutorum tuorum" ("Teach me, O Lord, the way of thy statues"), and "Statuta tua doce me" ("Teach me thy statutes") (Psalms 118:26, 33, 64). The psalm's focus on justice and its association with King David make it especially appropriate as a source text for a treatise on the prince's education.

With each of the English kings in its first five portraits shown at prayer with an open book on the *prie-dieu* before him, the Yale Law School *Nova statuta* manuscript offers visual reinforcement of the link between prayer and justice in Fortescue's treatise. One might see an additional parallel between the Yale Law School manuscript and Fortescue's *De laudibus* in the way that they both associate Henry VI with pious kingship and associate Edward IV with misused military might. Instead of the chronological order in which we find the two kings' images in the Yale manuscript, however, Fortescue's treatise presents the images of the two kings in reverse order: in its opening passage, Fortescue's treatise first associates the usurping Edward IV with the most unspeakable madness of civil war ("nephandissima rabie") and then praises Henry VI as the most pious king ("piissimus rex") (*De laudibus*, introduction [Chrimes 1942, 2–3]. The narrator's description of the deposed king sets up a parallel between Henry VI and the chancellor's depiction of the good kings of the Old Testament, who ruled wisely because they studied the book of Israel's laws, instituted by God. Finally, the details of the illustrations in the Yale manuscript that link the Lancastrian kings with wise advisors also parallel Fortescue's *De laudibus*, which depicts the wise king making judgments with the advice of his counselors. For example, in chapter 8 the chancellor explains that the prince will be able to consult with his judicial counselors about the fine points of the law when he is king (Chrimes 1942, 22–23), and in chapter 51 the chancellor describes how the wise king selects judges with the advice of his council (Chrimes 1942, 126–27).

While we do not have direct evidence of Fortescue's ownership or commission of a personal copy of the statutes, we know that he owned a collection of legal and historical texts that includes a copy of the *Modus tenendi Parliamentum*: Oxford, Bodleian Library MS Rawlinson C. 398, which dates from the mid-fifteenth century, bears a note indicating Fortescue's ownership in a later hand ("liber quondam Johannis Fortescue").[19] Fortescue's *De laudibus* does not explicitly advise the prince to have his own copy of this treatise; but in chapter 9 the chancellor explains to the prince that the English king does not have the authority to change the laws of his kingdom without the assent of his subjects, i.e., the assent of Parliament (Chrimes 1942, 24–25). Implied is the idea that the prince needs to understand how the king works with Parliament in order to provide just laws for his kingdom. The inclusion of the *Modus tenendi Parliamentum* in the Yale Law School *Nova statuta*, as well as the Latin treatise on the duties of the high steward or seneschal, provides yet another parallel between the *De laudibus* and the Yale *Nova statuta* manuscript and suggests that they might well have been intended as companion volumes for the education of Prince Edward.

Having served as a member of Parliament and as a judicial representative of the monarch in Parliament, Fortescue had good reason to know the practical as well as symbolic importance of the monarch's familiarity with the Statutes of the Realm. Fortescue's highlighting of the prince's interaction with the physical record of these laws in the *De laudibus* suggests that Fortescue appreciated the ways in which a manuscript's contextualization of a verbal text shapes the reader's engagement with the ideas the text contains. The chancellor's argument in the *De laudibus* that Prince Edward should read his own copy of the Statutes of the Realm reminds us of Fortescue's active involvement in shaping the manuscript records of the King's Bench while he was chief justice. The historiated initials that Fortescue commissioned for the *Coram rege* Rolls of 1460 (plates 72 and 73), which integrate images of the king with verbal allusions to the Bible, run parallel to the depictions of just rulership found in the *De laudibus* and in the Yale Law School *Nova statuta*.[20] The historiated initials in the *Coram rege* Rolls give the legal records in which they appear a link to the mirror for princes tradition, just as the historiated initials in the Yale *Nova statuta* manuscript help to transform a record of statutes into a mirror for princes. If Fortescue's addition of the initials to the King's Bench records served as a response to growing threats against the Lancastrian monarch in 1460, he may have used or encouraged the use of other legal texts in a similar manner at that time. It is Fortescue's *De laudibus legum Angliae*, however, that makes the most direct connection between the prince's education in kingship and reading the statutes of England, and the version of that treatise that survives probably dates from 1468–70. Whether Fortescue first made this argument in March 1460, when Prince Edward's formal education began, we cannot be certain.[21] Yet two things are clear. One is that Fortescue's emphasis on reading a personal copy of the statutes became an important part of his advice to the prince during their exile in France. The other is that the Yale Law School statutes manuscript would have fulfilled Prince Edward's needs in a manner consistent with Fortescue's ideas about kingship and law – if the manuscript ever reached the prince.

Both the evidence of the Yale *Nova statuta* and the known historical circumstances of 1470–71 suggest that the manuscript may never have been presented. No gift inscription or presentation miniature survives in the original parts of the Yale manuscript, which suggests that it remained incomplete when the Lancastrian line of kings came to an end in 1471. Despite Warwick's success in restoring Henry VI to the throne in October 1470, the Lancastrians could not maintain their power against the forces of Edward IV. When Queen Margaret and Prince Edward returned to England from exile in April 1471, Henry VI had been recaptured, and Warwick had been defeated and killed. By the end of May, the Lancastrian attempt to regain the throne had completely failed: Prince Edward and Henry VI were both dead, and Margaret of Anjou was Edward IV's prisoner. The other Lancastrians who remained alive, including Fortescue, needed pardons and reversals of attainder in order to regain their freedom and their property. Nevertheless, the clearly Lancastrian Yale *Nova statuta* manuscript survived, and its work continued.

FIVE

"Grace Be Our Guide"

THE CULTURAL SIGNIFICANCE OF A MEDIEVAL LAW BOOK

All indications are that the Yale *New Statutes* manuscript was still in production when the Lancastrian line of kings came to an end in May 1471. Only
with the death of Henry VI would a scribe who was working on a statutes
manuscript for a Lancastrian owner enter the rubric on fol. 356v: "Expliciunt
Statuta Regis Henrici Sexti" ("Here end the statutes of King Henry the
Sixth"). The manuscript's survival after the defeat of the Lancastrian cause
is testimony to its evolving significance as an historical artifact, as well as
legal resource, after 1471. Unless parts of the original manuscript are missing,
work appears to have ceased before the end of the statutes for 7 Edward IV,
though the decoration of these quires is complete. Whether or not the Yale
manuscript was made to be a gift for Prince Edward, it probably became an or-
phan in May 1471, since so many of those who had fought for the Lancastrian
cause had perished. Yet, unlike the Lancastrian survivors who were forced
to recant their support for Henry VI in order to receive pardons, the Yale
manuscript's Lancastrian loyalties remain intact. Somehow, the manuscript
passed into the hands of owners who preserved Margaret's coat of arms and
the critical portrayal of Edward IV – elements that made possession of the
manuscript potentially dangerous until public veneration of Henry VI as
a martyr grew so widespread that Richard III had the deposed king's body
moved to St. George's Chapel at Windsor Castle and Richard's successor,
Henry VII, sought to have Henry VI declared a saint. An unknown owner of
the manuscript after 1483 added an incomplete gathering of statutes from the
end of Edward IV's reign and beginning of Richard III's in a less formal hand

and format (see plates 16–18). Nevertheless, the inscriptions added to the Yale manuscript over the following two centuries offer insights into who owned the manuscript and how it was read. In particular, the Middle English inscriptions on two folios offer evidence of reader engagement with the manuscript's construction of justice and grace. Though printed copies of the *New Statutes of England* became available by the late fifteenth century, this manuscript continued to be used as a legal reference work and an historical document. From inscriptions, we learn that two women owned the manuscript, while other owners included eminent men, some trained in the law, some with appointments in royal service, and some who served in Parliament. The codex was transmitted as a personal gift for several generations, after which it was sold to private collectors of rare books and finally purchased for the collection of rare books and manuscripts now housed in Yale Law School's Lillian Goldman Library, making it more readily available for academic research and public display.

The reading of the *New Statutes* that the Yale manuscript suggests – that English law should be shaped by divine grace and justice – seems to have inspired responses from some of the earliest readers of the manuscript after the House of Lancaster failed in its final attempts to regain the English throne. On fol. 6r (plate 19), we find the Middle English phrase "Grace be oure gide" ("Grace be our guide"), followed by the initial *F*, inscribed next to a passage in the *Modus tenendi Parliamentum*. The English words appear to be in ink similar to that of the central text and are in a late fifteenth-century Bastard Anglicana hand; but the hand of the Middle English phrase differs from the hands of the treatises and the statutes, so the Middle English text appears to be an addition, rather than part of the manuscript's original contents. By definition, therefore, the English text is considered marginal. Nevertheless, the English text on this leaf might be seen as bridging the central texts and the margins of the manuscript: the hand is of professional quality, and the phrase has been inscribed within the central text block, rather than in the marginal space of the leaf. This suggests that the phrase shared a close relationship with the central text in the view of the inscriber. At the same time, the English text seems to have had significance beyond its relationship with the Latin text on this leaf, because the same phrase in a slightly different hand, followed by another initial, appears in the margin of fol. 235r (plate 20), next to the Latin incipit for the statutes enacted under Henry V. Taken together, the two English inscriptions create a bridge that links the Latin treatise that begins the manuscript to the *Nova statuta Angliae*, the central text in the manuscript.

"Grace be our guide" is an intriguing inscription. It might express advice, supplication, command, hope, or anxiety; yet it does not specify what kind of grace should be our guide. The word "grace" came into Middle English from French and could refer to the favor, gift, assistance, or mercy of God or of a human figure, including the beloved in medieval courtly discourse.[1] In addition, "grace" could refer to an attribute of courtly beauty or behavior, to good fortune, or to the thanks or recognition offered by the recipient of a gift or mercy. Several meanings of "grace" might thus be in play in this instance. In addition, we might ask why the inscriber commands, prays, or advises that grace be "our" guide, and not "my" guide: the community invoked by the first-person plural pronoun might link the inscriber to the people who participate in the sessions of Parliament discussed in the treatise, but in context the inscription could also link the inscriber to other readers of the manuscript. In addition, we must consider whether the initials that follow the two statements allude to the names of the inscribers of the English text or something else.

Some clue to the meaning of the English text might come from the Latin text it accompanies on fol. 6r; but the particular chapter of the *Modus* where the English phrase occurs does not make any direct reference to "grace":

> De Stationibus Loquencium in Parliamento
>   Omnes pares Parliamenti sedebunt, et nullus stabit nisi quando loquitur, ita quod quilibet de Parliamento eum audire valeat; nullus intrabit Parliamentum, nec exiet de Parliamento, nisi per unicum hostium; et quicumque loquitur rem aliquam que deliberari debet per Parliamentum, stabunt omnes loquentes; causa est ut audiantur a paribus, quia omnes pares sunt iudices et iusticiarii. (Pronay and Taylor 1980, 76–77)

> (Concerning the Position of Speakers in Parliament
>   All the peers of parliament will sit, and no one will stand except when he speaks in such a manner that everyone in parliament can hear him; no one will go in or out of parliament except by the one door. And whoever speaks on any matter which ought to be debated by parliament will stand as will all speakers. The reason for this is so that they may be heard by the peers, because all peers are judges and justices.) (Pronay and Taylor 1980, 89)

On one level, the passage seems to focus on very practical issues: who must sit and who must stand during sessions of Parliament and the restriction of entry to and exit from parliamentary sessions to one door. Perhaps the inscriber of the English text calls upon "grace" to guide the members of Parliament in their speaking and their listening to other speakers. This grace might be the courtly grace of knowing when to stand and when to sit, when to keep silent and when to speak loudly enough to be heard. Alternatively, the English phrase might call upon the grace of the king or his representatives to guide the members of Parliament in their speaking and listening to speakers.

Yet another option is that this inscription is a prayer for the guidance of divine grace. If this is an appeal to divine grace for guidance, it suggests that at least one reader of the *Modus* found a more significant issue in this passage than the protocols for entering and exiting, standing or sitting, speaking loudly or refraining from speaking during a parliamentary session. The inscriber of the phrase may have read the final words of the chapter – "quia omnes pares sunt iudices et iusticiarii" ("because all peers are judges and justices") – as a commentary on both the physical "standing" of members of Parliament and their legal, political, and moral standing: all the members of Parliament, from the king down to the citizens and burgesses, have the common role of "judges and justices" when they participate in Parliament. Perhaps the inscription "Grace be our guide" might be read as constructing a frame of divine grace for the Latin treatise's assertion of the judicial authority of the members of Parliament, just as the historiated initials in the Yale *Nova statuta* suggest that divine grace should frame the reading of England's statutes. The idea that divine guidance should be invoked to frame the deliberations of Parliament is inscribed in the *Modus* itself. The treatise states that, on one of the first days of the parliamentary session, a member of the clergy should preach a sermon to all those participating in the session, including the king, and lead them in prayer for the peace and tranquility of the king and the kingdom (Pronay and Taylor 1980, 71, 84). The treatise states further that, after the sermon, the king should address each group of the clergy and laity by name and ask them to deliberate on the business of Parliament so that their actions accord first with the will of God and second with the king's honor and their own (Pronay and Taylor 1980, 72, 84–85). The inscription "Grace be our guide" could be a reader's echo of these earlier passages, though an explicit reference to grace does not appear in either Latin passage. Nevertheless, by not specifying which grace should guide or who might be included in the first-person plural possessive pronoun, and also by using English instead of Latin or French to express the thought, this inscription of "Grace be oure gide" offers a more open vision of the human quest for justice than the one found in the text of the *Modus* or the historiated initials of the *New Statutes* in this manuscript.

The second appearance of "Grace be oure gide," on fol. 235r, continues that process of opening out its potential significance. Though the script of the second inscription is different from the first in using some Secretary let-ter forms, the hands are so similar that the second inscription is likely by the same writer at a later time, and the initial that follows the second inscription may well be an *F* that is missing its top stroke. In this case, the Middle En-glish phrase appears next to the Latin rubric for the beginning of the statutes for Henry V: "Incipiunt statuta apud Westminster edita anno primo Regis Henrici Quinti" ("Here begin the statutes issued at Westminster in the first year of King Henry the Fifth"). Finding an inscription referring to grace next to the text of the *Nova statuta Angliae* is not surprising. As we have noted already, divine grace and royal grace play prominent roles in the text of the statutes. The opening words of several of the reigns in the statutes text link the monarch's authority to divine authority by introducing the monarch as king "par la grace de Dieu" ("by the grace of God"), and many other passages in the statutes text refer to the grace of the king in authorizing an action. Yet the marginal inscriptions of "Grace be oure gide" broaden the discourses of grace in the manuscript, opening construction of the meaning of "grace" to all who read the manuscript. In this location, the phrase appears to be a comment on Henry V, the father of Henry VI, whose early death as a result of illness brought a tragic end to an illustrious career and caused consider-able anxiety, since his supporters presented Henry V's many achievements at home and abroad as validation of the legitimacy of the Lancastrian mon-archy. Critics of the Lancastrians suggested that the young king's death was divine retribution for the overthrow of Richard II in 1399, and the Lancas-trians responded with even greater idealization of Henry V.[2] As we have seen, Lancastrian attempts to depict Henry V's son as heir to his father's greatness became part of the political image-making of Henry VI's reign. It is interesting, therefore, to find the inscription "Grace be oure gide" next to the rubric for the opening of Henry V's statutes and not next to the rubric for the opening of the statutes for any of the other kings in the Yale manuscript, including Henry VI. Whereas the depiction of Henry VI in his historiated initial presents him as the most ideal of the kings shown (by its association of him, more than the others, with King David), the inscription on fol. 235r suggests a reconsideration of Henry VI's kingship through a new association of Henry V with royal and divine grace, as well as the English language and, by extension, other aspects of English culture. While the manuscript's earlier Lancastrian frames remain intact, the Middle English inscriptions added to the manuscript construct another frame that has linguistic, literary, and political dimensions.

Part of the rhetorical power of "Grace be oure gide" is its use of alliteration, which links the text with the medieval English poetic tradition, as well as English proverbs and family mottos. The fact that the same English text appears again later in the manuscript suggests that both the form and the content of the words were significant to the inscriber. While this phrase is not recorded as an English family motto or a proverb during the fifteenth century, it is very similar to a phrase that was part of the welcoming pageant for Margaret of Anjou at Leadenhall Market when she first arrived in London in 1445: "Grace conueie you forthe and be youre gide" ("Grace lead you forth and be your guide") (line 34).[3] In this pageant, Grace was depicted as the chancellor of the Heavenly King, who brought justice to earth through an alliance of the new queen and her people, represented as the estates of clergy, lords, and commons of England. Given that the initial after the first inscription of "Grace be oure gide" is an "F," perhaps the inscriber was Sir John Fortescue, Henry VI's chancellor-in-exile, advisor to Queen Margaret, and tutor to Prince Edward, who had suggested to the prince in *De laudibus legum Angliae* that he would receive divine grace if he had his own copy of the statutes of England to study every day. As chief justice of the King's Bench in 1445, Fortescue would almost certainly have attended the ceremonies involved in Margaret's coronation and may have been part of the procession bringing her through London to Westminster. If so, he would have witnessed Grace's pageant speech himself. If he was not personally present, he could also have read one of the transcriptions that were made as a record of the festivities.[4] Fortescue's personal connections with the royal family, as well as his professional role as interpreter of English law, make him a clear candidate for ownership of the Yale manuscript after 1471 and a possible inscriber of the English phrases.

The Yale *New Statutes* manuscript would not have been bound before 1471, when work on the original parts appears to have stopped before completion of the first set of statutes for Edward IV; the manuscript would have been kept in quires awaiting further instructions for its completion. The fact that the Lancastrian elements of the Yale manuscript were not painted over indicates that the manuscript's owners after 1471 continued to honor the Lancastrian royal line. Discretion about owning the manuscript would have been necessary, however, while Edward IV was on the throne: only by renouncing past support of the Lancastrian cause could survivors of the final battles in 1471, such as John Fortescue, George Ashby, and William Coote, receive a royal pardon. The king required Fortescue to compose a new treatise refuting his earlier written arguments against Edward's claim to the throne before issuing a pardon for him.[5] Since Edward IV then made Fortescue a member of the royal council, he continued to spend time in London and Westminster and would have been in a position to retrieve the Yale *Nova statuta* manuscript from those who had been working on it. As an official working closely with the royal family prior to Henry VI's deposition, as well as someone who had supervised the making of legal manuscripts in his role as chief justice of the King's Bench, Fortescue may have been the person who arranged to commission a statutes manuscript as a gift for the prince. Fortescue may also have been one of the few former Lancastrians who could have paid for the book when his property rights were restored, since he had considerable wealth prior to his attainder.[6] Fortescue could not have added the statutes from the 1480s to the manuscript, however, since he died around 1479.

Though Fortescue's possession of the Yale manuscript after 1471 must remain a matter of conjecture, it is a theory that finds support in the identity of the earliest documented owners of the manuscript. Lady Margaret Elyot's donation of the codex is recorded on fol. 1r (plate 21): "Liber Georgi Frevyle armigeri, ex dono domine Margarete Elyot vidue post mortem Ricardi Elyot militis defunct quondam viri sui" ("The book of George Frevyle esquire, a gift from Lady Margaret Elyot, widow, after the death of her former husband Richard Elyot, knight"). The inscription is incorrect, however, in describing Sir Richard Elyot as Lady Margaret's husband.

Though Lady Margaret may have received the manuscript from Sir Richard, who was her father-in-law, her husband was Sir Thomas Elyot, who inherited French and Latin books from his father. Sir Richard was a member of the Middle Temple Inn of Court who rose to become a member of Parliament, distinguished judge, and attorney general to Henry VII's queen, Elizabeth of York.[7] Henry VII's veneration of Henry VI had revived interest in the people associated with him. If Sir Richard knew of Fortescue's *De laudibus legum Angliae*, he may have recognized a link between this copy of the statutes and Fortescue's treatise. Sir Richard's first wife was Lady Alice Delamare, so he was probably responsible for the addition of the Elyot and Delamare coats of arms in the bottom roundels on the opening leaf of the statutes in the Yale manuscript (plate 1), mirroring the placement of Margaret of Anjou's arms with her husband's in the top roundels. The Elyot family arms also appear added to the border decoration on fols. 139r, 198r, 261r, and 358r (plates 2, 3, 5, and 6). Sir Richard and Lady Alice had two children, Thomas and Margery. Sir Thomas, who is thought to have been born in about 1490, had a distinguished career as a humanist scholar, author, assistant to Sir Thomas Cromwell, and diplomat for Henry VIII (Lehmberg 1960). Lady Margery married Robert Puttenham, and their son was George Puttenham, the author of *The Art of English Poesie*. When Sir Richard Elyot died in 1522, he left his French and Latin books to his son and his English books to his daughter.[8]

Sir Thomas Elyot and Lady Margaret Elyot have long been known as members of Sir Thomas More's humanist circle; yet scholars have not been aware of this manuscript's link to the couple and so have not explored the roles that the manuscript might have played in their intellectual and political lives. Sir Thomas Elyot's published works suggest that he was familiar with Fortescue's *De laudibus legum Angliae*, as well as with Fortescue's *Governance of England* and *De natura legis naturae*. Thomas Elyot himself composed two mirrors for princes, *The Boke Named the Governour* (published in 1531 and dedicated to Henry VIII) and *The Image of Governance* (published in 1541). Whereas the *New Statutes* manuscript Elyot received from his father uses indirect allusions to King David to present a biblical model of true kingship, grace, and justice, Elyot's *Boke Named the Governour* repeatedly uses King David to illustrate ideal kingly behavior. For example, Elyot's work depicts David as a "holy kynge," who was "predestinate to be a great kyng, and a great prophete" and who "for the soueraigne gyftes of grace and of nature, that he was endowed with, All mightye god sayde of him that he had founde a man after his harte and pleasure" (Croft 1883, 1:215, 219).[9] Both of Elyot's mirrors for princes also contain echoes of Fortescue's works.[10] The dating of Elyot's mirrors for princes becomes significant when we consider that he would have needed to consult a manuscript copy of Fortescue's *De laudibus legum Angliae* for the first and possibly the second of these treatises.[11] Since Sir Thomas Elyot inherited his father's Latin and French books, it may be that both the Yale *New Statutes* manuscript and copies of Fortescue's treatises came to Sir Thomas through his father.

Sir Richard Elyot was very well situated to have access to Fortescue's collection of books through his acquaintance with Fortescue's nephew, also Sir John. This John Fortescue served as esquire of the body to Edward IV and Richard III, but later joined the service of Henry VII and was knighted in 1485. He remained in royal service until his death in 1500. Although Sir Richard received his appointment as king's sergeant-at-law in 1503, he had received temporary commissions from the Crown in the 1490s and also served as a reader at New Inn, one of the Inns of Chancery that the elder Fortescue describes in *De laudibus*.[12] In addition, Richard Elyot's brother William and their cousin John Elyot held a lease on Clement's Inn, another of the Inns of

Chancery, where John Elyot was principal; and this property bordered on the property where the elder John Fortescue resided while serving as chief justice between 1442 and 1461 and again after his appointment to Edward IV's council in 1471.[13] After regaining ownership of his property through royal pardon and parliamentary reversal of his attainder, the elder John Fortescue gave the property next to St. Clement's Inn to his nephew in royal service, who left the property to his wife when he died. The younger John Fortescue therefore owned his uncle's home near the Inns of Chancery and served in Henry VII's court in the 1490s at the same time that Richard Elyot lectured at a nearby Inn of Chancery and entered royal service under the same king. Especially with his cousin John as principal of Clement's Inn, abutting the Fortescue property, Sir Richard had both opportunity and motive to become acquainted with the younger Sir John Fortescue. Since the elder Fortescue had used this home in St. Clement Danes parish during the many years he was chief justice and during his royal service after returning from exile, it is possible that he kept some of his legal books at that home and left them to his nephew along with the property at his death in about 1479. At this nephew's death in 1500, his family may have been willing to give or sell some of his books to a colleague, neighbor, and book collector like Sir Richard Elyot.

In 1507, Sir Richard inherited the lease on the Clement's Inn property from his brother; Richard then left the property to his son Thomas as part of his estate in 1522, along with his Latin and French books. Even if Sir Thomas did not recognize a connection between Fortescue's *De laudibus legum Angliae* and the copy of the *Nova statuta* he inherited from his father, the humanist scholar must have recognized the statute manuscript's connection with Margaret of Anjou, since it includes her coat of arms in the border decoration on three folios. Sir Richard Elyot's addition of Alice Delamare's arms to the manuscript, along with his own, in the lower border of the first leaf of the statutes, sets up a parallel between the two couples and their sons much as do the depictions of parents and children in the coats of arms used to decorate the copies of the *New Statutes* in the manuscript made for Sir Thomas Fitzwilliam and Philadelphia, Free Library MS Carson LC 14. 9.5 (plate 33).[14] The inclusion of Alice Delamare's arms on that leaf suggests a desire to continue this type of commemoration of a wife or mother's role in the history of a family and nation – a view of women that echoes Sir Thomas Elyot's own treatise, *A Defense of Good Women* (1540). There Elyot depicts several wise women of antiquity who became learned in languages, history, and philosophy, as evidence of women's capacity for education, virtue, and leadership. While Lehmberg (1960, 174–77) has interpreted Elyot's final example, the learned warrior queen Zenobia, as a veiled defense of Catherine of Aragon, many of the reasons given for admiring Zenobia could also apply to Margaret of Anjou, in regard to both fortitude under adversity and concern for the education of children.

A more positive view of Margaret's efforts on behalf of her husband and son may have resulted from Henry VII's cultivation of a saintly image for his Lancastrian predecessor in the 1480s and 1490s; but evidence of a sympathetic view of Margaret survives from the mid-1470s as well. Among the records of the Fraternity of Our Lady's Assumption, associated with the London Skinners' Company, we find, under the year 15 Edward IV (which began on 4 March 1475), the record of Margaret's admission to membership in the fraternity, a miniature that portrays the former queen kneeling before a *prie-dieu* on which rest a book, scepter, and crown (plate 76), and the description "The Qweene Margarete sumtyme wyff and Spowse to kyng Harry the sexthe" ("Queen Margaret former wife and spouse of King Harry the Sixth").[15] After imprisoning Margaret in the Tower of London in 1471, Edward IV released her to the custody of Lady Alice Chaucer, Dowager Duchess of Suffolk, and Margaret lived with the duchess at Wallingford Castle until January 1476. Margaret had been stripped of all her rights and property in England when she was attainted for treason in 1461, but she was still valuable to Edward IV as a bargaining chip with her cousin, Louis XI of France, who eventually agreed to the ransom that allowed Margaret to return to France (Maurer 2003, 202, 208). Just four years after the defeat of the Lancastrian forces, however, Margaret was again depicted with honor in England: membership in the Fraternity of Our Lady's Assumption brought her into "sisterhood" with Elizabeth Woodville, Edward IV's queen, whose admission to membership is inscribed in the record book just a few years earlier, also highlighted with a miniature (Laynesmith 2004, 33, illustration 4).

Elyot's positive views on the education and achievements of women reflect earlier humanist arguments, including those of Christine de Pizan, who praises Queen Zenobia in her *Livre de la cité des dames*.[16] Elyot's treatise also reflects the accomplishments of his wife, Margaret, whom he named sole executrix of his estate in his 1531 will (Lehmberg 1960, 182, 195). Both Sir Thomas and Lady Margaret Elyot participated in the gatherings of humanist scholars at the home of Sir Thomas More, where the leading intellectuals and artists of the period visited and worked, until More's opposition to Henry VIII's divorce led to his imprisonment and execution.[17] It was at More's home that Hans Holbein the Younger drew his portraits of the Elyots (plates 77 and 78), which now hang in the royal collection at Windsor Castle. Margaret's father, Sir Thomas Aborough or à Barrow, had sent her to More's home for her education, which was significantly more substantial than the education available to most women at the time (Dowling 1986, 222). Under the humanist scholar's supervision, Margaret's curriculum included reading classical Latin authors, writing and delivering presentations in Latin, and studying Greek (Dowling 1986, 221). Margaret Aborough's companion in study would have been More's own daughter Margaret, whose own scholarly achievements include translating Erasmus's treatise on the Lord's Prayer into English. Discussions of law, history, philosophy, and theology were part of the education that took place at More's home, so it is likely that Margaret Aborough continued to take an interest in these matters after her marriage to Thomas Elyot. Holbein's portrait of "The Lady Elyot" verifies that Margaret continued to participate in the humanist circle that met at More's home after her marriage. It was the turbulent political situation under Henry VIII that led to separation from the More family and several years of "retirement" from public office for Sir Thomas Elyot, during which time he composed his *Boke Named the Governour*. His time with his wife and his books was probably more extensive during this period than earlier in his career. Though we can only speculate that he may have consulted his *New Statutes* manuscript while composing his own mirror for princes, Elyot may well have considered whether Henry VIII followed the model of royal justice and grace represented by the first five kings depicted in his manuscript – or the model represented by the sword-wielding Edward IV.

It seems fitting that Margaret Elyot came into possession of the Yale *Nova statuta Angliae*, as the inscription on fol. 1r attests. The fact that she did not sell this manuscript along with her husband's books after his death in 1546 to raise money for charitable donations in his name, as his will instructed, suggests that the book had become hers prior to her husband's death. We can conjecture that Sir Thomas gave her the codex when he inherited it from his father in 1522, recognizing its commemoration of a more famous Margaret. Alternatively, with Sir Richard's appreciation of books as gifts, he may have given this copy of the *New Statutes* with the coats of arms of the Elyot and Delamare families to his son and daughter-in-law as a wedding present. However the manuscript came into her possession, Margaret decided not to sell it, but to bestow it as a gift. Without children of her own to educate, she gave the manuscript to a young member of the Middle Temple, the Cambridgeshire lawyer George Freville, as the inscription on fol. 1r indicates. In making the gift to a member of the Inn of Court where her father-in-law had been a member, Margaret may have described the manuscript to Freville as having been Sir Richard Elyot's, which would explain why the gift inscription mistakenly refers to her as Sir Richard's widow. Since Freville's record of the gift refers to the donor as Dame Margaret Elyot, she must have given Freville the statute manuscript before her marriage to Sir James Dyer, another member of the Middle Temple, which occurred before April 1551.[18]

After his education, Freville went on to a career as a lawyer and government official. He served as a justice of the peace for Cambridgeshire from 1539 until his death.[19] He served as a representative from Cambridgeshire in Parliament in 1547 and was retained as counsel to the duchy of Lancaster from 1548, which may have given him an interest in books associated with the Lancastrians. Freville's interest in education can be seen in his appointment as deputy high steward of Cambridge University in 1549; but he does not seem to have become an author like Sir Thomas Elyot. Nevertheless, like Elyot, Freville received a royal appointment. He must have been a highly regarded supporter of Elizabeth I, for in 1559 he received her appointment as third baron of the Exchequer and rose to second baron in 1564. Freville died in 1579.

The Yale manuscript came into the possession of another woman by 1581, as a partially defaced inscription on fol. 1r indicates: "This booke . . . mongest other bookes at her howse at Totenham High Crosse. 1581. Mense Augusti" ("This book [was found] . . . among other books at her house at Tottenham High Cross. 1581. The month of August") (plate 21). Unfortunately, the identity of the woman whose ownership is attested by this inscription remains hidden, as well as the identity of the person who owned the book immediately after her. In the sixteenth century, residence on the manor of Tottenham was a perquisite of members of the royal household, though they sometimes rented out their quarters (Woodworth 1945, 73); so it may be that this female owner of the Yale manuscript, or a husband or other relative, had a connection to the court and had either purchased the manuscript from Sir George Freville or received it as a gift from him. The reference to other books in this woman's house indicates that she owned at least a small collection of books in addition to the *New Statutes* manuscript.

Another inscription on the first leaf of the Yale manuscript reveals that the codex entered the marketplace by the early seventeenth century. Roger Nichols, a member of the Inner Temple, purchased the book in 1614: "Liber Rogeri Nichols Interioris Templi precium vi s. viii d. Anno Domini 1614" ("The book of Roger Nichols of Inner Temple, price 6 shillings 8 pence in the year of our Lord 1614"). A Roger Nichols of Willen, Buckinghamshire, was admitted to Inner Temple in November 1604 (Cooke 1877, 100). He was called to the bar in 1613–14 (Inderwick 1898, 78), which could explain his purchase of a statutes book in 1614. Though his name appears in several land transactions, Nichols seems to have had a more private career than the previous owners of the Yale manuscript. In 1646, he served as a justice of the peace for Buckinghamshire (Langley 1797, 16, 18). By 1667, Roger Nichols had died and his son, William Nichols of Woughton, was his heir.[20] Since the date of the next ownership inscription in the Yale manuscript is 1633, however, Roger Nichols must have sold or given the manuscript as a gift by then. The rest of this inscription is also defaced, which suggests that a later owner wished to remove evidence of earlier ownership, perhaps because of controversial political associations. Nevertheless, the manuscript's association with Margaret of Anjou remained intact throughout the transfers of ownership that the book underwent.

According to the inscription on the front paste-down of the Yale manuscript, the codex eventually became the property of "Sir Thomas Winnington, Baronet." This Sir Thomas Winnington might be the third baronet of Stanford Court, Worcestershire (1780–1839), or Sir Thomas Edward Winnington, Fourth Baronet of Stanford Court (1811–72).[21] Both of these men were antiquarians, as well as lawyers and politicians. The manuscript was certainly in the library at Stanford Court by 1870, when Alfred J. Horwood filed his report: Horwood lists a fifteenth-century manuscript of the *Modus tenendi Parliamentum* and a fifteenth-century manuscript of the *Nova statuta Angliae* with illuminated initials in the Winnington collection (Horwood 1870, 53), though this description does not make clear if the manuscript of the *Modus* was bound separately or is the one bound together with the statutes in the Yale manuscript. Another account indicates that the manuscript collection at Stanford Court contained a fifteenth-century illuminated copy of the *New Statutes* by 1862, and this account suggests that the manuscript may have passed into the family's ownership much earlier:

> The MSS. of various kinds preserved at Stanford Court, independently of those relating to the property, are considerable; many, it is believed, may have been derived from the ancient possessions of the Jefferies family, of Homme Castle, and some were collected by Sir Francis Winnington, Solicitor-General to Charles II. By the obliging courtesy of Sir Thomas Winnington [the fourth baronet] we were permitted to exhibit in the Museum two documents of great interest, not, however, connected with the county. One is

an illuminated MS of the Rolls of Parliament, written at the latter part of the fifteenth century, the other is an able State paper drawn up by the advisers of Queen Elizabeth to exonerate her from blame in the matter of the Queen of Scots. It is a valuable document, though not unknown in substance to the historical student, and Sir Thomas has kindly placed it at the disposal of the Camden Society, who are about to publish it. (Archaeological Institute 1862, 393)

Clearly, Sir Thomas Edward Winnington considered his *Nova statuta* manuscript one of the most important items in his collection, and it is interesting that he chose to highlight for the members of the Archaeological Institute two documents with links to English queens who came under fire for some of their actions. The account's information about the sources of manuscripts in the Stanford Court collection is intriguing. John Hamilton Baker also suggests that Sir Francis Winnington may have added the *Nova statuta* manuscript to the library at Stanford Court (Baker 1985, 74). Sir Francis Winnington (1634–1700) was a lawyer educated at Lincoln's Inn and a member of Parliament who became solicitor-general to Charles II in 1675, so he would have been able to appreciate and afford a manuscript like the Yale codex. A portrait of Sir Francis now hangs in the National Gallery in London (plate 79). Nevertheless, when Sir Francis purchased the Stanford Court estate from his wife's family, it had a collection of rare books and manuscripts in its library, so the statutes manuscript may have come to Stanford Court even earlier, perhaps soon after it passed from Roger Nichols's ownership.[22] The other suggested source in this account, the Jefferies (or Jeffreys) family, would mean that the manuscript probably came to Stanford Court no earlier than the early eighteenth century, when Sir Francis Winnington's third son, Edward Winnington, married the heiress of the Jefferies estate, added the surname of that family to his own, and took possession of Homme (or Ham) Castle (W. Williams 1897, 130).

Sir Francis's first son, Salway Winnington, inherited the Stanford Court estate and served in Parliament for many years; but it was Sir Francis's grandson, Sir Thomas Winnington (1696–1746), educated at Oxford and the Middle Temple, who had the more illustrious career in law and politics.[23] His portrait also hangs in the National Gallery in London (plate 80). This Thomas Winnington became a member of Parliament under Sir Robert Walpole and then received appointments as Lord Admiral, Lord of the Treasury, and privy counselor to the Crown. Sir Thomas is also known for his participation in the literary circle that included Henry Fielding (Battestin and Battestin

1993, 341–42; Urstad 1999, 72, 87). When Sir Thomas died without children, the Stanford Court estate passed to his cousin, Edward Winnington, whose son Sir Edward Winnington (1728–91) became the first baronet. Sir Edward Winnington was a member of Parliament from 1764 until 1791. His son, Sir Edward Winnington (1749–1805), the second baronet, also served in Parliament and in local offices in Worcestershire.

Through all these generations, the Winnington family continued to enhance its collection of rare books and manuscripts: the Franks Collection of British and American bookplates in the British Library contains nine examples from the Winningtons (Howe 1903, 228–29). Ownership of a *New Statutes* manuscript may have been a matter of historical interest and a symbolic link with the political institutions in which the Winnington men participated. Nevertheless, it is also possible that Margaret of Anjou's association with this manuscript of the *New Statutes* became an additional attraction for owners like the Winningtons. Despite Shakespeare's negative depiction of Margaret in *Henry VI, Part III*, and *Richard III*, positive depictions of Margaret as a courageous queen and mother appeared in England and France in the seventeenth, eighteenth, and nineteenth centuries. For example, portraits of Margaret began to circulate in the seventeenth century, including an anonymous engraving (London, National Portrait Gallery, NPG D23778) with a verse tribute to her:

> Amongst these worthyes Margaret may claime right,
> Who to support the red Rose gainst the white
> In seuerall pitcht fields Shee out dar'd her fate:
> Of mighty spirit Although unfortunate.

Literary depictions sympathetic to Margaret also began to appear in the eighteenth century. In the 1720s, Theophilus Cibber staged a revised version of Shakespeare's *Henry VI* that presents Margaret's defense of her son's claim to the throne as worthy of admiration and portrays Prince Edward as a valiant young knight who also wins the love of a young woman.[24] The anonymous *Biographium Faemineum: The Female Worthies*, published in 1766, describes Margaret as the heroic leader of the Lancastrian forces, who had "all the virtues of the men without their defects" (2:89).[25] In France, Antoine François Prévost published a sympathetic account of Margaret's life in his *Histoire de Marguerite d'Anjou, reine d'Angleterre* in 1740, and an English translation was published in 1755. An anonymous French playwright published the tragedy *Marguerite d'Anjou, reine d'Angleterre* in 1757. In the nineteenth century,

French public commemoration of Margaret's heroism focused on her role as mother, as can be seen in the statues of Margaret protecting her son at the chateau at Angers (1853) and in Luxembourg Gardens in Paris (1877). In England, several nineteenth-century artists and authors also presented sympathetic images of the queen. Margaret Holford's *Margaret of Anjou: A Poem in Ten Cantos* (1816) depicts Margaret as both courageous queen and mother of the ideal prince: "Young Edward on the saddle sate, / And ne'er did lovelier, braver lord / Ride forth to challenge Fate" (canto 1, stanza 27) (Holford 1816, 14). In this poem, Margaret's proud vision of Lancastrian glory is tempered by maternal love, making the loss of her child in pursuit of the throne the ultimate tragedy. Alexander Fraser Tytler, Lord Woodhouselee, in his *Universal History*, published posthumously in 1834, describes Margaret as "a woman of the most accomplished and manly spirit that, perhaps, ever appeared" (Tytler 1834, 5:114). While recognizing her cruelty to her enemies, Tytler's account presents the queen as one "whose greatness of soul was superior to all her misfortunes" and a "most intrepid and matchless woman" who "continued with unshaken firmness of mind to struggle against adversity" on behalf of her husband and son against the "barbarous" Edward IV (Tytler 1834, 5:118–20).

Whereas the presence of Margaret of Anjou's arms in this copy of the *New Statutes* may have been considered a liability in the eyes of some, the manuscript's links to the queen gave it added significance that most likely helped it survive through the centuries and perhaps gave it added financial value as well. The manuscript remained with the Winnington family from the nineteenth century into the twentieth, despite the loss of some of their collection of rare books and manuscripts in a fire at Stanford Court in December 1882.[26] After the death of the fifth baronet, Sir Francis Salwey Winnington, in 1931, his estate sold the manuscript, along with others from Stanford Court, through Hodgson and Co., at their sale on 26 May 1932.[27] The 1930s were difficult financial times in England as well as elsewhere, and many private owners sold rare books and manuscripts during this period. After leaving the Winnington family collection in 1932, the manuscript was sold through Sotheby's on 1 August 1933 and sold again at their sale on 12 April 1938 (Sotheby Auction House 1933, lot no. 427; Sotheby Auction House 1938, lot no. 312; Baker 1985, 74). The manuscript subsequently moved to a new continent and from private library to research library in the middle of the twentieth century. Yale Law School purchased the manuscript through C. A. Stonehill in 1955, and it is now available for study in the Paskus-Danziger Rare Book Room of the Lillian Goldman Law Library.

Over the centuries, owners have bestowed this *Nova statuta* manuscript as a gift or sold it as a rare book because of its cultural value, not just because it contains a copy of medieval English statutes. Beginning in the 1480s, readers who wished to own up-to-date copies of the *Nova statuta* could purchase printed versions (H. Bennett 1969, 80); yet the Yale manuscript continued to find sympathetic owners for centuries to come. As a personal gift, political statement, legal resource, artistic artifact, and historical document, the Yale manuscript offers an opportunity to discover how the discourses of kingship, queenship, justice, and grace that it employs continued to resonate over time. The manuscript's unique features – its paintings of kings and its use of Margaret of Anjou's coat of arms – made the codex valuable to owners over the centuries, but give the manuscript even more value to modern readers as an example of Lancastrian political discourse. Though the evidence that Margaret of Anjou commissioned this manuscript for her son remains indirect, this attribution is consistent with both the manuscript's content and the historical, political, literary, and iconographic contexts of its production and early ownership. Margaret was especially well situated to bring together the French and English literary and artistic traditions that shaped the manuscript's illustration and decoration. As Henry VI's queen and mother of Prince Edward, Margaret also provides the key to understanding the manuscript's reflection of arguments about just kingship found in works by Christine de Pizan, as well as Lancastrian authors, and use of them in defense of her husband and son. Fortescue's reference to Prince Edward's need for his own copy of the statutes in *De laudibus legum Angliae* and that text's depiction of just kingship in terms that parallel the imagery of the Yale manuscript support the idea that this manuscript of the *New Statutes of England* was made for Prince Edward and meant to be read as a mirror for princes, as well as a record of English laws.

Through its construction of multiple frames for the text of the Statutes of the Realm for later readers as well, the Yale Law School manuscript reveals how the *Nova statuta* could be read, not only as a legal reference work, but also as a narrative of English history and as a "parliament" giving voice to differing views of kingship, queenship, justice, and grace at play in fifteenth-century English culture. The Yale Law School manuscript of the *New Statutes* thus provides a striking example of the interaction of visual and verbal discourses utilized in medieval manuscript books and the role that these manuscripts can play in illuminating the culture that produced them. This manuscript offers an important example of the need for modern readers to recognize the diversity of voices from the past that await our discovery in medieval manuscripts. On the one hand, multiple surviving manuscript copies of a medieval work can reveal the different perspectives from which that work was read. On the other, a single manuscript can itself inscribe a "parliament" of voices – a textual space in which different ways of reading and differing ideas on a topic come into dialogue. The Yale manuscript demonstrates some of the ways in which medieval books, including law books, use visual and verbal marginal frames to shape a reader's perspective on the central texts these books contain, thereby opening these texts to new meanings for their original readers and for the readers who have followed them.

Chronology of Events

1321	Parliament persuades Edward II to exile his favorite, Hugh Despenser the Younger, and Hugh's father, Hugh Despenser the Elder
1322	Thomas, Earl of Lancaster, is executed for leading a baronial uprising against Edward II
	The Despensers return to England
1326	Queen Isabelle raises an army in France, invades England, and defeats the Despensers
	Edward II is captured and imprisoned; both Despensers are executed
1327	Edward II is forced to abdicate the throne and is later murdered in prison
	Edward II's eldest son becomes Edward III
	Parliament annuls Thomas of Lancaster's conviction for treason
1330	Edward III's first son, Edward of Woodstock, is born
1362	Edward III's fourth son, John of Gaunt, becomes Duke of Lancaster
1376	Edward of Woodstock, Prince of Wales, dies and his son Richard becomes Prince of Wales
1377	Edward III dies and his grandson becomes King Richard II at age ten
1398	Richard II exiles Henry Bolingbroke, eldest son of the Duke of Lancaster
1399	The Duke of Lancaster dies and Richard II seizes his property
	Henry Bolingbroke returns to England, defeats Richard II's forces, and imprisons the king
	Richard II is forced to abdicate the throne and is later murdered in prison
	Parliament declares Henry Bolingbroke king as Henry IV

1411 Henry IV dies and his son Henry V accedes to the throne

1420 The Treaty of Troyes makes Henry V heir to Charles VI of France through marriage to his daughter, Katherine of Valois

1421 Henry VI born (6 December)

1422 Henry V dies (August); Henry VI becomes king of England and heir to the throne of France

   Dukes of Bedford and Gloucester are appointed Protector and Defender of the Realm

   Charles VI dies (October); Henry VI becomes king of France by the Treaty of Troyes

   Charles VII claims the throne of France

1429 Charles VII is crowned king of France at Reims

   Henry VI is crowned king of England at Westminster (6 November)

1430 Margaret of Anjou is born (22 March)

1431 Henry VI is crowned king of France in Paris

1437 Katherine of Valois dies

   Henry VI establishes personal rule

1440 Henry VI founds Eton College

1441 Henry VI founds King's College, Cambridge

1444 Henry VI and Margaret of Anjou are betrothed as part of the Treaty of Tours

1445 Henry VI and Margaret of Anjou are married at Titchfield Abbey (23 April)

   Margaret of Anjou is crowned queen consort at Westminster (30 May)

   English begin surrender of captured territory to French

1447 Richard, Duke of York, is appointed lieutenant of Ireland

1448 English surrender Le Mans to French

1449 English surrender Rouen to French

1450 Cade's Rebellion

   Richard of York returns from Ireland

1451 French capture Bordeaux and English surrender Bayonne

1452 English recover Bordeaux

1453 Henry VI falls ill (August)

   Prince Edward is born (13 October)

1454 Prince Edward is designated Prince of Wales and Earl of Chester (15 March)

   Richard of York is appointed Protector of the Realm (27 March)

   Henry VI recovers (December)

1455   Richard of York resigns as Protector (February)

Henry VI is wounded at first Battle of St. Albans (22 May)

Council declares Henry VI incapacitated (11 November)

Richard of York is again appointed Protector of the Realm
(19 November)

1456   Richard of York resigns as Protector of the Realm (25 February)

1458   Reconciliation of the nobility is celebrated (25 March)

1459   Battle of Blore Heath (23 September)

Battle of Ludford Bridge (12 October)

Parliament convenes at Coventry and declares the York party
traitors (20 November)

1460   Henry VI is captured at the Battle of Northampton (10 July)

Queen Margaret and Prince Edward take refuge in Scotland

Henry VI (imprisoned in the Tower of London) designates the
Duke of York heir to the English throne (31 October)

Duke of York is killed at Battle of Wakefield (30 December)

1461   Battle of Mortimer's Cross (2 February)

Second Battle of St. Albans frees Henry VI, who knights Prince
Edward (17 February)

Edward of York claims crown of England (4 March)

Battle of Towton routs the Lancastrians (29 March)

Henry VI, Queen Margaret, and Prince Edward take refuge near
the Scottish border

Edward of York is crowned as Edward IV (28 June)

Charles VII of France dies; Louis XI accedes to throne of France
(22 July)

1463   Queen Margaret, Prince Edward, and supporters take refuge in
St. Mihiel, France

1465   Henry VI is captured and imprisoned in the Tower of London
(13 July)

1468   Richard Neville, Earl of Warwick, withdraws his support from
Edward IV and goes into exile in France

1470   Warwick joins forces with Margaret of Anjou and Prince Edward
(22 July)

Prince Edward is betrothed to Warwick's daughter, Anne Neville
(25 July)

Warwick's army lands in England (September)

Edward IV goes into exile (September)

Warwick defeats Edward IV's forces and reinstates Henry VI as
    king (3 October)

Prince Edward marries Lady Anne Neville (13 December)

1471   Edward IV returns to England (March)

Edward IV captures Henry VI and reclaims the throne (11 April)

Warwick is killed in the Battle of Barnet (14 April)

Prince Edward is killed in the Battle of Tewkesbury (4 May)

Margaret of Anjou is captured by Edward IV's forces

Henry VI is murdered in the Tower of London (21 May) and is
    buried at Benedictine abbey at Chertsey, Surrey

Margaret of Anjou is imprisoned in the Tower

1472   Margaret of Anjou is released to the custody of Alice Chaucer,
    Dowager Duchess of Suffolk, at Wallingford Castle

1476   Margaret of Anjou returns to France, after ransom by Louis XI
    (January)

1482   Margaret of Anjou dies at Chateau de Dampier, France (25 August),
    and is buried in Angers Cathedral

Codicological Description of New Haven, Yale Law School, Lillian Goldman Law Library MssG +St11 no.1

STRUCTURE

This manuscript has 392 vellum leaves, approximately 180 mm by 250 mm in size. Small holes appear in a few leaves (e.g., fols. 100 and 116). Truncated decoration in the outer and top margins of several leaves resulted from trimming during preparation for binding (plates 1 and 2). One paper pastedown appears at the front of the codex (plate 22). One paper flyleaf and a paper pastedown appear at the end of the codex. Modern pencil leaf numbers appear in the upper-right corners on 389 of the leaves, with 3 leaves missing numbers (between leaves 37 and 38, 64 and 65, and 282 and 283). The leaves of the manuscript are organized into 50 quires with the following structure: $1^{(1+8)}$, $2^{(8)}$ –$42^{(8)}$, $43^{(4-1)}$, $44^{(8)}$–$49^{(8)}$, $50^{(6+2)}$. In the final quire, fols. 383 and 389 are tipped in.

PREPARATION OF THE PAGE

Pricking for ruling remains visible in the bottom of fols. 2–9 (plates 7 and 8), the top of fol. 343 (plate 14), and the top and side margins of fols. 382–89 (plates 16–18). Most leaves during the statutes text show light brown ink ruling for a single column of text, with additional ruling for running heads in the top margin and ruling for regnal year notations in the outer margins (plates 10–13). Pencil ruling for the same layout appears on fols. 222r–224v and 246r–253v. The rulings appear slightly closer together on fols. 230–237. Similar light ink ruling appears during the treatises and subject index that precede the statutes proper (plates 7–9). During the subject index to the statutes, there are also vertical rulings for the subject headings. Up through fol. 381v, the text block is ruled for 38 lines; thereafter, the ruling is darker and less regular, with the number of lines of text varying from 34 to 38 (plates 16–18).

CONTENTS

This manuscript contains several legal texts in Latin and French:

HANDS

Three hands appear in the primary texts of the codex. Scribe A (fols. 2r–8v and 344v–381v) (plates 6–8, 15) and Scribe B (fols. 10r–344v) (plates 1–5, 9–15) use forms of Bastard Anglicana script for the body of the texts and Textura Semi-Quadrata script for headings at the top of the leaves, statute numbers in the margin, and the beginnings of statutes within the text block. The hands of Scribe A and Scribe B have many similarities and may represent work done by two scribes with similar training or by the same scribe at different times. Both hands retain many Anglicana letter forms (such as double-compartment *a*, *d*, and *g*), but show calligraphic treatment of minims. Both hands use long and short forms of *r* and *s*.

Nevertheless, several differences distinguish the two hands. Scribe A's work regularly demonstrates multiple forms for several additional letters: three forms of *v* or initial *u* (plate 8: "vt" in line 13, "vt" in line 30, and "vsque" in the final line), two forms of *w* (plate 6: "Edwardus" in line 1 and "Westminster" in line 11), two forms of *z* (plate 6: "venuz et assemblez" in line 12). Scribe A also regularly uses two forms of *t*, one of which is the split-stem *t* that Malcolm Parkes has associated with the scribe who copied at least parts of ten or more manuscripts of the *Nova statuta Angliae* (Parkes 2008, 44–45) (plate 6: "vnitee" in line 5 and "entierment" in lines 6–7). Scribe A uses only one form of abbreviation for the word *et* in French and Latin, with an approach stroke beginning well below the line of writing (plate 8: "et capient" in line 1 and "et ita" in line 7).

Scribe B uses fewer variations in letter forms: this scribe uses one form of *v* or initial *u* (plate 1: "voluntierment" and "vtlagez" in line 22; plate 9: "vexez" in line 11), one form of *z* (plate 1: "exilez disheritez et banuz" in line 13; plate 9: "saunz" in line 3), and one form of *w* (plate 1: "Edwardus" in lines 9, 20, and 26; plate 9: "allowance" in line 21), though very rarely another form will appear (see plate 5: "Citee Deuerwik" in line 21). Scribe B almost always uses one form of *et* abbreviation that differs from the one used by Scribe A (plate 3: "et de ffraunce" in lines 2–3 and "et concord" in line 6; plate 9: "briefs et" in line 33); but on rare occasions Scribe B uses both forms (plate 4: "Chiualers et Esquiers et autres" in line 21). Scribe B does not use the split-stem form of *t* except in very rare instances (plate 5: "temporelx" in lines 8–9). Initial letters in the headings at the top of some of the leaves copied by Scribe B have additional pen flourishes (plate 11).

During the *Modus tenendi Parliamentum* and *Tractatus de senescalsia Angliae*, Scribe A uses horizontal pairs of points at the outer ends of lines: these points differ from the double-stroke marks noting words that continue on the following line, and the points usually appear when there is also underlining of a word or letters within the line (plates 7 and 8). During the statutes text, Scribe B has sometimes made marginal corrections to the text (e.g., fols. 87*v* and 128*v*). Catchwords remain visible only on fols. 343*v* (plate 14), 351*v*, and 357*v*.

Hand C (fols. 382*r*–389*v*) (plates 16–18) uses a less formal Anglicana script in the body of the statutes, with many cursive elements, reserving a more formal script for the headings at the top of the leaves. Scribe C has a much less regular treatment of the text block on the right side, he does not place statute numbers in the outer margins, and he does not begin each statute with the first words in Textura script, only with a small space left for a paraph. Two notable details that distinguish Scribe C's letter forms from those of the previous hands in the manuscript are *v* with an unusually tall approach stroke (plate 17: "vintisme" in line 3 and "vexacious" in line 9) and *z* with a descender that veers sharply to the right (plate 16: "lez" and "mesmez" in line 21).

DECORATION AND ILLUSTRATION

The decoration and illustration of this codex seem to have been completed through fol. 381*v*, though it is possible that additional decoration might have been planned and not executed for the blank leaves that appear before the opening of the Latin treatises, subject index, and statutes texts. The decoration and illustration contribute to the reader's ability to locate information, as well as adding to the beauty and value of the book.

In the Latin treatises at the beginning of the manuscript, the openings of major sections are marked with gold initials (4–7 lines high) on painted fields divided blue and mauve, with white accents (plates 7 and 8). Sprays with small green leaves, gold pine cones, and small gold and green flowers extend from these initials into the borders of the leaf. Alternating red and blue paraph marks indicate subsections within the treatises. In the index to the statutes, similar gold initials (6 lines high) and sprays mark the first entry for each letter of the alphabet, and similar paraph marks mark each new subject and new statute under each subject (plate 9).

During the text of the statutes through fol. 381*v*, alternating red and blue paraph marks indicate the opening of each new statute, both within the text block and in the outer margins (see plates 2–6 and 10–15). Red and blue paraph marks also precede the headings at the top of each leaf. Occasionally, some of the paraph marks have been omitted, such as on fol. 139*v*.

Line-ending decoration in blue and red appears only during the statutes enacted during the reign of Henry IV (plate 12).

Gold initials five lines high mark the beginning of new parliaments during the statutes text through fol. 381*v*. These initials appear in two styles. The first is similar to the gold initials in the opening treatises and index, with the mauve and blue fields decorated with line designs made with white paint (plate 10). In the second style, found during the first two quires of statutes for

Henry IV, the gold initials have a square black line frame and a thin border in blue or mauve following the shape of the letter; the initials then have their inner spaces filled with blue and mauve fields and acanthus leaves in subtle white shading (plate 12).

The small border sprays that extend from the gold initials marking new sessions of parliament take several forms. The first style has feathery vines with round flowers or leaves in mauve and blue and a few small gold leaves, but the small round leaves have no paint (plate 10). The second style has small green leaves and larger triangular green leaves decorated with gold balls (plate 11). During the statutes for Henry IV (fols. 198r–356v), however, the small gold initials have more compact vine extensions with small green leaves and small flowers made of gold and white balls and penwork, as well as acanthus leaves in green, red, blue, and mauve (plate 12). A fourth style of border spray features vines with small green leaves, larger six-pointed and four-pointed leaves in mauve, blue, red, and green, and small flowers made of gold, green, and white balls (plate 13). The final style has small green leaves and small flowers made of gold and green balls (plate 14).

A large historiated initial, gold frame, and border decoration in paint and gold leaf mark the opening of the statutes for each of the first six reigns included in the manuscript. The historiated initials show the work of three illustrators (Scott 1980a, 46 n. 8): Illustrator A on fols. 55r and 139r; Illustrator B on fols. 198r, 235v, and 261r; and Illustrator C on fol. 358r. Scott has also suggested that each border accompanying an historiated initial was executed by a different border artist.

1. Fol. 55r (Opening of statutes for Edward III) (Plate 1)

This historiated initial is 18 lines high: its top half is blue and its bottom half is mauve, with similar white paint accents on both halves. The initial has a gold frame, with blue and mauve sections highlighted with white between the frame and initial. The scalloped edge of the gold frame is similar to that of the initial for the statutes of Edward III found on fol. 44r of another manuscript of the *Nova statuta Angliae* (Kew, National Archives MS E 164/10), which Kathleen Scott has dated to 1445/46 (Scott 2002, 64 and plate XVIII). The image inside this initial depicts a king kneeling to the left of a *prie-dieu*. The king wears a gold crown and a blue robe with ermine collar and decoration. He has brown hair and a short brown beard with two points. The *prie-dieu* is covered with a red cloth with gold decoration, and an open book lies on top, with the king's gold scepter lying across the book. The king's hands appear to be placed together, as if he is praying. Behind the king is a curtained rectangular green canopy, with red and gold decoration. The floor is green with gold decoration, and the background is red with gold decoration.

A full gold frame extends from the frame of the initial, with corner roundels holding coats of arms within red and gold inner frames: England quartered with France in top-left, Margaret of Anjou in top-right, Elyot in bottom-left, and Delamare in bottom-right. A roundel also appears at the bottom-left corner of the opening initial. Mauve and blue paint vines extending from the historiated initial follow the gold frame and roundels: these vines sprout acanthus leaves in blue, mauve, green, and red, with white paint highlights. Large flowers in mauve, blue, and red, with green stalks, sprout from the vines at the center of the right and bottom parts of the frame. Feathery sprays extend from some of the flowers and acanthus leaves. The sprays have unpainted small leaves, small flowers made of gold and unpainted balls, gold trefoil leaves, kidney-shaped and four-lobed painted leaves in blue and mauve with white highlights, and flowers with petals in blue and mauve with white highlights. The unpainted small leaves link these sprays to the ones that appear with the small gold initials in this section of the statutes (plate 10).

2. Fol. 139r (Opening of statutes for Richard II) (Plate 2)

This initial is 17 lines in height. Its top half is blue and its bottom half is mauve, both with white paint decoration. This initial has a gold bar frame, and the spaces between the letter and frame are filled with blue, mauve, or green paint. Inside the initial is a scene very similar to the one in the first historiated initial, except that the king's robe shows ermine ornament in the lower portion, and his right hand appears to be resting on the book open on the *prie-dieu* and also holding his gold scepter over his right shoulder. The red cloth on the *prie-dieu* also has a different gold design.

The gold frame of the historiated initial links to a full gold frame similar to that on fol. 55r, except that only two corners have roundels with coats of arms (England quartered with France on the left, the arms of Margaret of Anjou on the right), and a third roundel appears at the center of the bottom part of the frame, with the arms of the Elyot family. Blue and mauve vines extend from the initial and follow the gold frame. An extension of the gold frame at the center of the right side provides the field for entwined vines and acanthus leaves, and clusters of acanthus leaves make up right and left lower corner motifs. Feathery sprays extend from the gold frame into the borders of the leaf: the sprays include small green leaves and larger leaves of several shapes in blue, mauve, green, and red, accented with white or gold. The sprays are also decorated with small gold balls, leaves, and pine cones, as well as aroid flowers in blue, mauve, green, and red, accented with white.

3. Fol. 198r (Opening of statutes for Henry IV) (Plate 3)

This historiated initial is 18 lines high and divided into two mauve and two blue parts, each with white paint shading and decoration similar to that in the previous two initials. This initial differs from the previous two, however, in having a rectangular gold field surrounding it and acanthus leaves that intertwine with its top portion. Within the initial is an image of a kneeling king similar to the images in the previous two initials. In this case, however, the king's blue robe, the red fabric cover of the *prie-dieu,* and the green fabric of the canopy have additional gold and white designs. The king's gold scepter remains over his right shoulder; but the king's left hand holds the open book on the *prie-dieu,* and his right points to the book. In addition, a male figure in a red robe with ermine collar and decoration looks on from behind the curtain of the green canopy. A white mark is just visible on the left shoulder of this figure's robe, suggesting a stripe.

The gold field of the historiated initial links to a full gold frame that is followed by intertwining blue and mauve vines that emanate from the initial. This frame is similar to the previous frames, except that roundels with framed coats of arms only appear in the upper corners (the arms of England quartered with France on the left, the arms of Margaret of Anjou on the right). Vine and acanthus leaf clusters in mauve, blue, green, and red appear on gold fields at the bottom corners of the frame. Similar vine and acanthus leaf clusters on gold fields also appear at the mid-points of the left and right sections of the frame, and the arms of the Elyot family seem to have been painted over part of a flower at the center of the bottom section of the frame. Sprays extend from the gold frame into the margin on all four sides. Most of the small leaves have green paint, but some have been left empty. The sprays also have small gold leaves, gold trefoils, flowers made of small gold balls with unpainted balls and curlicues, and gold pine cones, as well as larger leaves and flowers in blue, mauve, green, and red, with gold or white highlighting.

4. Fol. 235v (Opening of statutes for Henry V) (Plate 4)

This historiated initial is 17 lines high, with its top half blue and its bottom half mauve, similar to the first two historiated initials. Like the initial on fol. 198r, however, this initial has a rectangular gold field surrounding it. Within the initial is a scene very similar to the previous image, except that the king's hands are joined in prayer and the red-robed figure now stands to the right of the king, behind the *prie-dieu*, with his arms extended toward the king, as if addressing him. This figure's robe has no white stripe on its left sleeve, but it does have additional ermine decoration.

As in the previous cases, the gold frame of this historiated initial is linked to a full gold bar-frame for the page, with blue and mauve vines that emanate from the initial and follow the gold bar-frame around the page. In this case, however, the frame includes only one roundel, in the upper-left corner, and this roundel has no inner frame or coat of arms, only acanthus leaves. Clusters of acanthus leaves on gold fields serve as the other three cornerpieces. Another gold field with an acanthus-leaf cluster and a large flower decorates the center of the bottom section of the frame. Feathery sprays emanate from the gold frame on all four sides, with small green leaves, small gold balls (some with green-painted curlicues), and gold pine cones, as well as larger mauve, blue, green, and red leaves in several shapes.

5. Fol. 261r (Opening of statutes for Henry VI) (Plate 5)

This initial is 18 lines tall, with its top half blue with white highlights and its bottom half mauve with white highlights, like most of the previous large initials. A narrow gold frame follows the outline of the initial. The image inside the initial, which is partially disrupted by the crossbar of the letter (A), shows a scene similar to the previous ones, but with some important differences. The king in this image is beardless, his hair is a lighter brown, and he wears an enclosed crown topped with a cross. He holds his scepter over his right shoulder, but his hands are placed together in prayer. The king's blue robe has no gold decoration, but has additional white accents. One figure in an ermine-decorated red robe with white horizontal stripes on his left sleeve stands to the right of the king's *prie-dieu*: he faces right, away from the king, with both hands raised. Immediately behind this figure, the head of another figure with a similar ermine collar and hairstyle is visible. In the top-right corner of the scene is a blue semi-circle with the outlines of a face in white and black, similar to images of the face of God in the heavens. The gold decoration in the red background in this initial shows lines emanating from the blue semi-circle.

The gold frame of this initial is linked to a three-quarter gold frame, extending around the left, bottom, and right sides of the page. Mauve and blue vines with acanthus leaves in blue, mauve, green, and red emanate from the initial itself and follow the gold frame, creating a roundel of acanthus leaves on a scalloped gold field in the lower-left corner of the frame. Clusters of acanthus leaves on scalloped gold fields also appear at the upper-left and lower-right corners of the frame, at the top end of the right side of the frame, and at the center of the right side of the frame. Feathery sprays also emanate from the gold frame into all four sides of the borders of the page. The sprays have small green leaves, four-pointed gold leaves, gold pine cones, and gold balls (some with green-painted curlicues), as well as acanthus leaves and flowers (aroid and round) in mauve, blue, green, and red paint. The coat of arms of the Elyot family has been painted over the border decoration at the center of the bottom frame.

6. Fol. 358r (*Opening of statutes for Edward IV*) (Plate 6)

This historiated initial is 11 lines high and is painted in blue with white shading and accents similar to the previous initials. The initial lies on a rectangular gold field. Within the initial is an image with significant differences from the previous initials, in terms of style and content. This scene is similar to the one described by Kathleen Scott as the standardized king-and-court scene that became widespread from the 1470s through the end of the century (Scott 1980a, 46, 49–50). At center sits a king facing forward between two groups of standing courtiers: tonsures and crosiers identify the group to the king's right as members of the clergy, while the group at his left appear to be secular lords. Most members of each group wear a red robe with white collar, but some have mauve or blue capes and some have ermine ornaments on their clothing. The foremost member of each group holds a scroll. One member of the secular lords has blond hair in a curled style. The hair of the other courtiers has light brown or black shading, and none wears a beard. All the faces in the image appear to have gray shading. The king is beardless and his hair appears to be white. His crown is gold and red. He wears a blue cape with ermine collar and lining, and underneath this he wears a red and gold robe, with ermine ornament at the edges of his sleeves. In his left hand, the king holds an upright sword, and his right hand points to the sword. The king sits on a brown-colored bench, on top of a light brown dais and below a green canopy with a short red and gold curtain around the top. The little background that is visible is red with gold decoration. The crossbar of the blue and white initial extends partway into the scene on both sides.

The gold field of the initial links to a full gold frame for the page. Blue and mauve vines with white highlights do not emanate from the initial, but follow the gold frame around the page, intertwining with the top of the initial at one point. Small clusters of acanthus leaves in green, blue, mauve, and red appear on gold extensions at the four corners of the frame, as well as at the centers of the right and bottom sides of the frame. The coat of arms of the Elyot family has been painted over the acanthus leaf cluster at the bottom of the frame. Feathery sprays extend from the gold frame, but these curve much less than the sprays in the previous borders. The sprays are decorated with small green leaves, small flowers made of gold balls with three small green balls, and gold pine cones, as well as larger flowers in blue, mauve, and red and leaves of different shapes (including heart-shaped) in blue, mauve, green, and red. The aroid flowers in the right margin are similar to the aroid flowers in the right margin of fol. 261r.

BINDING

The manuscript has a rebacked, sixteenth-century, dark brown leather binding over oak boards (see plates 23–24). The leather and wood of the front and back covers have become chipped and worn in many places. The older parts of the binding are blind-stamped, and an attempt was made to match the decoration on the new part of the back cover after the binding was repaired. At center on both covers is a quartered but empty shield surmounted by a crown. Surrounding the shield on each cover are multiple rectangular frames with foliage flourishes at the outer corners. Fleurs-de-lis appear at the inner corners of the innermost frame. One of the outer frames is filled with a diagonally striated design, while one of the inner frames is filled with a floral pattern, alternating large and small flowers. Remnants of two leather straps remain on the front cover, with two metal clasp holders remaining on the back cover.

ADDITIONS TO THE MANUSCRIPT

Many leaves contain marginal notes in Latin and Law French that suggest active readership of the manuscript for several centuries after its initial production. For example, a reader has added "de Hibernicis" ("on Ireland") in the margin on fol. 284*v*, and there are two pen drawings in the right margin of fol. 286*r*. A reader has also noted the incomplete ending of the statutes on fol. 389*v*, writing "hic desunt" ("here they fail") (plate 18). During the subject index to the statutes, a reader has added a symbol made up of two short parallel lines crossed diagonally by a third short line next to several entries, but no significant pattern emerges: this symbol appears next to the entries for war, petitions to the king, poundage, salaries for priests and chaplains, prohibitions, taxes, and the city of Winchester. Nevertheless, several inscriptions in the manuscript do offer concrete clues about its later ownership.

1. Fols. 6*r* (plate 19) and 235*r* (plate 20) – To the right of the chapter heading "De Stacionibus Loquencium in Parliament" ("Concerning the Standing of Speakers in Parliament") in the Latin treatise on holding Parliament (within the text block), there is a Middle English inscription in a late fifteenth-century Bastard Anglicana hand: "Grace be oure gide F" ("Grace be our guide F"). The same Middle English phrase appears next to a heading later in the statutes, "Incipiunt statuta apud Westminster edita anno primo Regis Henrici Quinti" ("Here begin the statutes issued at Westminster in the first year of King Henry the Fifth"). The hand in this inscription is similar to the hand of the earlier inscription; but the inscriber of the second phrase has used Secretary forms of the letters *g* and *d*, and the letter at the end of the Middle English phrase takes a different form, looking more like an *I* or an *L*, or possibly an *F* with its top stroke missing. The hands in these inscriptions are smaller than the hands of the primary texts in the manuscript, and the letter forms do not match any of the hands of the primary texts in the manuscript. Since the phrases also do not take a traditional form for scribal signatures, but seem more like a motto, the phrases might be inscriptions of ownership, perhaps by two members of the same family, or comments on the text by one or two readers.

2. Fols. 55*r*, 139*r*, 198*r*, 261*r*, and 358*r* (plates 1–3, 5, and 6) – On fol. 55*r*, a late fifteenth-century hand has written "Arma Elyot" and "arma delamare" below the coats of arms that have been added in the bottom roundels in the border decoration. The same hand has written "Arma Elyot" or "Elyot" under the coat of arms added in the bottom part of the border decoration on fols. 139*r*, 198*r*, 261*r*, and 358*r*. The added coats of arms and inscriptions suggest that the manuscript was owned by Sir Richard Elyot (d. 1522) and his wife, Lady Alice Delamare.

3. Fol. 1*r* (plate 21) – The first folio of the manuscript contains several early ownership inscriptions:

    a) A seventeenth-century inscription at the top of the leaf states, "Liber Rogeri Nichols Interioris Templi precium vi s. viii d. Anno Domini 1614" ("The book of Roger Nichols of Inner Temple, price 6 shillings 8 pence in the year of our Lord 1614"), followed by two or three more illegible words. Roger Nichols of

Willen, Buckinghamshire, was admitted to Inner Temple in November 1604 (Cooke 1877, 100) and called to the bar in 1613–14 (Inderwick 1898, 78).

b) A sixteenth-century inscription below this states, "Liber Georgi Frevyle armigeri, ex dono domine Margarete Elyot vidue post mortem Ricardi Elyot militis defunct quondam viri sui" ("The book of George Frevyle esquire, a gift from Lady Margaret Elyot, widow, after the death of her former husband Richard Elyot, knight"). Sir George Freville (d. 1579) was a Cambridgeshire lawyer and member of the Middle Temple who served as a justice of the peace for Cambridgeshire from 1539 until his death.[1] He represented Preston in Parliament in 1547 and was retained as counsel to the duchy of Lancaster from 1548. He served as third baron of the exchequer in 1559 and rose to second baron in 1564. Freville's inscription helps verify the earliest documented ownership of the manuscript, by Sir Richard Elyot. Freville's inscription is incorrect, however, in identifying Lady Margaret Elyot as Richard's wife. Dame Margaret Elyot was the wife of Sir Thomas Elyot, the son of Richard Elyot and his wife Alice Delamare. Margaret Elyot may have received the book as a gift from her father-in-law or from her husband. She served as executrix of her husband's will when he died in 1546 (Lehmberg 1960, 196).

c) Another sixteenth-century inscription, partially defaced, follows: "This booke [three lines defaced] mongest other bookes at her howse at Totenham High Crosse. 1581. Mense Augusti" ("This book . . . amongst other books at her house at Tottenham High Cross. 1581. The month of August"). Unfortunately, the identity of the woman whose ownership is attested by this inscription remains hidden, as well as that of the person who owned the book after her.

d) Below this, there is another defaced inscription, followed by "September 1633."

4. Front paste-down (plate 22) – Several more records of ownership are on the front paste-down:

a) Centered near the top is "Sir Thomas Winnington, Baronet" in pencil. This Sir Thomas Winnington might be the third baronet of Stanford Court, Worcestershire (1780–1839), or Sir Thomas Edward Winnington, fourth baronet of Stanford Court (1811–72).[2] Alfred J. Horwood lists a fifteenth-century manuscript of the *Modus tenendi Parliamentum* and a fifteenth-century manuscript of the *Nova statuta Angliae* with illuminated initials in the library of Sir Thomas Edward Winnington at Stanford Court, though the description indicates that the second manuscript contains the statutes from 1 Edward III to 1 Edward IV (Horwood 1870, 53). Sir Thomas Edward Winnington was succeeded by his son, Sir Francis Salwey Winnington, fifth baronet, who died in 1931. The manuscript was sold by the estate of Sir Francis Salwey Winnington through Hodgson and Company on 26 May 1932 (Hodgson and Company 1932, lot no. 463; Baker 1985, 74).

b) Below this is written "#10851" in pencil.

c) Centered on the page is a Yale Law Library bookplate indicating purchase with funding established by John Hoober in honor of Arthur Woodburne Chambers.

d) At the bottom of the page, in pencil, is Yale Law Library's shelf number: "Gr. Brit. Laws, statutes, etc. Collections / Statuta angliae nova / MssG / St 11 / no. 1."

5. Back paste-down – A modern hand has noted the Yale Law Library purchase in pencil: "55-1 / Chambers Trust / Jan. 4, 1955."

PROVENANCE

No direct evidence about commission of the manuscript, its scribes or artists, or its presentation as a gift remains in the original text of this manuscript. From the manuscript's contents and connections with other copies of the *Nova statuta Angliae*, however, it seems clear that the Yale manuscript was produced in the London area in the third quarter of the fifteenth century. From the evidence of the additions to the manuscript, moreover, the owners of the manuscript can be documented from at least the beginning of the sixteenth century through the twenty-first, with only a few gaps. Sir Richard Elyot, who may have owned the book before the death of his first wife Alice Delamare in 1510, gave it to Sir Thomas Elyot and/or Lady Margaret Elyot by 1522. Lady Margaret Elyot gave the book to Sir George Freville, probably shortly after the death of her husband Sir Thomas in 1546. By 1581, the book belonged to a woman who lived near Tottenham High Crosse, but her name has been defaced. The next known owner is Roger Nichols, who purchased the book in 1614. By 1633, the book apparently had a new owner, but that person's inscription has also been defaced.

The next known owner of the manuscript is Sir Thomas Winnington, baronet of Stanford Court; but it is unclear whether this is the third baronet (d. 1839) or the fourth (d. 1872). Both of these men were antiquarians, as well as lawyers and politicians. It may be that the manuscript passed into the family's ownership as early as the time of Sir Francis Winnington (1634–1700), who purchased Stanford Court.[3] The manuscript seems to have been in the Winnington collection at Stanford Court by 1862, when it was exhibited during a meeting of the Archaeological Institute of Great Britain and Ireland; the manuscript was also at Stanford Court in 1870, when Horwood made his report for the Royal Commission on Historical Manuscripts (Archaeological Institute 1862, 393; Horwood 1870, 53). If the manuscript was physically at Stanford Court in December 1882, we are very lucky to have it at all, since some of the rare books and manuscripts in that library were destroyed in a fire that month.[4]

After the sale by Sir Francis Salwey Winnington's estate in 1932, the manuscript passed through several hands before it arrived at Yale Law School: the manuscript was sold through Sotheby's on 1 August 1933 and again on 12 April 1938 (Sotheby Auction House 1933, lot no. 427; Sotheby Auction House 1938, lot no. 312; and Baker 1985, 74). Yale Law School purchased the manuscript through C. A. Stonehill in 1955. It is now housed in the Paskus-Danziger Rare Book Room of the Lillian Goldman Law Library.

SUMMARY TABLE

Quire	Foliation	Contents, Scribes, Illustrators, and Comments
1	1–9	Fols. 2r–7r: *Modus tenendi Parliamentum* (Scribe A). Fol. 1 (blank except for added inscriptions) tipped in before four bifolia. Fols. 7r–8v: *De senescalsia Angliae* (Scribe A) Fols. 9r–v blank.
2	10–17	Fol. 10r: Subject index for *Nova statuta Angliae* begins (Scribe B).
3	18–25	
4	26–33	
5	34–40	
6	41–48	
7	49–54	Fols. 53v–54v blank.
8	55–62	Fol. 55r: *Nova statuta Angliae* for Edward III begin (Scribe B). Historiated initial (Illustrator A)
9	63–69	
10	70–77	
11	78–85	
12	86–93	
13	94–101	
14	102–109	
15	110–117	
16	118–125	
17	126–133	
18	134–141	Fol. 139r: *Nova statuta Angliae* for Richard II begin (Scribe B). Historiated initial (Illustrator A)
19	142–149	
20	150–157	
21	158–165	
22	166–173	

Quire	Foliation	Contents, Scribes, Illustrators, and Comments
23	174–181	
24	182–189	
25	190–197	
26	198–205	Fol. 198r: *Nova statuta Angliae* for Henry IV begin (Scribe B). Historiated initial (Illustrator B)
27	206–213	
28	214–221	
29	222–229	
30	230–237	Fol. 235v: *Nova statuta Angliae* for Henry V begin (Scribe B). Historiated initial (Illustrator B)
31	238–245	
32	246–253	
33	254–261	Fol. 261r: *Nova statuta Angliae* for Henry VI begin (Scribe B). Historiated initial (Illustrator B)
34	262–269	
35	270–277	
36	278–284	
37	285–292	
38	293–300	
39	301–308	
40	309–316	
41	317–324	
42	325–332	
43	333–335	Fols. 334v–335v blank (two bifolia, with leaf removed).
44	336–343	(Catchword on fol. 343v)
45	344–351	(Scribe A begins again midway on fol. 344v) (Catchword on fol. 351v)
46	352–357	Fol. 357r–v blank (except for catchword on fol. 357v).
47	358–365	Fol. 358r: *Nova statuta Angliae* for Edward IV begin (Scribe A). Historiated initial (Illustrator C)
48	366–373	
49	374–381	
50	382–389	Fols. 382r–389v: Scribe C (no rubrication, decoration, or illustration)
		Fol. 386r: *Nova statuta Angliae* for Richard III begin.
		(Three bifolia plus two tipped-in leaves: fols. 383 and 389)

Notes

INTRODUCTION

1. The manuscript's shelf mark is MssG +StII no.1. The *New Statutes* text has this title to distinguish it from texts presenting laws enacted prior to 1327, which are called the *Old Statutes* (*Statuta antiqua* or *Vetera statuta*). See Pronay and Taylor 1980, 18–19.

2. For the earliest published discussions, see Horwood 1870, 53; Hodgson and Company 1932, lot no. 463 and accompanying plate; Sotheby Auction House 1933, 56–57, lot 427 and accompanying plate; Sotheby Auction House 1938, lot 312 and accompanying plate; and Faye and Bond 1962, no. 20.

3. A preliminary version of parts of this analysis appeared in McGerr 2006. New information in this study allows for a more detailed assessment of the manuscript's production, intertextual relationships, and significance.

4. Bakhtin's theories about heteroglossia and the carnivalesque nature of the novel have been translated from Russian into English in several forms: see Bakhtin 1981, 1984, and 1993.

5. Van Gennep's 1909 landmark work *Les rites de passage* (translated into English as van Gennep 1960) greatly influenced the theories of Victor Turner (see Turner 1969).

6. Much has been written about the definition, origins, battles, and leaders of the so-called "Wars of the Roses": see, for example, Wolffe 1981, Carpenter 1997, R. Griffiths 1981, and Lander 2007. See appendix 1 for a chronology of important dates.

7. See, for example, Lawton 1987, Patterson 1993, Pearsall 1994, Strohm 1998, and Nuttall 2007.

8. See Walker 2004. Griffiths begins his study of Henry VI with an introduction subtitled "The Making of a Reputation" (R. Griffiths 1981, 1–8).

9. Richard Firth Green also discusses John Lydgate's role as an apologist for Henry VI's monarchy: see Green 1980, 186–90.

10. See Binski 1995 and 1999, Stanton 2001, and Scheifele 1999.

11. Recent reassessments of Margaret's role include Maurer 2003 and Laynesmith 2004.

12. For a detailed discussion of this passage, see chapter 3.

13. A presentation manuscript of Fortescue's *De laudibus legum Angliae* has not been identified, but the text takes the

form of a Latin dialogue with the prince: see Chrimes 1942 and Gross 1996. Edward IV's history book is now London, British Library MS Royal 15 E iv. On the concurrent use of Latin, French, and English in literature in England during the fourteenth and fifteenth centuries, see Yeager 2000 and Petrina 2004, 72–90.

14. On the concurrent use of French, English, and Latin as languages of legal record in the fourteenth and fifteenth centuries, see Fisher 1996, 26–35, 43–46; Ormrod 2003; and Giancarlo 2007, 218–21.

15. See Skemer 1999, 113. Manuscript copies of the *Nova statuta* in English include Cambridge, Cambridge University Library MS Ff. 3. 1; London, British Library MS Additional 81292; London, British Library MS Harley 4999; Nottingham, Nottingham University Library, Willoughby Family Papers MS Mi L 2/2; and Oslo and London, Martin Schøyen Collection MS 1355. For *Nova statuta* manuscripts in which the language of the statutes begins as French and changes to English, see London, British Library MS Additional 15728 and London, Lincoln's Inn Library MS Hale 183.

16. See Scott 1980a, 45–59, 66–68; and Scott 1989, 32–34. Don Skemer argues that most of the surviving copies of the *Nova statuta* manuscripts were made during Henry VI's reign, but the high point in *Nova statuta* production was probably the third quarter of the fifteenth century (Skemer 1999, 130).

17. On Henry IV's writ, see Strohm 1998, 40–45; for the writ's text, see Given-Wilson 2005, 8:109. See also Giancarlo's reading of Thomas Paunfield's 1414 petition to Parliament, which allegorizes

his opponent (Giancarlo 2007, 222–28), and Nuttall's reading of the exchange of documents between Commons and Henry IV in January 1401, in which both sides use metaphors to associate financial credit and political loyalty (Nuttall 2007, 98–99).

18. See, for example, the discussions by Berges 1938, Genet 1977, Green 1980, Nederman 1998, Briggs 1999, and Grassnick 2006.

19. See also Harriss 1985; Patterson 1993; Pearsall 1994; Watts 1996, 16–39; Fletcher 2004; and Grassnick 2006.

20. See Nuttall 2007, 27.

I. THE YALE *NEW STATUTES* MANUSCRIPT AND MEDIEVAL ENGLISH STATUTE BOOKS

1. A full presentation of the physical details of the manuscript appears in appendix 2.

2. See Scott 1980a, 45–49, 66–68; 1980b; 1989, 32–34; and 1996, 2:300, 346, 354.

3. See, for example, Robinson 2003, 57; and Parkes 2008, 45n.

4. Before his untimely death, Jeremy Griffiths proposed linking the Yale scribe to other manuscripts of the *Nova statuta*, as well as manuscripts of other texts. He generously communicated some of his findings in correspondence with me.

5. See Skemer 1999, 121; and Elton 1979, 1–2.

6. See also Skemer's discussion of reference to archival copies of statutes (Skemer 1999, 120–22).

7. Ker describes the hands used in several manuscripts of the *New Statutes* as "legal anglicana" (Ker 1969–2002, l:19, 87).

8. For the text of the treatise and a list of surviving manuscripts, see Pronay and Taylor 1980, 67–91, 202–209.

9. See, for example, J. Taylor 1968, Pronay and Taylor 1974, and Weber 1998.

10. For the text of this treatise, see Harcourt 1907, 164–67.

11. On the decoration of manuscripts of the older statutes, see the evidence provided in A. Bennett 1986, especially 1–4.

12. On Plimpton 273, see Baker 1985, 5. On Petyt 505, see Davies 1972, 176–79.

13. On Lansdowne 468, see Ellis and Douce 1819, no. 468. On Additional 81292, a Middle English translation of the *New Statutes*, see the description and two plates in Christie Auction House 2005, lot 19, and the report on the manuscript in Baker 2006, 208. Three Latin inscriptions indicate that the manuscript was owned by Sir William Coote of Coningsby, Lincolnshire, a lawyer and Lancastrian loyalist. Because this copy ends with the statutes for 20 Henry VI (1441–42), it may have been made shortly thereafter; but the limitation of the contents may just represent the extent of the English translation available to the copyist, since English versions of the statutes appear to have been unusual.

14. On Carson LC 14. 10, see Baker 1985, 60. On the Harvard Law School Library manuscripts, see Baker 1985, 16, 21, 24, 33. On Lansdowne 470, see Ellis and Douce 1819, 130. On National Archives MS E 164/10, see Scott 2002, 64 and plate XVIII.

15. Unfortunately, nothing is known about the ownership of this manuscript until the seventeenth century. See British Museum 1834–40, 96–97.

16. See Baker 1985, 28, 36.

17. This manuscript may therefore be a presentation copy for Richard II. See Sandler 1986, no. 156; Robinson 1988, 1:85, no. 291, and 2: plate 174; and Binski and Panayotova 2005, no. 134.

18. Though the leaf with the opening of Edward III's reign has been removed, traces of its decoration remain on the verso of the previous leaf. See Dutschke 1989 and Scott 1996, 1: plates 80, 82, 83, and 2: plates 84, 85.

19. On Stowe 389, see British Museum 1895–96, 1: no. 389. On Harvard Law School Library MS 21, see Baker 1985, 18.

20. On Hale 194, see Hunter 1838, 150–51; Ker 1969–2002, 1:140; Scott 1980a, 67; Scott 1996, 2:300, 346, 354; and Robinson 2003, 1: no. 107 and 2: plate 156. MS Yates Thompson 48 is not included in the published catalogues of this collection, since Yates Thompson purchased it in 1924, after the catalogues were published. According to the British Library's website, MS 48 was given to the British Library by Mrs. Yates Thompson in 1941 (http://www.bl.uk/catalogues/illuminatedmanuscripts/record.asp?MS ID=6503&CollID=58&NStart=48).

21. On Harley 5233, see Wright 1972, 87–88.

22. On Carson LC 14. 9.5, see Scott 1980a, 46; and Baker 1985, 59–60. On MS E 164/11, see Scott 2002, 110–13 and plates XXXVIIa and XXXVIIb. On Holkham Hall MS 232, see Scott 1980a, 47–48, and Scott 1996, 2:347, 354. On Cotton Nero C i, see Scott 1980a, 47; and Pronay and Taylor 1974, 14–15. On Hargrave 274, see Scott 1980a, 66–67; and Scott 1996, 1: plates 479–80, and 2:347. London, British Library MS Lansdowne 522 has all six of its large initials

cut out, which suggests that they were historiated; but it is not clear whether the manuscript used the standardized image in any or all of its initials (Scott 1980a, 67).

23. On Hatton 10, see Bodleian Library 1967, 40–41 and plate V; Pächt and Alexander 1973, 3: no. 1168 and plates CVIIa–d; and Scott 1980a, 47.

24. On Richardson 40, see Scott 1980a, 66; Wieck 1983, 96 and plate; and Baker 1985, 39. On St. John's College MS 257, see Scott 1980a, 68.

25. On Sir Thomas Fitzwilliam and the heraldic iconography of the Fitzwilliam *New Statutes* manuscript, see Higgins 1900–1901, with plates showing four initials; and Sotheby Auction House 1958, with a plate showing one initial. The manuscript was once owned by William Morris and then became part of the Dyson Perrins Collection, before being sold at Sotheby Auction House on 9 December 1958. The manuscript's current location is unknown. Fitzwilliam was a member of Inner Temple (Baker 1999, 422; Baker 2003, 505).

26. On MS Hale 71, see Ker 1969–2002, 1:126; Baker 2002, 505; and Robinson 2003, 1:57, 64, and 2: plates 219, 220, 226, and 227. Like Thomas Fitzwilliam, Adgore was a member of Inner Temple.

27. See, for example, Scott's discussion of the influence of patrons on the illustration of fifteenth-century English manuscripts (Scott 1989, 19–63).

28. See Scott 1980a, 47; and Baker 1985, 54. The *Modus* was also sometimes copied with other legal texts that have been found bound together, as well as in statutes books: for example, San Marino, Huntington Library MS EL 35 B 61 contains copies of the English corona-

tion rite and the *Modus*, with matching initials and border decoration. This manuscript includes space left for a coat of arms in the border decoration of the first leaf of each treatise, suggesting that it was made on speculation and the purchaser would then have his or her arms painted in (Baker 1985, 41).

29. On the Metropolitan Archives MS (*olim* Corporation of London, Guildhall, "Cartae Antiquae"), see Scott 1996, 1: plates 481–83, and 2:346.

30. Jeremy Griffiths believed that he had found this same scribe's work in at least ten additional manuscripts, but his identifications have not yet been verified by other paleographers, except for London, Lincoln's Inn Library MS Hale 71. See also Scott 1980a, 46–48.

31. Ker's original list (Ker 1969–2002, 1:18–19, 87, 140, 190) did not include the Yale Law School manuscript.

32. Robinson argues that MS Hale 194 is the product of a single scribe who is not the scribe of MS Petyt 505 (Robinson 2003, 1:58, and 2: plate 156).

33. According to Scott, these two manuscripts share another illustrator, who executed initials on fols. 98, 131, 153*v*, and 168*v* in Hale 194 and one on fol. 236*v* in the Metropolitan Archives MS.

34. Gross 1996, 39. For example, the capture of agents bearing letters from the Lancastrians in France in 1468 led to arrests, imprisonments, torture, and executions (see Kekewich et al. 1995, 88–92).

35. On some leaves, one of the two shields has been filled in with the same coat of arms (fols. 147*v*, 162*v*, 222*v*), but all the others remain blank.

36. Robinson 1988, 1:85; Baker and Ringrose 1996; and Binski and Panayotova 2005, no. 134.

37. The additional coats of arms include those of Sir John Holme of Paull-Holme, Yorkshire (d. 1438), and either his wife, Elizabeth Wastneys, or their son, John, who served as baron of the exchequer in 1446–49 (Dutschke 1989).

2. ROYAL PORTRAITS AND ROYAL ARMS

1. On the history of coats of arms, see Woodcock and Robinson 1988.

2. For a discussion of the illustration of this prayer roll by the London artist William Abell, see Alexander 1972, 166–72; and Scott 1996, 2:264, 266–68.

3. Information about this psalter's origins and extensive use of heraldic imagery can be found in Sandler 2003, 221–32.

4. See, for instance, Boos 2004, 8, 14; and Wagner 1950, 73.

5. For example, Jane Hayward makes this argument in her comments about the Yale Law School manuscript in the catalogue for an exhibit in which the manuscript appeared at the Cloisters Museum: see Hayward 1975, 142–43.

6. See the accounts in Wolffe 1981, 180–83; Maurer 2003, 17–23; and Laynesmith 2004, 74–86.

7. See Mandach 1974a and 1974b, and Bossy 1998.

8. On Lancastrian depictions of Richard's *demerita notoria*, see Nuttall 2007, 1–16.

9. See also Walker 2004.

10. London, British Library MS Additional 18002, which traces the kings of England from Noah to Henry VI, is thought to have been compiled in 1422, the year Henry VI inherited the throne from his father. London, British Library MS Additional 29504 depicts Henry VI's descent from the Anglo-Saxon king Athelstan and was made around the time of Henry VI's coronation in 1429. London, British Library MS Additional 21058, which was made in 1453, the year in which Henry VI's son was born, traces Henry VI's heritage back to the British king Constans in 446. Winchester, Winchester College Library MS 13B was also made shortly after Prince Edward's birth and traces Henry's ancestry to Adam and Eve. Another roll that begins with Noah (London, British Library MS Royal 14 B viii) was made in 1454 or shortly after, since it includes Henry VI's son and refers to him as Prince of Wales.

11. On the ambivalent nature of Lancastrian texts, see also Patterson 1993, 95.

12. On the *Brut* continuations in the fifteenth century, see Gransden 1996, 220–48; and Matheson 1998, 8–29. When Henry VI was two, his uncle, the duke of Bedford, commissioned a French poem from Laurence Calot about Henry's inheritance of the two crowns, with a painting of the young king's pedigree that may be the source for the genealogy of Henry VI in London, British Library MS Royal 15 E vi, as well as Cambridge, Cambridge University Library MS Ll. v. 20. See Rowe 1933; McKenna 1965, 151–52; and Patterson 1993, 89–92.

13. Lydgate's poem survives in more than thirty manuscripts. It addresses an English audience, but has links to Lydgate's translation of Calot's French poem on Henry VI's claim to the French and English thrones. See Mooney 1989.

14. This copy of Hardyng's chronicle includes a dedication to Henry VI and illustrations of the kings. The copy in

London, British Library MS Harley 661 gives the genealogical descent of the English kings from St. Louis, with a prose explanation of their right to the French crown. See Edwards 1987, 75, 83; Scott 1996, 2:206, 218–19, and fig. 1; and Gransden 1996, 276–77.

15. Brown 2003, 233. The other works of Lancastrian art Brown sees as part of this group are stained glass windows at All Souls College in Oxford and at St. Mary's Hall in Coventry and the statues of kings on the *pulpitum* in Christ Church Cathedral in Canterbury. There has been much debate on the dating of the York screen. Some scholars argue that the statues on the screen were planned to celebrate Henry V's victory at Agincourt in 1415, with seven kings on each side; but Henry V's death in 1422 led the planners to add Henry VI, requiring eight kings on the right side. Other scholars argue that the fact that the statue of Henry VI holds a book suggests it was made in the late 1440s, after Henry VI founded Eton and King's College, Cambridge, but the statue of Henry VI now on display is a nineteenth-century replacement: the original statue of Henry VI may have been removed because it became an object of veneration when miracles were ascribed to the deposed king after his death in 1471. See also Vallance 1947, 83–88, fig. 14; and Bond 1908, 156.

16. See, for instance, the thirteenth-century manuscripts discussed in Collard 2007.

17. Scott 1980a, 45–59, 66–68; Scott 1980b, 103–105; Scott 1989, 32–34; Scott 1996, 2:300, 345–46, 354; and J. Griffiths 1980 and personal correspondence.

18. This manuscript was in the pos-session of Edward IV's brother Richard of Gloucester before he became Richard III in 1483, but we don't know when it arrived in England.

19. See Scott 1996, 2:101, 135, 204. This illustration comes at the opening of the Book of Wisdom, so it probably depicts King Solomon. The illustration that opens the Book of Ecclesiastes depicts an enthroned king holding orb and scepter, but without advisors (fol. 163*v*).

20. On the striped sleeves worn by medieval lawyers, see Hodges 2000, 112–19. On bars of white miniver on red robes as the ceremonial attire of dukes, earls, and barons in Parliament, see Butt 1989, 265; and Pollard 1920, 382.

21. William of Malmesbury 1998, book 2, section 162.

22. See, for instance, Pearsall 1994, 389; Grassnick 2006, 171; and Nuttall 2007, 3–4.

23. Prudence's precepts on choosing royal counselors lead her to advise seeking justice through law, rather than war. See the comments by Scanlon 2007, 211–14. On discussions of choosing wise counselors in other mirrors for princes and Lancastrian self-representation, see, for example, Pearsall 1994; Watts 1996, 25–29; Ferster 1996; Perkins 2001; and Hedeman 2001, 7, 31.

24. On the depositions of Edward II and Richard II, see Saul 1997, 405–34; and Valente 1998.

25. For accounts of the role of Parliament in Richard of York's attempts to establish his claim to the throne, see Wolffe 1981, 280–88, 295–98; R. Griffiths 1981, 715–71; and Maurer 2003, 95–123.

26. On the king as embodiment of the law (*lex animata*), see Kantorowicz

1957, 127–42; Ullmann 1975, 60–61, 92; and Mayali 1988.

27. On the role of the sword in the iconography of justice, see Curtis and Resnik 1987, 1729–30, 1754–55; and Resnik and Curtis 2007, 143–45.

28. See Barron 2004, 113–14.

29. See, for example, Gillingham 1999, 179, fig. 1b, and 180, fig. 2a.

30. On Cotton Julius E iv, see Scott 1996, 1: plates 297–300, 2:221–23. On Harvard Law School Library MS 58, see Baker 1985, 28. On Scheide Collection MS 30, see A. Bennett 1986, 5 and fig. 10.

31. For reproductions, see Saul 1997, 254, plate 21, and cover; and Binski 1999, 80–83 and plate 2. Discussions of this portrait include Whittingham 1971, 20–21; Alexander 1997, 197–206; Scheifele 1999, 264–65; and Barr 2002, 81–82.

32. For additional examples, see Owens 1989, 23–38; and the scenes described as David "at prayer" and "communicating with God" in Hourihane 2002.

33. On British Library MS Arundel 109, see Ker 1964, 221; and Scott 1995, 153–56.

34. On Bodleian Library MS Don. d. 85, see Scott 1996, 1: plates 168–71, and 2: no. 39; Pächt and Alexander 1973, 3: no. 803, and plates LXXVI–VII; and de la Mare and Barker-Benfield 1980, no. 17.3, and figs. 44, 49. As mentioned before, British Library MS Royal 1 E ix may be the "great Bible" made for either Richard II or Henry IV. See Scott 1996, 1: plate 121, and 2:101, 135, 204.

35. See, for instance, Kantorowicz 1958, 56–59, 64; Tudor-Craig 1989, 183–205; Hen 1998, 277–89; and Hobbs 2003, 102–28.

36. Webb 1909, 2:378, translated in Nederman 1990, 209.

37. See Schröder 1971 and Rorimer and Freeman 1949.

38. See Macaulay 1899.

39. On the interplay of verbal and visual images of kingship in this manuscript, see Camille 1993. Genet points out that this treatise also survives in London, British Library MS Cotton Cleopatra B x and Rouen, Bibliothèque municipale MS 939 (I.36) (Genet 1977, x).

40. See Dutton and Kessler 1997, 7–8, 43–44, 87–99.

41. See Scott 1989, 42–46, 61 n. 70.

42. For detailed discussions of this manuscript and its illustrations, see Meiss 1967, figs. 83–176; Avril, Dunlopp, and Yapp 1989; and Manion 1991.

43. See Hedeman 2001, 3–5, 70, and figs. 15, 16.

44. See, for example, the illustration in New York, Pierpont Morgan Library MS M359, fol. 69r.

45. On the decoration of these charters, see Alexander 1972 and Danbury 1989a, 167.

46. In the copy of the *New Statutes of England* in London, British Library MS Yates Thompson 48, which contains statutes through 1451, three of the five kings portrayed (Henry IV, Henry V, and Henry VI) wear a closed crown topped with a cross, perhaps to distinguish the Lancastrian kings from their predecessors.

47. See the accounts of miracles attributed to Henry VI in Knox and Leslie 1923; Grosjean 1935; McKenna 1974; and Wolffe 1981, 4–15.

48. See Spencer 1978; and Spencer 1998, 189–92.

49. See Lovatt 1981, 438–39; and Lovatt 1984.

50. See also R. Griffiths 1981, 217–28.

51. McKenna extrapolates from the copy of the pedigree in London, British Library MS Royal 15 E vi.

52. See Epstein 2006, 364.

53. "Roundel at the Coronation of Henry VI" and "Ballade to Henry VI at his Coronation" in MacCracken 1934, 622, 625. See McKenna 1965, 153–56; Nolan 2005, 74; and Winstead 2007, 134.

54. See also McKenna 1965, 157; and Epstein 2006, 361–62.

55. There is some evidence that parts of the manuscript were made earlier in the century and perhaps originally intended for a French dauphin, such as Charles VI's eldest son, Louis of Guyenne; but, in its current form, the manuscript depicts Henry VI at about the age at which he was crowned king of France.

56. Auerbach discusses the decoration of the *Coram rege* Rolls under Henry VI and Edward IV as examples of experimentation in royal portraiture that led to the traditions used by artists under the Tudor monarchs: see Auerbach 1954, 18–23.

57. The first *Coram rege* Roll to begin with a highly decorated initial, the one for Easter session, 1443 (Kew, National Archives MS KB 27/728), does not present the image of the monarch, but holds a blank shield, which Auerbach reads as a play on Fortescue's name: family tradition held that their name and motto ("Forte scutum salus ducam") were gained because their ancestor, Sir Richard le Forte, protected William the Conqueror (Duke of Normandy) at the battle of Hastings by holding a shield in front of him. Perhaps Fortescue envisioned the role of chief justice as one of protecting the king's reputation for upholding justice and, by extension, protecting the king's ability to rule.

58. Though some medieval copies of Psalm 57 in the Vulgate Bible read "recta iudicate," other medieval copies of Psalm 57 use "recte iudicate" instead: see, for example, the opening of Psalm 57 in the St. Albans Psalter (Pächt, Dodwell, and Wormald 1960) and Richard Rolle's commentary on Psalm 57 (Rolle 1884, 204).

59. The judges' caps fit the description found in Baker 1984, 72.

60. As Hall points out, Glanville here follows the *Institutes* attributed to Emperor Justinian, and several other Latin works on English law echo Glanville's statement in their own prefaces, so the theme was well established in legal literature by the fifteenth century.

61. On Henry VI's capture and imprisonment in the Tower of London, see Scofield 1923, 1:380–84; and Ross 1974, 61–62.

62. See the discussions of this manuscript and reproductions of its images in Sutton and Visser-Fuchs 1997, 137–41; Radulescu 2003, 65; and Strohm 2005, 2–3. Another manuscript that associates Edward IV with quotations from the Bible is Philadelphia, Free Library MS Lewis E201. See Scott 1996, 2:288–89 and illustrations 393–94; and Scott 2001.

3. THE QUEEN AND THE LANCASTRIAN CAUSE

1. All quotations and English translations of this account in the following discussion come from *The Statutes of the Realm*, 1 Edward III (Raithby 1810–28, 1:251–52). For the beginning of this passage in the Yale manuscript, see plate 1.

2. The same can be said for the Parliament Roll itself: as Seymour Phillips and Mark Ormrod put it, "Edward II had been airbrushed out of the record" (in Given-Wilson 2005, 4:8). For detailed discussions of Edward's deposition, see Fryde 1979, 195–206; and Haines 2003, 177–218.

3. See Menache 1984, 112–17; Lord 2002, 45; and Weir 2007, xviii.

4. See Michael 1985 and Stanton 2001, 194–240.

5. Dunn 2000, 147. Margaret is called "She-Wolf of France" by Richard, Duke of York, in Shakespeare's play *Henry VI, Part 3*, act 1, scene 4, line 111. Thomas Gray uses the epithet for Isabelle in his 1757 poem "The Bard" (line 57). W. Mark Ormrod also discusses these two queens as victims of demonization in their own centuries as part of efforts to sanitize the reputations of their husbands (Ormrod 2005).

6. Quotations come from Gordon Kipling's reconstruction of the pageants based on the two surviving manuscripts: London, British Library MSS Harley 542 and Harley 3869 (Kipling 1982, 19–27).

7. On the appearance of the Four Daughters of God in medieval liturgies, literature, and visual arts, see Traver 1907 and Newman 2003.

8. *Middle English Dictionary*, under "chaunceler" (n. (1)), definition 2(a).

9. See McGerr 1990.

10. There is some ambiguity in the phrase "the Lawes commendable" (line 49). At some points, Kipling's commentary suggests that "Lawes" refers to lawyers or legal scholars, who are depicted as joining with the clergy and knights in approving the counsels of Grace; but he also suggests that the first part of this line ("Clergie, Knyghthode") refers to two of the three traditional "estates" of medieval society. If the passage is meant to allude to parliamentary ratification, representing the unified voice of the people, one would expect some reference to the Commons as the third group joining with the clergy and knights, as in the English Parliament, to approve the teachings of Grace as law, especially in a pageant presented by the city of London. As a result, I read "Lawes" as a variant spelling of "Lowes," which in Middle English could refer to the lower ranks of society. See the *Middle English Dictionary*, under "loue" (adj.), definition 5a, and verification of the spelling variant.

11. See Calabi 2004, 169; and Picard 2005, 49, 148.

12. See Myers 1957–58, 94–95; and R. Griffiths 1981, 262.

13. See the discussions by Monro 1863, 111–12; and R. Griffiths 1981, 259–62.

14. Coote first appears in the *Calendar of the Patent Rolls* as the "king's servant" with an annuity for life granted in 1439, then as justice of the peace for Lincoln (Parts of Kesteven) in 1448. In 1452, he was appointed to a royal commission investigating crimes in Lincolnshire. Reference to Coote as Margaret's attorney general in Chancery comes in July 1459. Coote seems to have continued his service to the Lancastrian party until its final defeat, since he was one of those who received a general pardon from Edward IV in July 1471. See *Calendar of the Patent Rolls: Henry VI*, vol. 3, *1436–41*, 291, 495; *Calendar of the Patent Rolls: Henry VI*, vol. 5, *1446–52*, 579, 591; *Calendar of the Patent Rolls: Henry VI*, vol. 6, *1452–61*, 104, 507; and *Calendar of the Patent Rolls:*

Edward IV, Henry VI, vol. 2, 1467–77, 261. For additional information about British Library MS Additional 81292, see Christie Auction House 2005, lot 19.

15. See Gross 1996, 46–56; Watts 1996, 305–62; Maurer 2003, 67–111; Laynesmith 2004, 11, 140–43; and Lee 1986. Scholars continue to debate the causes of Henry's physical and mental illness: see R. Griffiths 1981, 715–18; and Wolffe 1981, 267–86.

16. See, for example, the account in R. Griffiths 1981, 719–25.

17. See, for example, Prendergast 2002.

18. See, for example, Watts 1996, 337; Maurer 2003, 134–35; and Laynesmith 2004, 151–52.

19. Laynesmith 2004, 140, 143. Although there is no evidence that Margaret herself had a hand in planning the Coventry pageants, members of her staff may have indicated topics that would please the queen. See also Laynesmith 2003.

20. See Maurer 2003, 23; Jansen 2002, 36–37, 59; and Vale 1974.

21. Quotations of the Old French text come from the edition by Christine Laennec in her 1988 dissertation; the English translations are my own. Critical discussions of Christine's treatise in light of French and English politics include Teague 1991, Willard 1999, Forhan 2002, and Le Saux 2004. On *Knyghthode and Bataile,* see the discussion in chapter 4.

22. See the discussion of London, British Library MS Royal 15 E vi in chapter 2.

23. See also Willard 1999, 12–13.

24. Some manuscripts read "xiiii" instead of "xiii"; see Willard 1999, 30.

25. See Forhan 2002, 110–32; and Teague 1991, 28.

26. See McGrady 1998. On Jean of Berry's role as one of Christine's chief patrons, see Meiss 1967, 1:50, and 2: figs. 833–36.

27. On Alice Chaucer's ownership of a copy of the *Livre de la cité des dames,* see Meale 1996.

28. See Myers 1957–58, 92; and Maurer 2003, 133–34.

29. On Booth's career, see Reeves 1998.

30. On the conventions of educating noble children in the late Middle Ages, see Given-Wilson 1987, 3; and Orme 2001, 68.

31. For descriptions of some of the elaborate ceremonies that accompanied the knighting of a medieval prince, see Vale 2001, 130–31, 210–11.

32. These tapestries of the Nine Worthies now hang in the Cloisters Museum in New York. See Rorimer and Freeman 1949.

33. See plate 60 and the discussion of the depictions of the duke at prayer in his manuscripts in chapter 2.

34. See Robin 1985. Art historians have suggested that René may have assisted Margaret's uncle, Charles VII, in commissioning illustrations for the Duke of Berry's *Très riches heures,* which remained unfinished at the duke's death (Cazelles and Rathofer 1988, 218, 224).

35. Discussions of Margaret as a book owner can be found in Dunn 1995, 112–14; and Michalove 2004, 66–68.

36. Hatton 73 has an inscription indicating that it previously belonged to "Queen Margaret." See Laynesmith 2004, 253; and Madan et al. 1895–1953, no. 4119.

37. Oxford, Bodleian Library MS Jesus College 124 is actually a roll, rather than a codex, and it was illustrated by the London artist William Abell, who also illustrated charters granted by Henry VI and several statutes books. See Scott 1996, 2:264, 266–68; and Laynesmith 2004, 253 and plate 2.

38. See Alexander and Kauffmann 1973, no. 70; and Michalove 2004, 75. A catalogue of the manuscript collection of Robert Hoe in 1909 lists Margaret of Anjou as the owner of a fifteenth-century book of hours (Shipman 1909, 59–61); but the attribution of ownership is not very strong, being based on the appearance of a noblewoman in prayer before the Virgin Mary.

39. London, British Library MS Additional 40851, called "Thomas Jenyns's Ordinary of Arms," has Margaret's full-page coat of arms at the front. See Boos 2004. For the connection between the College of Arms and copies of the *Nova statuta*, see Pronay and Taylor 1974, 17.

40. See Means 1992, 600.

41. See Chastellain 1988, 13–15, 85–87; and Michalove 2004, 75. The Vatican manuscript heading for the text refers to the deaths of Henry VI and Prince Edward, which took place in May 1471. The manuscript appears to be a new copy made for Margaret when she returned to France after her imprisonment in England in 1475. Several other manuscript copies of this text retain opening miniatures that depict Margaret, but no other miniature shows the author presenting his book to the queen.

4. EDUCATING THE PRINCE

1. See Scanlon 1990, 235; Pearsall 1994, 389–90; and Briggs 1999, 63–65.

2. See, for example, Saygin 2002, 58.

3. See the discussion and edition of this treatise by Genet 1977, 40–173; as well as Briggs 1999, 68.

4. One author refers to both Henry VI and Prince Edward as the audience for his text: when he dedicates the first version of his *Chronicle* to Henry VI in 1457, John Hardyng expresses the hope that the prince will also read it. See Kingsford 1912, 462–82.

5. See Gilson 1911 for the text of the *Somnium vigilantis*. This tract (in English, Latin, and French) survives in a unique manuscript (London, British Library MS Royal 17 D xv, fols. 302–11), which also contains a treatise against the Yorkists' claims by Fortescue. For the dating of the tract, see Kekewich 2007, 25–30. Some scholars have suggested that Fortescue had a hand in composing this text: see, for example, Lander 1961, 120; McCulloch and Jones 1983, 133; Gross 1996, 58–59; and Strohm 2005, 145. Meyer-Lee suggests that Ashby is just as likely a candidate for its authorship (Meyer-Lee 2004, 711).

6. This passage is found on fol. 6r in the Yale manuscript (plate 19).

7. Passages from the Middle English text are cited from the edition by Dyboski and Arend 1935; translations into modern English are my own. This work has sometimes been attributed to a priest named Robert Parker, while others argue for different authorship: see Watts 1996, 349–54; Bowers 2002, 355; Wakelin 2004; and Wakelin 2007, 81. On Viscount Beaumont, see also Laynesmith 2004, 151–52.

8. English texts from earlier in the century also depict the king's legal authority in parallel with God's justice: see, for example, Osberg 1986.

9. Passages from Ashby's Middle English poem are cited from Bateson 1899; the modern English translations are my own. The unique copy of Ashby's poem has a Latin prose preface. Ashby's *Dicta*, a collection of Latin quotations with English translations that follows *On the Active Policy of a Prince*, may be an appendix to Ashby's poem, rather than a separate work (Scattergood 1990, 171–74; Meyer-Lee 2007, 149).

10. For recent discussions of Ashby's administrative career and poems, see Scattergood 1996, 258–74; Kekewich 1990; Summers 2004, 142–43; Meyer-Lee 2004; and Meyer-Lee 2007, 138–67.

11. *Calendar of the Patent Rolls: Henry VI*, vol. 3, *1436–41*, 550; *Calendar of the Close Rolls: Henry VI*, vol. 3, *1435–41*, 419; and Summers 2004, 142. King's (or queen's) serjeants were appointed by royal patent from the larger group of serjeants-at-law. See Baker 1986.

12. Ashby's name does not appear in contemporary accounts of the Lancastrian exiles or in the accounts of the Lancastrians who died in battle or were captured by Edward IV's forces when Queen Margaret and Prince Edward returned to England with other exiles in the spring of 1471. At the same time, Meyer-Lee's reading of the *Active Policy* might not require Ashby's physical presence with the prince and queen, since records indicate that Lancastrian loyalists in England had secret correspondence with the exiles. See, for example, Gross 1996, 39; and Kekewich et al. 1995, 88–92. Yorkist capture of agents bearing

letters from the Lancastrians in France in 1468 led to arrests, imprisonments, and executions.

13. This document survives in London, British Library MS Additional 48031, a compilation attributed to John Vale and thought to have been made ca. 1480. Scholars attribute the composition of the seven principles to Fortescue because they have close links with his treatise *On the Governance of England*. See the discussions in Kekevich et al. 1995, 222–25; Gross 1996, 83–85; and Strohm 2005, 143.

14. Charles Arrowood also suggests that Ashby's poem and Fortescue's treatise date from 1468–70; but Arrowood only links the works together in their purpose of educating Prince Edward (Arrowood 1935, 404).

15. On Fortescue's life, see the *Oxford Dictionary of National Biography*, rev. ed., article by E. W. Ives; Cromartie 2004, 48–49; and Chrimes 1942, lix–lxvii.

16. See the recent discussions of Fortescue's recantation by Landman 2001, 143–48, 165–70; and Strohm 2005, 134–45.

17. For John of Salisbury's text, see Keats-Rohan 1993, lines 2797, 2871–76; and Nederman 1990, 36, 41.

18. Chrimes (1942, xcii–xciii) contends that the *De natura* could have been written at any point after 1460. Gill (1971, 334) maintains that Fortescue composed it during his exile in Scotland, before July 1463.

19. See Pronay and Taylor 1974, 17; Matheson 1998, 16; Clarke 1936, 357; and Kingsford 1913, 310.

20. See the discussion of these images in chapter 2.

21. See the discussion of Prince Edward's early education in chapter 3.

5. "GRACE BE OUR GUIDE"

1. See the *Middle English Dictionary*, under "grace" (n).

2. On the biographies of Henry V that appeared during his lifetime and in the aftermath of his death, see Gransden 1996, 194–217.

3. Quoted from Kipling 1982, 19–27. See the discussion of this pageant in chapter 3.

4. See Kipling 1982, 7–13 for a discussion of the surviving documents. Kipling argues that these pageants represent an important innovation in English civic drama because they were the first to include speeches by characters in the scenes.

5. See the discussions by Kekewich et al. 1995, 53–66; and Strohm 2005, 134–54.

6. Before fleeing to Scotland to join Margaret of Anjou and Prince Edward in 1461, Fortescue arranged for some of his property to be used to support his wife; but Edward IV awarded many of Fortescue's estates to Yorkist supporters. (See Scofield 1912 and Roskell 2005, 257–58.) Nevertheless, Fortescue regained his estates after the reversal of his attainder. Because his only son Martin died in 1471 and his wife died in 1472, Fortescue bequeathed most of his estates to Martin's sons (Chrimes 1942, lxxv).

7. On Sir Richard Elyot, see the *Oxford Dictionary of National Biography*, rev. ed., article by Richard Schoeck.

8. For Richard Elyot's will, see Lehmberg 1960, 25.

9. For additional references to King David in *The Boke Named the Governour*, see Croft 1883, 1:14, 39, 95, 214.

10. See the discussion of Elyot's use of Fortescue's treatises in Croft's edition of *The Boke Named the Governour* (Croft 1883, 1:132n–133n), as well as in McLaren 1996.

11. Because of its critical depiction of Edward IV, Fortescue's treatise did not circulate openly during that monarch's reign. The two manuscript copies that survive appear to date from the sixteenth century. The treatise was not printed until Edward Whitechurche's edition, which is undated; scholars have hypothesized that this edition dates from 1537 (Hill 1997, 361), 1543 (Simpson 2004, 281), or 1546 (Wood 1994, 44).

12. For Fortescue's discussion of the Inns of Chancery in *De laudibus*, see Chrimes 1942, 114–21.

13. For information about the Elyot family's holding of the Clement's Inn property, see E. Williams 1927, 2: nos. 1467, 1466–68, 1506, and 1510–13A. Information on Fortescue property holdings is contained in E. Williams 1927, 1:24 and 2:1466–67, 1474, 1498, and 1506; see also Wedgwood 1938, 349.

14. For more information about these manuscripts, see chapter 1.

15. See the discussions by Scott 1996, 1: plate 464 and 2:343; Laynesmith 2004, 172 and illustration 3; and Meale 1989, 212–13 and illustration 22.

16. Christine presents Zenobia's story in part 1, chapter 20. For a discussion of Elyot's text in relationship to Christine's work, see D. O'Brien 1993.

17. See Lehmberg 1960, 16–19; and Dowling 1986, 221.

18. On Lady Margaret's marriage to Dyer, see Lehmberg 1960, 182. Dyer became a member of Parliament for

Cambridgeshire, speaker of the House of Commons, legal historian, and chief justice of the Common Pleas. On Dyer, see the *Oxford Dictionary of National Biography*, rev. ed., article by John Hamilton Baker.

19. On Freville, see the *Oxford Dictionary of National Biography*, rev. ed., article by John Hamilton Baker.

20. Roger is listed as deceased with William as his heir in a deed from 22 July, 19 Charles II (1667): see Archives of the Center for Buckinghamshire Studies, Ivinghoe Manor and Newport Pagnell Deeds, D 27/99.

21. On Sir Thomas Winnington, third baronet, and Sir Thomas Edward Winnington, fourth baronet, see Mosley 2003, 3:4,221–24.

22. On Sir Francis Winnington, see the *Oxford Dictionary of National Biography*, rev. ed., article by Paul D. Halliday; and Horwood 1870, 53.

23. On Sir Thomas Winnington, see the *Oxford Dictionary of National Biography*, rev. ed., article by W. P. Courtney (rev. by M. E. Clayton).

24. For example, Cibber's play adds sympathy for Prince Edward with scenes of the prince falling in love with Warwick's daughter, Lady Anne, and of the parting vows of faithful love between the prince and his bride (Cibber 1724, 45, 53–54).

25. Earlier, the passage on Margaret describes her as "a princess who had, to the beauties of her body, added all the perfections of the mind. She was endowed with an excellent understanding; sagacity, and prudence; very reasonable and considerate, diligent in all her designs, and with her other admirable qualities, was perfectly handsome" (*Biographium faemineum* 1766, 2:80).

26. On the fire at Stanford Court, see Walford 1883, 97–98.

27. See Hodgson and Co. 1932, lot no. 463; and Baker 1985, 74.

APPENDIX 2

1. On Freville, see the *Oxford Dictionary of National Biography*, rev. ed., article by John Hamilton Baker.

2. On Sir Thomas Winnington, third baronet, and Sir Thomas Edward Winnington, fourth baronet, see Mosley 2003, 3:4,221–24.

3. On Sir Francis Winnington, see the *Oxford Dictionary of National Biography*, rev. ed., article by Paul D. Halliday; and Horwood 1870, 53.

4. On the fire at Stanford Court, see Walford 1883, 97–98. Some reports indicate that the whole collection was lost in the fire, but other reports verify that at least some of the manuscripts were saved: see Royal Archaeological Institute of Britain and Ireland 1882, 483.

Bibliography and
Manuscripts Cited

Alexander, Jonathan J. G. 1972. "William Abell 'Lymnour' and Fifteenth-Century English Illumination." In *Kunsthistorische Forschungen: Otto Pächt zu seinem 70. Geburtstag*, ed. Artur Rosenauer and Gerold Weber, 166–72. Saltzburg: Residenz Verlag.

———. 1983. "Painting and Manuscript Illumination for Royal Patrons in the Later Middle Ages." In *English Court Culture in the Later Middle Ages*, ed. V. J. Scattergood and J. W. Sherborne, 141–62. New York: St. Martin's Press.

———. 1997. "The Portrait of Richard II in Westminster Abbey." In *The Regal Image of Richard II and the Wilton Diptych*, ed. Dillian Gordon, Lisa Monnas, and Caroline Elam, 197–206. London: Harvey Miller.

Alexander, Jonathan J. G., and Claus M. Kauffmann. 1973. *English Illuminated Manuscripts, 700–1500*. Brussels: Bibliothèque royale Albert Ier.

Archaeological Institute of Great Britain and Ireland. 1862. "Proceedings at the Annual Meeting, 1862: Held at Worcester, July 22 to July 29." *Archaeological Journal* 19:370–401.

Arrowood, Charles F. 1935. "Sir John Fortescue on the Education of Rulers." *Speculum* 10:404–10.

Auerbach, Erna. 1954. *Tudor Artists: A Study of Painters in the Royal Service and of Portraiture on Illuminated Documents from the Accession of Henry VIII to the Death of Elizabeth I*. London: Athlone Press.

Avril, François, Louisa Dunlopp, and Brunsdon Yapp. 1989–90. *Les petites heures du Duc de Berry*. 2 vols. Lucerne: Faksimile-Verlag.

Backhouse, Janet. 1997. *The Illuminated Page: Ten Centuries of Manuscript Painting*. London: British Library.

Baker, John Hamilton. 1978. "A History of English Judges' Robes." *Costume: The Journal of the Costume* 12:27–39.

———. 1984. *The Order of Serjeants at Law: A Chronicle of Creations, with Related Texts*. London: Selden Society.

———. 1985. *English Legal Manuscripts in the United States of America: A Descriptive List*. Vol. 1, *Medieval and Renaissance Period*. London: Selden Society.

———. 1986. "The English Legal Profession, 1450–1550." In *The Legal Profession and the Common Law: Historical Essays*, 75–98. London: Hambledon Press.

———. 1990. *Manual of Law French*. 2nd ed. Aldershot, UK: Scolar Press.

———. 1999. "The Books of the Common Law." In *The Cambridge History of the Book in Britain, Vol. 3: 1400–1557*, ed. Lotte Hellinga and J. B. Trapp, 411–32. Cambridge: Cambridge University Press.

———. 2000a. *The Common Law Tradition: Lawyers, Books, and the Law.* London: Hambledon Press.

———. 2000b. *Readers and Readings in the Inns of Court and Chancery.* London: Selden Society.

———. 2002. *An Introduction to English Legal History.* 4th ed. London: Butterworths.

———. 2003. *The Oxford History of the Laws of England, Volume 6: 1483–1558.* Oxford: Oxford University Press.

———. 2006. "Migration of Manuscripts, 2005." *Journal of Legal History* 27 (2): 199–209.

Baker, John Hamilton, and Jayne S. Ringrose. 1996. *A Catalogue of English Legal Manuscripts in Cambridge University Library.* Woodbridge, UK: Boydell Press.

Bakhtin, Mikhail. 1981. *The Dialogic Imagination: Four Essays.* Ed. Michael Holquist. Trans. Caryl Emerson and Michael Holquist. Austin: University of Texas Press.

———. 1984. *Problems of Dostoevsky's Poetics.* Ed. and trans. Caryl Emerson. Minneapolis: University of Minnesota Press.

———. 1993. *Rabelais and His World.* Trans. Hélène Iswolsky. Bloomington: Indiana University Press.

Barr, Helen. 2002. *Socioliterary Practice in Late Medieval England.* New York: Oxford University Press.

Barron, Caroline M. 2004. "The Political Culture of Medieval London." In Clark and Carpenter 2004, 111–34.

Bartlett, Anne Clark. 2005. "Translation, Self-Representation, and Statecraft: Lady Margaret Beaufort and Caxton's *Blanchardyn and Eglantine* (1489)." *Essays in Medieval Studies* 22:53–66.

Bateson, Mary, ed. 1899. *George Ashby's Poems.* Reprint, Early English Text Society, extra series 76. London: Oxford University Press, 1965.

Battestin, Martin C., and Ruthe R. Battestin. 1993. *Henry Fielding: A Life.* London: Routledge.

Bennett, Adelaide. 1980. "The Windmill Psalter: The Historiated Letter B of Psalm One." *Journal of the Warburg and Courtauld Institutes* 43:52–67.

———. 1986. "Anthony Bek's Copy of *Statuta Anglicana.*" In *England in the Fourteenth Century: Proceedings of the 1985 Harlaxton Symposium*, ed. W. M. Ormrod, 1–27. Woodbridge, UK: Boydell Press.

Bennett, Henry Stanley. 1969. *English Books and Readers, 1475 to 1557: Being a Study in the History of the Book Trade from Caxton to the Incorporation of the Stationers' Company.* 2nd ed. Cambridge: Cambridge University Press.

Benson, Larry, ed. 1987. *The Riverside Chaucer.* 3rd ed. Boston: Houghton Mifflin.

Berges, Wilhelm. 1938. *Die Fürstenspiegel des hohen und späten Mittelalters.* Monumenta Germaniae historica, Schriften des Reichsinstituts für ältere deutsche Geschichtskunde 2. Leipzig: K. W. Hiersemann.

Biblia sacra iuxta Vulgatam Clementinam. 1965. 4th ed. Ed. Alberto Colunga and Laurentio Turrado. Madrid: Biblioteca de autores cristianos.

Binski, Paul. 1986. *The Painted Chamber at Westminster.* London: Society of Antiquaries.

———. 1995. *Westminster Abbey and the Plantagenets: Kingship and the Representation of Power, 1200–1400.* New Haven, Conn.: Yale University Press.

———. 1999. "Hierarchies and Orders in English Royal Images of Power." In *Orders and Hierarchies in Late Medieval and Renaissance Europe,* ed. Jeffrey H. Denton and David E. Smith, 74–93. Toronto: University of Toronto Press.

Binski, Paul, and Stella Panayotova, eds. 2005. *The Cambridge Illuminations: Ten Centuries of Book Production in the Medieval West.* London: Harvey Miller.

Biographium faemineum: The Female Worthies, or, Memoirs of the Most Illustrious Ladies, of all Ages and Nations. 1766. 2 vols. London: S. Crowder, J. Payne, J. Wilkie, W. Nicoll and J. Wren.

Bodleian Library. 1967. *Heraldry: Catalogue of an Exhibition Held in Connection with the English Heraldry Society.* Oxford: Bodleian Library.

Bond, Francis. 1908. *Screens and Galleries in English Churches.* London: Oxford University Press.

Boos, Emmanuel de. 2004. *L'armorial ordonné de la reine Marguerite, al. Livre de Thomas Jenyns: D'après le manuscrit de Londres, British library, Ms Add. 40851.* Documents d'héraldique médiévale 6. Paris: Le Léopard d'Or.

Bossy, Michel-André. 1998. "Arms and the Bride: Christine de Pizan's Military Treatise as a Wedding Gift for Margaret of Anjou." In Desmond 1998, 236–56.

Bowers, John M. 2002. "Thomas Hoccleve and the Politics of Tradition." *Chaucer Review* 36:352–69.

Breviarium ad usum insignis Ecclesie Eboracensis, vol. 1. 1880. Ed. Stephen Willoughby Lawley. Surtees Society, vol. 71. Durham, UK: Andrews and Co.

Briggs, Charles F. 1999. *Giles of Rome's "De regimine principum": Reading and Writing Politics at Court and University, c. 1275–c. 1525.* Cambridge Studies in Palaeography and Codicology. Cambridge: Cambridge University Press.

British Museum. 1834–40. *Catalogue of Manuscripts in the British Museum, New Series, Part 1: The Arundel Manuscripts.* London: British Museum.

———. 1895–96. *Catalogue of the Stowe Manuscripts in the British Museum.* 2 vols. London: British Museum.

Brown, Sarah. 2003. *York Minster: An Architectural History, ca. 1220–1500.* Swindon: English Heritage.

Butt, Ronald. 1989. *A History of Parliament: The Middle Ages.* London: Constable.

Cahn, Walter, and James Marrow. 1978. *Medieval and Renaissance Manuscripts at Yale: A Selection.* Special issue of the *Yale University Library Gazette* 52 (4).

Calabi, Donatella. 2004. *The Market and the City: Square, Street and Architecture in Early Modern Europe.* Trans. Marlene Klein. Farnham, UK: Ashgate.

Calendar of the Close Rolls Preserved in the Public Record Office. 1892–1963. 61 vols. London: Her Majesty's Stationery Office.

Calendar of the Patent Rolls Preserved in the Public Record Office. 1891–1916. 52 vols. London: Her Majesty's Stationery Office.

Camille, Michael. 1992. *Image on the Edge: The Margins of Medieval Art*. Cambridge, Mass.: Harvard University Press.

———. 1993. "The King's New Bodies: An Illustrated Mirror for Princes in the Morgan Library." In *Künstlerischer Austausch/Artistic Exchange: Akten des 28. Internationalen Kongresses für Kunstgeschichte, Berlin, 15–20 Juli 1992*, ed. Thomas W. Gaehtgens, 393–405. Berlin: Akademie Verlag.

———. 1998. *Mirror in Parchment: The Luttrell Psalter and the Making of Medieval England*. Chicago: University of Chicago Press.

Carpenter, Christine. 1997. *The Wars of the Roses: Politics and the Constitution in England, c. 1437–1509*. Reprint, Cambridge: Cambridge University Press, 2002.

Cazelles, Raymond, and Johannes Rathofer. 1988. *Illuminations of Heaven and Earth: The Glories of the "Très riches heures du Duc de Berry."* With a forward by Umberto Eco. New York: Harry N. Abrams; Luzern: Faksimile-Verlag.

Chance, Jane. 1998. "Gender Subversion and Linguistic Castration in Fifteenth-Century English Translations of Christine de Pizan." In *Violence against Women in Medieval Texts*, ed. Anna Roberts and Anna Klosowska, 161–94. Gainesville: University Press of Florida.

Chastellain, Georges. 1988. *Le temple de Boccace*. Ed. Susanna Bliggenstorfer. Berne: Francke.

Cherry, John, and Neil Stratford. 1995. *Westminster Kings and the Medieval Palace of Westminster*. London: British Museum.

Chrimes, Stanley B[ertram], ed. and trans. 1942. *De laudibus legum Anglie*. By Sir John Fortescue. Cambridge: Cambridge University Press.

Christie Auction House. 2005. *Valuable Printed Books and Manuscripts, Including Maps and Atlases*. London: Christie.

Cibber, Theophilus. 1724. *King Henry VI, a Tragedy: As It Is Acted at the Theatre-Royal in Drury-Lane, by His Majesty's Servants. Altered from Shakespear, in the Year 1720*. 2nd ed. London: W. Chetwood.

Clark, Linda, and Christine Carpenter, eds. 2004. *Political Culture in Late Medieval Britain*. Woodbridge, UK: Boydell Press.

Clarke, Maude Violet. 1936. *Medieval Representation and Consent: A Study of Early Parliaments in England and Ireland, with Special Reference to the "Modus tenendi Parliamentum."* London: Longmans.

Cockerell, Sydney Carlyle. 1908. *Exhibition of Illuminated Manuscripts*. London: Burlington Fine Arts Club.

Collard, Judith. 2007. "*Effigies ad Regem Angliae* and the Representation of Kingship in Thirteenth-Century English Royal Culture." *Electronic British Library Journal*, article 9. http://www.bl.uk/eblj/2007articles/pdf/ebljarticle92007.pdf (accessed 1 November 2010).

Cooke, William H. 1877. *Students Admitted to Inner Temple, 1547–1660*. London: Clowes and Sons.

Croft, Henry Herbert Stephen, ed. 1883. *The Boke Named the Governour, devised by Sir Thomas Elyot, Knight*. 2 vols. London: Kegan Paul, Trench, and Co.

Cromartie, Alan. 2004. "Common Law, Counsel and Consent in Fortescue's Political Theory." In Clark and Carpenter 2004, 45–68.

Curtis, Dennis, and Judith Resnik. 1987. "Images of Justice." *Yale Law Journal* 96:1727–72.

Danbury, Elizabeth. 1989a. "The Decoration and Illumination of Royal Charters in England, 1250–1509: An Introduction." In *England and Her Neighbours, 1066–1453: Essays in Honour of Pierre Chaplais*, ed. Michael Jones and Malcolm Vale, 157–79. London: Hambledon Press.

———. 1989b. "English and French Artistic Propaganda during the Period of the Hundred Years War: Some Evidence from Royal Charters." In *Power, Culture and Religion in France, c. 1350–c. 1550*, ed. Christopher Allmand, 75–97. Woodbridge, UK: Boydell Press.

Davies, James Conway. 1972. *Catalogue of Manuscripts in the Library of the Honourable Society of the Inner Temple: Vol. 1, The Petyt Collection, Manuscripts 502–533*. London: Oxford University Press.

de la Mare, A[lbinia], and B[ruce] C. Barker-Benfield, eds. 1980. *Manuscripts at Oxford: An Exhibition in Memory of Richard William Hunt (1908–1979), Keeper of Western Manuscripts at the Bodleian Library, Oxford, 1945–1975, on Themes Selected and Described by Some of His Friends*. Oxford: Bodleian Library.

Derolez, Albert. 2003. *The Palaeography of Gothic Manuscript Books*. Cambridge: Cambridge University Press.

Desmond, Marilynn, ed. 1998. *Christine de Pizan and the Categories of Differ-* ence. Minneapolis: University of Minnesota Press.

Dockray, Keith. 2000. *Henry VI, Margaret of Anjou and the Wars of the Roses*. Stroud, UK: Sutton Publishing.

Dodd, Gwilym. 2007. *Justice and Grace: Private Petitioning and the English Parliament in the Late Middle Ages*. Oxford: Oxford University Press.

Dowling, Maria. 1986. *Humanism in the Age of Henry VIII*. London: Routledge.

Dunn, Diana E. S. 1995. "Margaret of Anjou, Queen Consort of Henry VI: A Reassessment of Her Role, 1445–53." In *Crown, Government and People in the Fifteenth Century*, ed. Rowena E. Archer, 107–43. Stroud, UK: Alan Sutton.

———. 2000. "The Queen at War: The Role of Margaret of Anjou in the Wars of the Roses." In *War and Society in Medieval and Early Modern Britain*, ed. Diana Dunn, 141–61. Liverpool: Liverpool University Press.

Dutschke, C[onsuelo] W., with the assistance of R. H. Rouse, et al. 1989. *Guide to Medieval and Renaissance Manuscripts in the Huntington Library*. San Marino, Calif.: Huntington Library.

Dutton, Paul Edward, and Herbert L. Kessler. 1997. *The Poetry and Paintings of the First Bible of Charles the Bald*. Ann Arbor: University of Michigan Press.

Dyboski, Roman, and Zygfryd Marjan Arend, eds. 1935. *Knyghthode and Bataile*. Early English Text Society, original series 201. Reprint, London: D. S. Brewer, 1995.

Eden, Frederick Sydney. 1933. *Ancient Stained and Painted Glass*. 2nd ed. Cambridge: Cambridge University Press.

Edwards, A. S. G. 1987. "The Manuscripts and Texts of the Second Version of John Hardyng's Chronicle." In *England in the Fifteenth Century: Proceedings of the 1986 Harlaxton Symposium,* ed. David Williams, 75–84. Woodbridge, UK: Boydell Press.

Ellis, Henry, and Francis Douce. 1819. *A Catalogue of the Lansdowne Manuscripts in the British Museum.* Reprint, London: Harvester Press, 1976.

Elton, Geoffrey R. 1979. "The Rolls of Parliament, 1449–1547." *Historical Journal* 22:1–29.

Epstein, Robert. 2006. "Eating Their Words: Food and Text in the Coronation Banquet of Henry VI." *Journal of Medieval and Early Modern Studies* 36:355–77.

Faye, Christopher Undahl, and William Henry Bond, eds. 1962. *Supplement to the Census of Medieval and Renaissance Manuscripts in the United States and Canada.* New York: Bibliographical Society of America.

Fell, Christine. 1971. *Edward, King and Martyr.* Leeds: University of Leeds, School of English.

Ferguson, Arthur B. 1959. "Fortescue and the Renaissance: A Study in Transition." *Studies in the Renaissance* 6:175–94.

Ferster, Judith. 1996. *Fictions of Advice: The Literature and Politics of Counsel in Late Medieval England.* Philadelphia: University of Pennsylvania Press.

Fisher, John H. 1996. *The Emergence of Standard English.* Lexington: University Press of Kentucky.

Fletcher, Christopher D. 2004. "Narrative and Political Strategies at the Deposition of Richard II." *Journal of Medieval History* 30:323–41.

Forhan, Kate Langdon. 2002. *The Political Theory of Christine de Pizan.* Aldershot: Ashgate.

Fryde, Natalie. 1979. *The Tyranny and Fall of Edward II, 1321–1326.* Reprint, Cambridge: Cambridge University Press, 2004.

Gambier Howe, E. R. J. See Howe, E. R. J. Gambier.

Genet, Jean-Philippe. 1977. *Four English Political Tracts of the Later Middle Ages.* London: Royal Historical Society.

Giancarlo, Matthew. 2007. *Parliament and Literature in Late Medieval England.* Cambridge: Cambridge University Press.

Gill, Paul E. 1971. "Politics and Propaganda in Fifteenth-Century England: The Polemical Writings of Sir John Fortescue." *Speculum* 46:333–47.

Gillingham, John. 1999. *Richard I.* New Haven, Conn.: Yale University Press.

Gilson, Julius. 1911. "A Defence of the Proscription of the Yorkists in 1459." *English Historical Review* 26:512–25.

Gilson, Julius, and George Warner. 1921. *Catalogue of Western Manuscripts in the Old Royal and Kings Collections.* 4 vols. London: British Museum.

Given-Wilson, Chris. 1987. *English Nobility in the Late Middle Ages: The Fourteenth-Century Political Community.* Reprint, London: Routledge, 1996.

———, ed. 2005. *The Parliament Rolls of Medieval England, 1275–1504.* 16 vols. Woodbridge, UK: Boydell Press; London: National Archives.

Gordon, Dillian, et al. 1993. *Making and Meaning: The Wilton Diptych.* London: National Gallery of Great Britain.

Gransden, Antonia. 1996. *Historical Writing in England.* Reprint, London: Routledge, 2000.

Grassnick, Ulrike. 2006. "'O Prince, Desyre to Be Honorable': The Deposition of Richard II and Mirrors for Princes." In Jeffrey S. Hamilton, ed., *Fourteenth-Century England IV*, 159–74. Woodbridge, UK: Boydell and Brewer.

Green, Richard Firth. 1980. *Poets and Princepleasers: Literature and the English Court in the Late Middle Ages*. Toronto: University of Toronto Press.

Griffiths, Jeremy. 1980. "The Production of Manuscripts in London at the End of the Fifteenth Century and the Introduction of Printing, with Particular Attention to the Copies of the Statutes." Unpublished paper (Gordon Duff Prize Essay).

———. 1995. "Unrecorded Middle English Verse in the Library at Holkham Hall, Norfolk." *Medium aevum* 64:278–84.

Griffiths, Ralph A. 1981. *The Reign of King Henry VI: The Exercise of Royal Authority, 1422–1461*. Berkeley: University of California Press.

Grosjean, P[aul], ed. 1935. *Henrici VI Angliae regis miracula postuma ex codice Musei Britannici Regio 13. C. VIII*. Brussels: Société des Bollandistes.

Gross, Anthony. 1996. *The Dissolution of the Lancastrian Kingship: Sir John Fortescue and the Crisis of Monarchy in Fifteenth-Century England*. Stamford, UK: Paul Watkins.

Haines, Roy Martin. 2003. *King Edward II*. Montreal: McGill-Queen's University Press.

Hall, George D. G., ed. and trans. 1965. *The Treatise on the Laws and Customs of the Realm of England Commonly Called Glanvill*. Reprint, Oxford: Oxford University Press, 2002.

Harcourt, Leveson William Vernon. 1907. *His Grace the Steward and Trial of Peers: A Novel Inquiry into a Special Branch of Constitutional Government*. London: Longmans, Green and Co.

Hardy, Thomas D., ed. and trans. 1846. *"Modus tenendi Parliamentum": An Ancient Treatise on the Mode of Holding the Parliament in England*. London: Eyre and Spottiswoode.

Harf-Lancner, Laurence. 1998. "Image and Propaganda: The Illustration of Book I of Froissart's *Chroniques*." In *Froissart across the Genres*, ed. Donald Maddox and Sara Sturm-Maddox, 221–50. Gainesville: University Press of Florida.

Harris, Mary Dormer, ed. 1907. *The Coventry Leet Book, or Mayor's Register, Part I*. Early English Text Society, original series 134. London: Kegan Paul, Trench, Trübner, and Co.

Harriss, G[erald] L[eslie]. 1985. "The Exemplar of Kingship." Introduction to *Henry V: The Practice of Kingship*, ed. G. L. Harriss. Oxford: Oxford University Press.

Hayward, Jane. 1975. "Guilds and Civic Affairs." In *The Secular Spirit: Life and Art at the End of the Middle Ages*, Metropolitan Museum of Art, 126–43. New York: E. P. Dutton.

Hedeman, Anne D. 1991. *The Royal Image: Illustrations of the "Grandes chroniques de France," 1274–1422*. Berkeley: University of California Press.

———. 2001. *Of Counselors and Kings: The Three Versions of Pierre Salmon's "Dialogues."* Urbana: University of Illinois Press.

Hen, Yitzhak. 1998. "The Uses of the Bible and the Perception of Kingship in Merovingian Gaul." *Early Medieval Europe* 7:277–89.

Higgins, Alfred. 1900–1901. "On an Illuminated and Emblazoned Copy of the Statutes from Edward III to Henry VI, Illustrating the Genealogy of the Family of Fitzwilliam of Mablethorpe, Co. Lincoln." *Archaeologia* 57:1–10.

Hill, Christopher. 1997. *Intellectual Origins of the English Revolution Revisited*. New York: Oxford University Press.

Hoak, Dale. 1995. "The Iconography of the Crown Imperial." In *Tudor Political Culture*, ed. Dale Hoak, 54–103. Cambridge: Cambridge University Press.

Hobbs, R. Gerald. 2003. "Bucer's Use of King David as Mirror of the Christian Prince." *Reformation & Renaissance Review: Journal of the Society for Reformation Studies* 5:102–28.

Hodges, Laura Fullerton. 2000. *Chaucer and Costume: The Secular Pilgrims in the General Prologue*. Cambridge: Cambridge University Press.

Hodgson and Co. 1932. *A Catalogue of Interesting Mss. and Rare Books, Including a Selection from an Old Country House Library . . . Which Will Be Sold by Auction by Messrs. Hodgson & Co. . . . on Wednesday, May 25th, 1932, and Two Following Days*. London: Hodgson and Co.

Holford, Margaret. 1816. *Margaret of Anjou: A Poem in Ten Cantos*. London: John Murray.

Holt, James Clarke. 1992. *Magna Carta*. Cambridge: Cambridge University Press.

Horwood, Alfred J[ohn]. 1870. *First Report of the Royal Commission on Historical Manuscripts*. Reprint, London: George Edward Eyre and William Spottiswoode, 1874.

Hourihane, Colum, ed. 2002. *King David in the Index of Christian Art*. Princeton, N.J.: Princeton University Press.

Howe, E. R. J. Gambier. 1903. *Franks Bequest: Catalogue of British and American Book Plates Bequeathed to the Trustees of the British Museum by Sir Augustus Wollaston Franks*. 3 vols. London: British Museum.

Hunter, Joseph. 1838. *A Catalogue of the Manuscripts in the Library of the Honourable Society of Lincoln's Inn*. London: Eyre and Spottiswoode.

Inderwick, Frederick Andrew. 1898. *A Calendar of the Inner Temple Records: Vol. 2, 1 James I (1603)–Restoration (1660)*. London: Henry Sotheran and Co.

James, M[ontegue] R., and E[ric] G. Millar. 1936. *The Bohun Manuscripts*. Oxford: Roxburghe Club.

Jansen, Sharon L. 2002. *The Monstrous Regiment of Women: Female Rulers in Early Modern Europe*. London: Palgrave Macmillan.

Johnstone, Hilda. 1936–37. "Isabella the She-Wolf of France." *History* 21:208–19.

Jones, Michael K., and Malcolm G. Underwood. 1993. *The King's Mother: Lady Margaret Beaufort, Countess of Richmond and Derby*. Cambridge: Cambridge University Press.

Kantorowicz, Ernst. 1957. *The King's Two Bodies: A Study in Mediaeval Political Theology*. Reprint, with introduction by William Chester Jordan. Princeton, N.J.: Princeton University Press, 1997.

————. 1958. *Laudes Regiae: A Study in Liturgical Acclamations and Medieval Ruler Worship*. University of California Publications in History 33. 2nd ed. Berkeley: University of California Press.

Keats-Rohan, Katharine S. B., ed. 1993. *Policraticus (Books I–IV)*, by John of Salisbury. Corpus Christianorum Continuatio Medievalis 118. Turnhout: Brepols.

Kekewich, Margaret Lucille. 1990. "George Ashby's *The Active Policy of a Prince*: An Additional Source." *Review of English Studies*, new series, 41:533–35.

———. 2007. "The Attainder of the Yorkists in 1459: Two Contemporary Accounts." *Historical Research* 55:25–34.

Kekewich, Margaret Lucille, Colin Richmond, Anne F. Sutton, Livia Visser-Fuchs, and John L. Watts. 1995. *The Politics of Fifteenth-Century England: John Vale's Book*. Gloucester, UK: Alan Sutton Publishing.

Ker, N[eil] R[ipley]. 1964. *Medieval Libraries of Great Britain: A List of Surviving Books*. 2nd ed. Royal Historical Society Guides and Handbooks 3. London: Royal Historical Society.

———. 1969–2002. *Medieval Manuscripts in British Libraries*. 5 vols. Oxford: Oxford University Press.

Kingsford, Charles Lethbridge. 1912. "The First Version of Hardyng's Chronicle." *English Historical Review* 27:462–82.

———. 1913. *English Historical Literature in the Fifteenth Century*. Oxford: Clarendon Press.

Kipling, Gordon. 1982. "The London Pageants for Margaret of Anjou: A Medieval Script Restored." *Medieval English Theatre* 4:5–27.

———. 1986–87. "'Grace in This Lyf and Aftirwarde Glorie': Margaret of Anjou's Royal Entry into London." *Research Opportunities in Renaissance Drama* 29:77–84.

Kirschbaum, Engelbert, ed. 1968–76. *Lexikon der christlichen Ikonographie*. 8 vols. Rome: Herder.

Knox, Ronald, and Shane Leslie, eds. 1923. *The Miracles of King Henry VI: Being an Account and Translation of Twenty-three Miracles Taken from the Manuscript in the British Museum (Royal 13 c. viii)*. Cambridge: Cambridge University Press.

König, Eberhard. 2004. *Die Belles Heures des Duc de Berry: Sternstunden der Buchkunst*. Stuttgart: Konrad Theiss.

Laennec, Christine Moneera. 1988. "An Edition of BN MS 603, *Le livre des fais d'armes et de chevallerie*." Vol. 2 of her Ph.D. diss., Yale University.

Lander, J[ack] R[obert]. 1961. "Attainder and Forfeiture, 1453 to 1509." *Historical Journal* 4:119–51.

———. 2007. *The Wars of the Roses*. Rev. ed. Stroud, UK: Sutton Publishing.

Landman, James H. 2001. "Pleading, Pragmatism, and Permissible Hypocrisy: The 'Colours' of Legal Discourse in Late Medieval England." *New Medieval Literatures* 4:139–70.

Langley, Thomas. 1797. *The History and Antiquities of the Hundred of Desborough and Deanery of Wycombe in Buckinghamshire*. London: R. Faulder and B. and J. White.

Lawton, David. 1987. "Dullness and the Fifteenth Century." *English Literary History* 54:761–99.

Laynesmith, J[oanna] L. 2003. "Constructing Queenship at Coventry: Pageantry and Politics at Margaret of Anjou's 'Secret Harbour.'" In *The Fifteenth Century III: Authority and Subversion*, ed. Linda Clark, 137–47. Woodbridge, UK: Boydell and Brewer.

———. 2004. *The Last Medieval Queens: English Queenship, 1445–1503*. Oxford: Oxford University Press.

Le Saux, Françoise. 2004. "War and Knighthood in Christine de Pizan's *Livre des faits d'armes et de chevallerie*." In *Writing War: Medieval Literary Responses to Warfare*, ed. Corinne J. Saunders, Françoise Hazel Marie Le Saux, and Neil Thomas, 93–105. Woodbridge, UK: Boydell and Brewer.

Lee, Patricia Ann. 1986. "Reflections of Power: Margaret of Anjou and the Dark Side of Queenship." *Renaissance Quarterly* 39:183–217.

Lehmberg, Stanford. 1960. *Sir Thomas Elyot, Tudor Humanist*. Austin: University of Texas Press.

Lewis, Katherine J. 2005. "Edmund of East Anglia, Henry VI and Ideals of Kingly Masculinity." In *Holiness and Masculinity in the Middle Ages*, ed. P. H. Cullum and Katharine J. Lewis, 158–73. Toronto: University of Toronto Press.

Litzen, Veikko. 1971. *A War of Roses and Lilies: The Theme of Succession in Sir John Fortescue's Works*. Helsinki: Academia Scientiarum Fennica.

Lord, Carla. 2002. "Queen Isabella at the Court of France." In *Fourteenth Century England II*, ed. Chris Given-Wilson, Nigel Saul, and W. M. Ormrod, 45–52. Woodbridge, UK: Boydell and Brewer.

Lovatt, Roger. 1981. "John Blacman: Biographer of Henry VI." In *The Writing of History in the Middle Ages: Essays Presented to Richard William Southern*, ed. Ralph Henry, C. Davis, and John Michael Wallace-Hadrill, 415–44. Oxford: Clarendon Press.

———. 1984. "A Collector of Apocryphal Anecdotes: John Blacman Revisited." In *Property and Politics: Essays in Later Medieval English History*, ed. Anthony J. Pollard, 172–97. Gloucester, U.K.: Alan Sutton.

Macaulay, G. C., ed. 1899. *The Complete Works of John Gower: French Works*. Oxford: Clarendon Press.

MacCracken, Henry Noble, ed. 1934. *The Minor Poems of John Lydgate, Part Two: Secular Poems*. Early English Text Society, original series 192. Reprint, London: Oxford University Press, 1961.

Madan, Falconer, et al., eds. 1895–1953. *A Summary Catalogue of Western Manuscripts in the Bodleian Library*. 7 vols. in 8. Reprint with corrections, Munich: Kraus Reprints, 1980.

Mahoney, Dhira. 1996. "Middle English Renderings of Christine de Pizan." In *The Medieval "Opus": Imitation, Rewriting, and Transmission in the French Tradition*, ed. Douglas Kelly, 405–27. Amsterdam: Rodopi.

Mandach, André de. 1974a. "L'anthologie chevaleresque de Marguerite d'Anjou (B. M. Royal 15 E VI) et les officines de Saint-Augustin de Canterbury, Jean Wauquelin du Mons, et David Aubert de Hesdin." In *VIe Congrès international de la Société Rencesvals: Actes*, ed. Jean Subrenat, 317–50. Aix-en-Provence: Université de Provence.

———. 1974b. "A Royal Wedding Present in the Making: Talbot's Chivalric Anthology (Royal E VI) for Queen Margaret of Anjou and the 'Laval-Middleton' Anthology of Nottingham." *Nottingham Medieval Studies* 18:56–76.

Manion, Margaret M. 1991. "Art and Devotion: The Prayer Books of Jean de

Berry." In *Medieval Texts and Images: Studies of Manuscripts from the Middle Ages*, ed. Margaret M. Manion and Bernard J. Muir, 177–200. Philadelphia: Harwood Academic Publishers.

Marguerite d'Anjou, reine d'Angleterre: Essai tragique en cinq actes. 1757. Paris: Prault.

Marks, Richard. 1993. *Stained Glass in England during the Middle Ages*. London: Routledge.

Matheson, Lister M. 1998. *The Prose Brut: The Development of a Middle English Chronicle*. Tempe, Ariz.: Medieval and Renaissance Texts and Studies.

Maurer, Helen. 2003. *Margaret of Anjou: Queenship and Power in Late Medieval England*. Woodbridge, UK: Boydell Press.

Mayali, Laurent. 1988. "'Lex animata': Rationalisation du pouvoir politique et science juridique (XIIème–XIVème siècles)." In *Renaissance du pouvoir législatif et genèse de l'état*, ed. André Gouron and Albert Rigaudière, 155–64. Publications de la Société d'histoire du droit et des institutions des anciens pays de droit écrit 3. Montpellier: Université de Montpellier.

McCulloch, Diarmaid, and Evan David Jones. 1983. "Lancastrian Politics, the French War, and the Rise of the Popular Element." *Speculum* 58:95–138.

McGerr, Rosemarie, ed. 1990. *The Pilgrimage of the Soul: A Critical Edition of the Middle English Dream Vision*. Vol. 1. Garland Medieval Texts 16. New York: Garland.

———. 2006. "A Statutes Book and Lancastrian Mirror for Princes: The Yale Law School Manuscript of the *Nova statuta Angliae*." *Textual Cultures: Text, Contexts, Interpretation* 1 (2): 6–59.

McGrady, Deborah. 1998. "What Is a Patron? Benefactors and Authorship in Harley 4431, Christine de Pizan's Collected Works." In Desmond 1998, 195–214.

McKenna, J[ohn] W. 1965. "Henry VI of England and the Dual Monarchy: Aspects of Royal Political Propaganda, 1422–32." *Journal of the Warburg and Courtauld Institutes* 28:145–62.

———. 1974. "Piety and Propaganda: The Cult of Henry VI." In *Chaucer and Middle English Studies in Honour of Rossell Hope Robbins*, ed. Beryl Rowland, 72–88. Kent, Ohio: Kent State University Press.

McLaren, Anne N. 1996. "Delineating the Elizabethan Body Politic: Knox, Aylmer and the Definition of Counsel, 1558–88." *History of Political Thought* 17:224–52.

Meale, Carole. 1989. "Patrons, Buyers and Owners: Book Production and Social Status." In *Book Production and Publishing in Britain, 1375–1475*, ed. Jeremy Griffiths and Derek Pearsall, 201–38. Cambridge: Cambridge University Press.

———. 1996. "Reading Women's Culture in Fifteenth-Century England: The Case of Alice Chaucer." In *Mediaevalitas: Reading the Middle Ages; The J. A. W. Bennett Memorial Lectures, Ninth Series, Perugia, 1995*, ed. Piero Boitani and Anna Torti, 81–101. Cambridge: D. S. Brewer and Boydell and Brewer.

Means, Laurel. 1992. "'Ffor as moche as yche man may not haue þe astrolabe': Popular Middle English Variations on the Computus." *Speculum* 67 (3): 595–623.

Meiss, Millard. 1967. *French Painting in the Time of Jean de Berry: The Late Fourteenth Century and the Patronage of the Duke.* 2 vols. London: Phaidon Press.

———. 1973. *The Rohan Master: A Book of Hours.* New York: G. Braziller.

Menache, Sophia. 1984. "Isabelle of France, Queen of England: A Reconsideration." *Journal of Medieval History* 10:107–24.

Meyer-Lee, Robert. 2004. "Laureates and Beggars in Fifteenth-Century English Poetry: The Case of George Ashby." *Speculum* 79:688–726.

———. 2007. *Poets and Power from Chaucer to Wyatt.* Cambridge: Cambridge University Press.

Michael, Michael A. 1985. "A Manuscript Wedding Gift from Philippa of Hainault to Edward III." *Burlington Magazine* 127 (990): 582–99.

———. 1994. "The Iconography of Kingship in the Walter of Milemete Treatise." *Journal of the Warburg and Courtauld Institutes* 57:35–47.

———. 1997. "The Privilege of 'Proximity': Towards a Re-definition of the Function of Armorials." *Journal of Medieval History* 23:55–74.

Michalove, Sharon. 2004. "Women as Book Collectors and the Dissemination of Culture in Late Medieval Europe." In *Reputation and Representation in Fifteenth-Century Europe,* ed. Douglas Biggs, Sharon D. Michalove, and Albert Compton Reeves, 57–79. Leiden: Brill.

Mohr, Richard. 2005. "Enduring Signs and Obscure Meanings: Contested Coats of Arms in Australian Jurisdic-

tions." In *Contemporary Issues of the Semiotics of Law: Cultural and Symbolic Analyses of Law in a Global Context,* ed. Farid Samir, Benavides Vanegas, and Anne Wagner, 179–95. Portland, Ore.: Hart Publishing.

Monro, Cecil, ed. 1863. *Letters of Queen Margaret of Anjou and Bishop Beckington and Others: Written in the Reigns of Henry V and Henry VI.* Camden Society, old series 86. London: Nichols and Sons.

Mooney, Linne R. 1989. "Lydgate's 'Kings of England' and Another Verse Chronicle of the Kings." *Viator: Medieval and Renaissance Studies* 20:255–89.

Mosley, Charles, ed. 2003. *Burke's Peerage, Baronetage and Knightage, 107th edition.* 3 vols. Stokesley: Burke's Peerage.

Muir, Lynette. 1995. *The Biblical Drama of Medieval Europe.* Cambridge: Cambridge University Press.

Musson, Anthony. 2001. *Medieval Law in Context: The Growth of Legal Consciousness from Magna Carta to the Peasants' Revolt.* Manchester: Manchester University Press.

———. 2004. "Law and Text: Legal Authority and Judicial Accessibility in the Late Middle Ages." In *The Uses of Script and Print, 1300–1700,* ed. Julia C. Crick and Alexandra Walsham, 95–115. Cambridge: Cambridge University Press.

Myers, Alec Reginald. 1957–58. "The Household Accounts of Queen Margaret of Anjou, 1452–3." *Bulletin of the John Rylands Library* 40:79–113, 391–432. Reprint in *Crown, Household, and Parliament in Fifteenth-Century England,* ed. Cecil H. Clough, 93–229 (London: Hambledon Press, 1985).

Nederman, Cary J., ed. 1990. *Policraticus.* By John of Salisbury. Cambridge: Cambridge University Press.

———. 1998. "The Mirror Crack'd: The *Speculum principium* as Political and Social Criticism in the Late Middle Ages." *European Legacy* 3:18–38.

Newman, Barbara. 2003. *God and the Goddesses: Vision, Poetry, and Belief in the Middle Ages.* Philadelphia: University of Pennsylvania Press.

Nicolas, Harris, ed. 1834–37. *Proceedings and Ordinances of the Privy Council of England.* 7 vols. London: G. Eyre and A. Spottiswoode, for the Great Britain Record Commission.

Nolan, Maura. 2005. *John Lydgate and the Making of Public Culture.* Cambridge: Cambridge University Press.

Nuttall, Jennifer. 2007. *The Creation of Lancastrian Kingship: Literature, Language and Politics in Late Medieval England.* Cambridge: Cambridge University Press.

O'Brien, Bruce R. 1999. *God's Peace and King's Peace: The Laws of Edward the Confessor.* Philadelphia: Pennsylvania University Press.

O'Brien, Dennis J. 1993. "Warrior Queen: The Character of Zenobia According to Giovanni Boccaccio, Christine de Pizan, and Sir Thomas Elyot." *Medieval Perspectives* 8:53–68.

O'Meara, Carra Ferguson. 2001. *Monarchy and Consent: The Coronation Book of Charles V of France, British Library, Cotton MS Tiberius B. VIII.* London: Harvey Miller.

Orme, Nicholas. 1984. *From Childhood to Chivalry: The Education of the English Kings and Aristocracy, 1066–1530.* London: Methuen.

———. 2001. *Medieval Children.* Reprint, New Haven, Conn.: Yale University Press, 2003.

Ormrod, W. Mark. 2003. "The Use of English: Language, Law, and Political Culture in Fourteenth-Century England." *Speculum* 78:750–87.

———. 2005. "Monarchy, Martyrdom and Masculinity: England in the Later Middle Ages." In *Holiness and Masculinity in the Middle Ages,* ed. P. H. Cullum and Katherine J. Lewis, 174–91. Toronto: University of Toronto Press.

Osberg, Richard. 1986. "The Jesse Tree in the 1432 London Entry of Henry VI: Messianic Kingship and the Rule of Justice." *Journal of Medieval and Renaissance Studies* 16:213–32.

Owens, Margareth Boyer. 1989. "The Image of King David in Prayer in Fifteenth-Century Books of Hours." *Imago musicae* 6:23–38.

Pächt, Otto, and Jonathan J. G. Alexander. 1973. *Illuminated Manuscripts in the Bodleian Library, Oxford.* 3 vols. Oxford: Bodleian Library.

Pächt, Otto, Charles Reginald Dodwell, and Francis Wormald. 1960. *The St Albans Psalter.* Studies of the Warburg Institute 25. London: The Warburg Institute, University of London.

Palliser, Fanny [Mrs. Bury Palliser]. 1870. *Historic Devices, Badges, and War-Cries.* London: Sampson Lowe.

Parkes, Malcolm B. 1969. *English Cursive Book Hands, 1250–1500.* Reprint, Berkeley: University of California Press, 1980.

———. 1976. "The Influence of the Concepts of *Ordinatio* and *Compilatio* on the Development of the Book." In *Medieval Learning and Literature:*

Essays Presented to Richard William Hunt, ed. Jonathan J. G. Alexander and Margaret T. Gibson, 115–41. Oxford: Clarendon Press.

———. 2008. *Their Hands before Our Eyes: A Closer Look at Scribes.* Farnham, UK: Ashgate.

Parkes, Malcolm B., and Anthony I. Doyle. 1978. "The Production of Copies of the *Canterbury Tales* and the *Confessio Amantis* in the Early Fifteenth Century." In *Medieval Scribes, Manuscripts and Libraries: Essays Presented to N. R. Ker,* ed. Malcolm B. Parkes and Andrew G. Watson, 163–210. London: Scolar Press.

Patterson, Lee. 1993. "Making Identities: Henry V and Lydgate." In *New Historical Literary Study: Essays on Reproducing Texts, Representing History,* ed. Jeffrey N. Cox and Larry J. Reynolds, 69–106. Princeton, N.J.: Princeton University Press.

Pearsall, Derek. 1994. "Hoccleve's *Regement of Princes:* The Poetics of Royal Self-Representation." *Speculum* 69:386–410.

Perkins, Nicholas. 2001. *Hoccleve's Regiment of Princes: Counsel and Constraint.* Cambridge: D. S. Brewer.

Petrina, Alessandra. 2004. *Cultural Politics in Fifteenth-Century England: The Case of Humphrey, Duke of Gloucester.* Leiden: Brill.

Picard, Liza. 2005. *Elizabeth's London: Everyday Life in Elizabethan London.* London: Macmillan.

Pollard, Albert Frederick. 1920. *The Evolution of Parliament.* London: Longmans, Green, and Co.

Porcher, Jean. 1945. "Two Models for the 'Heures de Rohan.'" *Journal of the Warburg and Courtauld Institutes* 8:1–6.

Prendergast, Thomas A. 2002. "The Invisible Spouse: Henry VI, Arthur, and the Fifteenth-Century Subject." *Journal of Medieval and Early Modern Studies* 32:305–26.

Prévost, Antoine François. 1740. *Histoire de Marguerite d'Anjou, reine d'Angleterre.* 2 vols. Amsterdam: François Desbordes.

———. 1755. *The History of Margaret d'Anjou, Queen of England.* Anonymous translation. 2 vols. London: J. Payne.

Pronay, Nicholas, and John Taylor. 1974. "The Use of the *Modus tenendi Parliamentum* in the Middle Ages." *Bulletin of the Institute of Historical Research* 47:11–23.

———, eds. 1980. *Parliamentary Texts of the Later Middle Ages.* Oxford: Clarendon Press.

Radulescu, Raluca. 2003. *The Gentry Context for Malory's "Morte Darthur."* Cambridge: D. S. Brewer.

Raithby, John, ed. 1810–28. *The Statutes of the Realm, Printed by Command of His Majesty King George the Third: In Pursuance of an Address of the House of Commons of Great Britain; From Original Records and Authentic Manuscripts.* 11 vols. London: Eyre and Strahan.

Reeves, A. Compton. 1998. "Lawrence Booth: Bishop of Durham (1457–76), Archbishop of York (1476–80)." In *Estrangement, Enterprise and Education in Fifteenth-Century England,* ed. S. D. Michalove and A. C. Reeves, 63–88. Stroud, UK: Alan Sutton.

Resnik, Judith, and Dennis Curtis. 2007. "Representing Justice: From Renaissance Iconography to 21st-Century Courthouses." *Proceedings of the American Philosophical Society* 151:139–83.

Robin, Françoise. 1985. *La cour d'Anjou-Provence: La vie artistique sous le règne de René.* Paris: Picard.

Robinson, Pamela R. 1988. *Catalogue of Dated and Datable Manuscripts c. 737–1600 in Cambridge Libraries.* 2 vols. Cambridge: Cambridge University.

———. 2003. *Catalogue of Dated and Datable Manuscripts c. 888–1600 in London Libraries.* 2 vols. London: British Library.

Rolle, Richard. 1884. *The Psalter, or Psalms of David and Certain Canticles.* Ed. Henry Ramsden Bramley. Oxford: Clarendon Press.

Rorimer, James J., and Margaret B. Freeman. 1949. "The Nine Heroes Tapestries at the Cloisters." *The Metropolitan Museum of Art Bulletin,* May, 243–60. Reprinted as *The Nine Heroes Tapestries at the Cloisters* (New York: Metropolitan Museum of Art, 1960).

Roskell, John Smith. 2005. *Parliament and Politics in Late Medieval England,* Vol. 2. London: Continuum International Publishing Group.

Ross, Charles Derek. 1974. *Edward IV.* Reprint, New Haven, Conn.: Yale University Press, 1997.

Rowe, Benedicta Jeannette Hanbury. 1933. "King Henry VI's Claim to France: In Picture and Poem." *The Library,* 4th series, 13:77–88.

Royal Archaeological Institute of Britain and Ireland. 1882. "Archaeological Intelligence." *Archaeological Journal* 39:481–83.

Sandler, Lucy Freeman. 1985. "A Note on the Illuminators of the Bohun Manuscripts." *Speculum* 60:364–72.

———. 1986. *Gothic Manuscripts, 1285–1385: A Survey of Manuscripts Illumi-* nated in the British Isles, Vol. 5. 2 vols. New York: Oxford University Press.

———. 2003. "Lancastrian Heraldry in the Bohun Manuscripts." In *The Lancastrian Court: Proceedings of the 2001 Harlaxton Symposium,* ed. Jenny Stratford, 221–32. Harlaxton Medieval Studies, new series, 13. Donington, UK: Shaun Tyas.

Saul, Nigel. 1997. *Richard II.* New Haven, Conn.: Yale University Press.

Saygin, Susanne. 2002. *Humphrey, Duke of Gloucester (1390–1447) and the Italian Humanists.* Leiden: Brill.

Scanlon, Larry. 1990. "The King's Two Voices: Narrative and Power in Hoccleve's *Regement of Princes.*" In *Literary Practice and Social Change in Britain, 1380–1530,* ed. Lee Patterson, 216–47. Berkeley: University of California Press.

———. 2007. *Narrative, Authority and Power: The Medieval Exemplum and the Chaucerian Tradition.* Cambridge: Cambridge University Press.

Scattergood, John. 1990. "The Date and Composition of George Ashby's Poems." *Leeds Studies in English* 21:167–76.

———. 1993. "George Ashby's *Prisoner's Reflections* and the Virtue of Patience." *Nottingham Medieval Studies* 37:102–109.

———. 1996. *Reading the Past: Essays on Medieval and Renaissance Literature.* Dublin: Four Courts Press.

Scheifele, Eleanor. 1999. "Richard II and the Visual Arts." In *Richard II: The Art of Kingship,* ed. Anthony Goodman and James L. Gillespie, 255–71. Oxford: Oxford University Press.

Schröder, Horst. 1971. *Der Topos der Nine Worthies in Literatur und bil-*

dender Kunst. Göttingen: Vandenhoek & Ruprecht.

Scofield, Cora Louise. 1912. "Sir John Fortescue in February 1461." *English Historical Review* 27 (106): 321–23.

———. 1923. *The Life and Reign of Edward the Fourth.* 2 vols. London: Longmans, Green, and Co.

Scott, Kathleen L. 1980a. "Additions to the Oeuvre of the English Border Artist: The *Nova statuta*" and Appendix B. In *The Mirroure of the Worlde: MS Bodley 283 (England c. 1470–80).* Oxford: Roxburghe Club.

———. 1980b. "A Late Fifteenth-Century Group of *Nova statuta* Manuscripts." In de la Mare and Barker-Benfield 1980, 103–105.

———. 1989. "*Caveat Lector*: Ownership and Standardization in the Illustration of Fifteenth-Century English Manuscripts." *English Manuscript Studies, 1100–1700* 1:19–63.

———. 1995. "Limning and Book-Producing Terms and Signs *in situ* in Late-Medieval English Manuscripts: A First Listing." In *New Science out of Old Books: Studies in Manuscripts and Early Printed Books in Honour of A. I. Doyle,* ed. Richard Beadle and Alan J. Piper, 142–88. Aldershot, UK: Scolar Press.

———. 1996. *Later Gothic Manuscripts: 1390–1490 (A Survey of Manuscripts Illuminated in the British Isles, Part 6).* 2 vols. London: Harvey Miller.

———. 2001. "The Edward IV Roll." In *Leaves of Gold: Treasures of Manuscript Illumination from Philadelphia Collections,* ed. James R. Tanis and Jennifer A. Thompson, 228–32. Philadelphia: Philadelphia Museum of Art.

———. 2002. *Dated and Datable English Manuscript Borders, c. 1395–1499.* London: British Library.

Sherman, Claire Richter. 1969. *The Portraits of Charles V of France (1338–1380).* New York: New York University Press for the College Art Association of America.

Shipman, Carolyn. 1909. *A Catalogue of Manuscripts Forming a Portion of the Library of Robert Hoe.* Privately printed.

Simpson, James. 2004. "Reginald Pecock and John Fortescue." In *A Companion to Middle English Prose,* ed. Anthony S. G. Edwards, 271–87. Cambridge: D. S. Brewer.

Skemer, Don C. 1995. "From Archives to the Book Trade: Private Statute Rolls in England, 1285–1307." *Journal of the Society of Archivists* 16:193–206.

———. 1997. "Sir William Breton's Book: Production of *Statuta Angliae* in the Late Thirteenth Century." *English Manuscript Studies, 1100–1700* 6:24–51.

———. 1999. "Reading the Law: Statute Books and the Private Transmission of Legal Knowledge in Late Medieval England." In *Learning the Law: Teaching and the Transmission of Law in England, 1150–1900,* ed. Jonathan A. Bush and Alain A. Wijffels, 113–31. London: Hambledon Press.

Sotheby Auction House. 1933. *Catalogue of Valuable Printed Books, Illuminated and Other Manuscripts, Autograph Letters and Historical Documents, etc. . . . Which Will Be Sold by Auction . . . on Monday, the 31st of July, 1933, and the Following Day.* London: Sotheby and Co.

———. 1938. *Catalogue of Valuable Printed Books, Illuminated and Other Manuscripts, Autograph Letters and*

Historical Documents . . . : Which Will Be Sold by Auction . . . on Monday, April 11th, 1938, and Following Day. London: Sotheby and Co.

——. 1958. *Catalogue of Forty-five Exceptionally Important Illuminated Manuscripts of the 9th to the 18th century.* London: Sotheby and Co.

Spencer, Brian. 1978. "King Henry of Windsor and the London Pilgrim." In *Collectanea Londiniensia: Studies in London Archaeology and History Presented to Ralph Merrifield,* ed. Joanna Bird, Hugh Chapman, and John Clark, 235–64. London and Middlesex Archaeological Society, special paper no. 2. London: London and Middlesex Archaeological Society.

——. 1998. *Pilgrim Souvenirs and Secular Badges.* London: Stationery Office.

Stanton, Anne Rudloff. 2001. *The Queen Mary Psalter: A Study of Affect and Audience.* Philadelphia: American Philosophical Society.

Steiner, Emily. 2003. *Documentary Culture and the Making of Medieval English Literature.* Cambridge: Cambridge University Press.

Strohm, Paul. 1998. *England's Empty Throne: Usurpation and the Language of Legitimation, 1399–1422.* New Haven, Conn.: Yale University Press.

——. 2005. *Politique: Languages of Statecraft between Chaucer and Shakespeare.* South Bend, Ind.: University of Notre Dame Press.

Strong, Patrick. 1981. "The Last Will and Codicils of Henry V." *English Historical Review* 96:79–102.

Summers, Joanna. 2004. *Late-Medieval Prison Writing and the Politics of Autobiography.* Oxford: Oxford University Press.

Sutton, Anne, and Livia Visser-Fuchs. 1997. *Richard III's Books.* Gloucester, UK: Sutton Publishing.

Taylor, Andrew. 2002. *Textual Situations: Three Medieval Manuscripts and Their Readers.* Philadelphia: University of Pennsylvania Press.

Taylor, John. 1968. "The Manuscripts of the *Modus tenendi Parliamentum.*" *English Historical Review* 83:673–88.

——. 1987. *English Historical Literature in the Fourteenth Century.* Oxford: Oxford University Press.

Teague, Frances. 1991. "Christine de Pizan's *Book of War.*" In *The Reception of Christine de Pizan from the Fifteenth through the Nineteenth Centuries,* ed. Glenda K. McLeod, 25–41. Lewiston: Edwin Mellen Press.

Thomas, Marcel. 1979. *The Golden Age: Manuscript Painting at the Time of Jean, Duke of Berry.* Trans. Ursele Molinaro and Bruce Benderson. New York: George Braziller.

Tomlins, T. Edlyn, et al. 1811–28. *The Statutes of the Realm, 1225–1713.* 11 vols. Reprint, London: Dawsons Publishing, 1963.

Traver, Hope. 1907. *The Four Daughters of God: A Study of the Versions of This Allegory, with Special Reference to Those in Latin, French, and English.* Philadelphia: John C. Winston.

Tribble, Evelyn B. 1993. *Margins and Marginality: The Printed Page in Early Modern England.* Richmond: University of Virginia Press.

Tudor-Craig, Pamela. 1989. "Henry VIII and King David." In *Early Tudor England: Proceedings of the 1987 Harlaxton Symposium,* ed. Daniel Williams, 183–205. Woodbridge, UK: Boydell Press.

Turner, Victor. 1969. *The Ritual Process: Structure and Anti-structure.* Chicago: Aldine Press.

Twigg, John. 1987. *A History of Queens' College, Cambridge, 1448–1986.* Woodbridge, UK: Boydell Press.

Tytler, Alexander Fraser, Lord Woodhouselee. 1834. *Universal History: From the Creation of the World to the Beginning of the Eighteenth Century.* 6 vols. London: John Murray.

Ullmann, Walter. 1975. *Law and Politics in the Middle Ages: An Introduction to the Sources of Medieval Political Ideas.* London: Hodder and Stoughton.

Urstad, Tone Sundt. 1999. *Sir Robert Walpole's Poets: The Use of Literature as Pro-government Propaganda, 1721–1742.* Newark: University of Delaware Press.

Vale, Malcolm. 1974. *Charles VII.* Berkeley: University of California Press.

———. 2001. *The Princely Court: Medieval Courts and Culture in North-West Europe, 1270–1380.* Reprint, Oxford: Oxford University Press, 2003.

Valente, Claire. 1998. "The Deposition and Abdication of Edward II." *English Historical Review* 113:852–81.

———. 2003. *The Theory and Practice of Revolt in Medieval England.* Farnham, UK: Ashgate.

Vallance, Aymer. 1947. *Greater English Church Screens, Being Great Roods, Screenwork and Rood-Lofts in Cathedral, Monastic and Collegiate Churches in England and Wales.* London: Batsford.

van Gennep, Arnold. 1960. *The Rites of Passage.* Trans. M. B. Vizedom and G. L. Caffee. Chicago: University of Chicago Press.

Wagner, Anthony Richard. 1950. *A Catalogue of English Mediaeval Rolls of Arms.* Oxford: Society of Antiquaries.

———. 1956. *Heralds and Heraldry in the Middle Ages: An Inquiry into the Growth of the Armorial Function of Heralds.* 2nd ed. Oxford: Oxford University Press.

Wakelin, Daniel. 2004. "The Occasion, Author, and Readers of *Knyghthode and Bataile.*" *Medium Aevum* 73:260–72.

———. 2007. *Humanism, Reading and English Literature, 1430–1530.* Oxford: Oxford University Press.

Walford, Edward. 1883. "Antiquarian News and Notes." *The Antiquarian Magazine and Bibliographer* 3:94–99.

Walker, Simon. 2004. "Remembering Richard: History and Memory in Lancastrian England." In Clark and Carpenter 2004, 21–32.

Watts, John. 1996. *Henry VI and the Politics of Kingship.* Cambridge: Cambridge University Press.

Webb, Clement Charles Julien, ed. 1909. *Policraticus.* By John of Salisbury. 2 vols. Oxford: Clarendon Press.

Weber, W. C. 1998. "The Purpose of the English *Modus tenendi Parliamentum.*" *Parliamentary History* 17:149–77.

Wedgwood, Josiah C. 1938. *History of Parliament, 1439–1509: Biographies.* London: His Majesty's Stationery Office.

Weir, Alison. 2007. *Queen Isabella: Treachery, Adultery, and Murder in Medieval England.* London: Random House. (Originally published in 2005 as *Isabella: She-Wolf of France, Queen of England.*)

Whittingham, Selby. 1971. "The Chronology of the Portraits of Richard II." *Burlington Magazine* 113:12–21.

Wieck, Roger S. 1983. *Late Medieval and Renaissance Illuminated Manuscripts (1350–1525) in the Houghton Library.*

Cambridge, Mass.: Harvard College Library.

Willard, Charity Cannon, ed. 1999. *The Book of the Deeds of Arms and of Chivalry*, by Christine de Pizan. Trans. Sumner Willard. University Park: Pennsylvania State University Press.

William of Malmesbury. 1998. *Gesta regum Anglorum: The History of the English Kings*. Vol. 1. Ed. and trans. Roger Aubrey Baskerville Mynors, Rodney M. Thomson, and Michael Winterbottom. Oxford: Clarendon Press.

Williams, Elijah. 1927. *Early Holborn and the Legal Quarter of London*. 2 vols. London: Sweet and Maxwell.

Williams, William Retlaw. 1897. *The Parliamentary History of the County of Worcester: Including the City of Worcester, and the Boroughs of Bewdly, Droitwich, Dudley, Evesham, Kidderminster, Bromsgrove and Pershore, from the Earliest Times to the Present Day, 1213–1897; With Biographical and Genealogical Notices of the Members*. Hereford: Jakeman and Carver.

Wilson, William Burton, ed. and trans. 1992. *Mirour de l'omme (The Mirror of Mankind)*. By John Gower. Rev. by Nancy Wilson Van Baak. East Lansing, Mich.: Colleagues Press.

Winstead, Karen Anne. 2007. *John Capgrave's Fifteenth Century*. Philadelphia: University of Pennsylvania Press.

Wolffe, Bertram. 1981. *Henry VI*. Reprint, New Haven, Conn.: Yale University Press, 2001.

Wood, Neal. 1994. *Foundations of Political Economy: Some Early Tudor Views on State and Society*. Berkeley: University of California.

Woodcock, Thomas, and John Martin Robinson. 1988. *The Oxford Guide to Heraldry*. Reprint, Oxford: Oxford University Press, 1990.

Woodworth, Allegra. 1945. "Purveyance for the Royal Household in the Reign of Queen Elizabeth." *Transactions of the American Philosophical Society*, new series, 35 (1): 1–98.

Wormald, Francis. 1951. "The Yates Thompson Manuscripts." *British Museum Quarterly* 16:4–5.

Wormald, Patrick. 1999. *The Making of English Law: King Alfred to the Twelfth Century*. Reprint, Oxford: Blackwell Publishers, 2000.

Wright, Cyril Ernest. 1972. *Fontes Harleiani: A Study of the Sources of the Harleian Collection of Manuscripts in the British Museum*. London: British Museum.

Yeager, Robert F. 2000. "Politics and the French Language in England during the Hundred Years' War: The Case of John Gower." In *Inscribing the Hundred Years' War in French and English Cultures*, ed. Denise Nowakowski Baker, 127–57. Albany: State University of New York Press.

Yonge, Charlotte Mary. 1877. *Cameos from English History: The Wars of the Roses*. London: Macmillan.

Zajkowski, Robert. 2002. "Henry VI of England: The Ritual Education of an Adolescent Prince." In *The Premodern Teenager: Youth in Society, 1150–1650*, ed. Konrad Eisenbichler, 111–29. Toronto: Centre for Reformation and Renaissance Studies.

MANUSCRIPTS CITED

Austin, Texas
University of Texas, Harry Ransom Humanities Research Center, MS HRC 5

Cambridge, Massachusetts
Harvard Law School Library, MS 10
Harvard Law School Library, MS 21
Harvard Law School Library, MS 29
Harvard Law School Library, MS 30
Harvard Law School Library, MS 42
Harvard Law School Library, MS 58
Harvard Law School Library, MS 163
Harvard Law School Library, MS 177
Harvard University, Houghton Library,
　MS Richardson 40

Cambridge, United Kingdom
Cambridge University, Fitzwilliam Museum, MS 38-1950
Cambridge University, King's College
　Library, MS KC/18
Cambridge University, St. John's College
　Library, MS A. 7
Cambridge University Library, MS Ff. 3. 1
Cambridge University Library, MS Ll.
　v. 20
Cambridge University Library, MS Mm.
　iv. 42

Cape Town, South Africa
National Library of South Africa, MS
　Grey 4 c 5

Chantilly, France
Musée Condé, MS 65

Chicago, Illinois
Newberry Library, MS 32.1

Durham, United Kingdom
Durham Cathedral Library, MS 1. 2.
　Reg. 6a

Geneva, Switzerland
Bibliothèque publique et universitaire,
　MS fr. 165

Holkham, Norfolk, United Kingdom
Holkham Hall, Library of the Earl of
　Leicester, MS 232

Kew, United Kingdom
National Archives of the United Kingdom, MS E 164/10
National Archives of the United Kingdom, MS E 164/11
National Archives of the United Kingdom, MS KB 27/728
National Archives of the United Kingdom, MS KB 27/796
National Archives of the United Kingdom, MS KB 27/798
National Archives of the United Kingdom, MS KB 27/819
National Archives of the United Kingdom, MS KB 27/820

London, United Kingdom
British Library, MS Additional 15728
British Library, MS Additional 18002
British Library, MS Additional 21058
British Library, MS Additional 24079
British Library, MS Additional 27342
British Library, MS Additional 29504
British Library, MS Additional 40851
British Library, MS Additional 81292
British Library, MS Arundel 109
British Library, MS Arundel 331
British Library, MS Cotton Cleopatra
　A xiii
British Library, MS Cotton Cleopatra
　B x
British Library, MS Cotton Domitian
　A xvii
British Library, MS Cotton Julius E iv
British Library, MS Cotton Nero C i
British Library, MS Cotton Nero D vi
British Library, MS Egerton Charter 2132
British Library, MS Egerton Charter
　2129
British Library, MS Hargrave 274
British Library, MS Harley 542
British Library, MS Harley 661
British Library, MS Harley 937

British Library, MS Harley 2287
British Library, MS Harley 3869
British Library, MS Harley 4431
British Library, MS Harley 4999
British Library, MS Harley 5233
British Library, MS Harley 7353
British Library, MS Harley Charter 51
H 6
British Library, MS Lansdowne 204
British Library, MS Lansdowne 468
British Library, MS Lansdowne 470
British Library, MS Royal 1 E ix
British Library, MS Royal 2 B vii
British Library, MS Royal 14 B viii
British Library, MS Royal 15 E iv
British Library, MS Royal 15 E vi
British Library, MS Royal 17 D xv
British Library, MS Royal 18 D ii
British Library, MS Royal 20 C vii
British Library, MS Stowe 389
British Library, MS Yates Thompson 48
City of London Corporation, London
Metropolitan Archives, MS COL/
CS/01/007
City of London Corporation, London
Metropolitan Archives, Guildhall
Library, MS 31692
Inner Temple Library, MS Petyt 505
Leathersellers' Company, 1444
Charter
Lincoln's Inn Library, MS Hale 71
Lincoln's Inn Library, MS Hale 183
Lincoln's Inn Library, MS Hale 194
Westminster Abbey, MS 38

New Haven, Connecticut
Yale Law School, Lillian Goldman Law
Library, MssG +StII no.1

New York, New York
Columbia University, Rare Book and
Manuscript Library, Plimpton MS
273

Metropolitan Museum of Art, The
Cloisters Museum, Acc. No. 54.1.1
New York Public Library, MS 32
Pierpont Morgan Library, MS M102
Pierpont Morgan Library, MS M253
Pierpont Morgan Library, MS M359
Pierpont Morgan Library, MS M456

Nottingham, United Kingdom
Nottingham University Library, Willoughby Family Papers, MS Mi L 2/2
Nottingham University Library, Wollaton Antiphonal

Oslo, Norway, and London, United Kingdom
Martin Schøyen Collection, MS 1355

Oxford, United Kingdom
Oxford University, Bodleian Library, MS
Digby 36
Oxford University, Bodleian Library, MS
Don. d. 85
Oxford University, Bodleian Library, MS
Hatton 10
Oxford University, Bodleian Library, MS
Hatton 73
Oxford University, Bodleian Library, MS
Jesus College 124
Oxford University, Bodleian Library, MS
Rawlinson C. 398
Oxford University, St. John's College,
MS 257

Paris, France
Bibliothèque nationale de France, MS
lat. 1
Bibliothèque nationale de France, MS
lat. 17294
Bibliothèque nationale de France, MS
lat. 18014

Philadelphia, Pennsylvania
Free Library of Philadelphia, MS Carson
LC 14. 9.5

Free Library of Philadelphia, MS Carson
  LC 14. 10
Free Library of Philadelphia, MS Carson
  LC 14. 20.5
Free Library of Philadelphia, MS Lewis
  E201

Princeton, New Jersey
Princeton University Library, Scheide
  Collection, MS 30

Rouen, France
Bibliothèque municipale, MS 939

San Marino, California
Huntington Library, MS EL 35 B 61
Huntington Library, MS HM 19920

Shrewsbury, United Kingdom
Guildhall, Corporation Muniments,
  Charter of 1389

Turin, Italy
Biblioteca Nazionale Universitaria,
  MS I. I. 9

Vatican City
Vatican Library, MS Reginense latino
  1520

Winchester, United Kingdom
Winchester College Library, MS
  13B

Windsor, United Kingdom
Eton College Archives, MS 39/57

Current location unknown
Nova statuta Angliae made for Sir
  Thomas Fitzwilliam of Mablethorpe
  (formerly part of Dyson Perrins
  Collection, sold at Sotheby Auction
  House, 9 December 1958)

Index

Abbey of Saint Martin, Tours, 57

Abel (Abell), William, 60, 165n2, 170n37

Aborough, Margaret. *See* Elyot, Margaret

Aborough (à Barrow), Thomas, 132

Adam, 165n10

Adgore, Gregory, 21–22, 32, 164n26

Agincourt, Battle of, 166n15

Alexander the Great, 91

All Souls College, Oxford, 166n15

Angers, France, 137

Antiqua statuta Angliae. See *Vetera statuta Angliae*

Archaeological Institute of Great Britain and Ireland, 135, 157

arms. *See* coats of arms

Arrowood, Charles F., 172n14

Ashby, George, 12, 104, 106–112, 117, 127, 171n5, 172n9, 172n10, 172n12, 172n14

Ashby, Margaret, 109

Athelstan, King of England, 165n10

Auerbach, Erna, 67, 69, 71, 168n56, 168n57

Austin, Texas: University of Texas, Harry Ransom Humanities Research Center, MS HRC 5, 56, *plate 57*

authority, 9, 11, 56, 71, 75, 86, 91, 100; divine, 56, 58, 106, 114, 126; judicial, 53, 67; of Parliament, 65, 125; royal, 6–7, 10, 12, 39, 51–52, 54–55, 60, 67, 70, 73, 77, 88, 91–92, 97, 119, 126; textual, 2–3, 74

L'Avis aus roys, 57, 64, 167n39

Baker, John Hamilton, 10, 15, 22–24, 135

Bakhtin, Mikhail, 3, 161n4

Baldocke, Robert, 78–80

Bartlett, Anne Clark, 4, 10, 101

Bateson, Mary, 110

Beauchamp, Richard, Earl of Warwick, 103

Beaufort, Edmund, Duke of Somerset, 92

Beaufort, Thomas, Duke of Exeter, 103

Beaumont, John, Viscount, 105, 171n7

Bedford. *See* John of Lancaster, Duke of Bedford

Bekynton, Thomas, 109

Bennett, Adelaide, 52

Bible (Vulgate), 48, 55–58, 63, 66, 69, 71–74, 82, 84, 86, 102, 115–116, 118, 120; Deuteronomy, 115–116; Ecclesiastes, 166n19; Ephesians, 53; Genesis, 83–84; Isaiah, 84–85; 1 Kings, 52–55; Psalms, 5, 53, 55–57, 59, 63–64, 66, 68–70, 72–74, 85–87, 118–119, 168n58; Wisdom, 115, 166n19

Binski, Paul, 34, 54

Biographium Faemineum: The Female Worthies, 136, 174n25

Rosemarie McGerr is Remak Professor of Comparative Literature and Director of the Medieval Studies Institute at Indiana University. Her publications include *Chaucer's Open Books: Resistance to Closure in Medieval Discourse* (1998) and *The Pilgrimage of the Soul: A Critical Edition of the Middle English Dream Vision* (1990).